Administrative Thinkers

Published by:
Saurabh Publishing House

Administrative Thinkers

Ashok Kumar

Saurabh
Publishing House
4735/22, Prakash Deep Building,
Ansari Road, Daryaganj,
New Delhi- 110002

Published by :
SAURABH PUBLISHING HOUSE

Distributed by :
Lotus Press Publishers & Distributors
Unit No. 220, 2nd Floor, 4735/22, Prakash Deep Building,
Ansari Road, Darya Ganj, New Delhi- 110002
Ph.: 41325510, 09811838000
• E-mail : lotuspress1984@gmail.com
www.lotuspress.co.in

Saurabh Publishing House is an imprint of
Lotus Press Publishers & Distributors

Administrative Thinkers

ISBN: 978-81-89005-25-2 (HB)

Printed by & Published : **Lotus Press Publishers & Distributors, Delhi**

PREFACE

As the human society evolved and the people started living in organised societies, need for administration was felt. Slowly and steadily social, economic and political problems began to become complex and complicated and with that the headache of administrators to run smooth administration too increased. Thus the beginning of administrative thought can be traced back with the origin of civilised society.

Not much attention was paid to the need of the study of administrative thought till the middle of the last century, when some attention began to be paid to this subject. It was only thereafter that more attention began to be paid to it and for this various causes were responsible. Gradually the functions of the state considerably increased and these became complex. The state became quite powerful and many political thinkers pleaded that it should be placed on high pedestals and worshipped It was forcefully argued by them that individual should completely merge himself in the state.

A very significant contribution in the growth of administrative thought in our modern time was made by political thinkers like Karl Marx who strongly pleaded that the workers who form vast majority of population in very country are being denied a share in the running of their own administration both in the government and industry. Karl Marx and many other intellectuals came forward with their ideas about administration and role of administrators in society. Mention among others may be made about Woodrow Wilson, Henri Fayol, F. W. Taylor, Max Weber, Urwick, L.

Gulick, M.P. Follet, Chester I. Bernard, Likert, Dror, Gregor etc. Then came various political philosophies like Individualism, Socialism, Anarchism, Syndicalism etc . Each school of political though gave its own views about the role of administrators and state administration in the life of the citizens.

This book deals with the topics of—Introduction to Administrative Thought; Kautilya; Victor H. Vroom; D. Waldo; Henry Fayol; Woodrow Wilson; George Elton Mayo; David G. Mc Clelland; Max Weber; Fredrick W. Taylor; Rensis Likert; Peter F. Drucker; Herbert A. Simon; Fred W. Riggs; Frederick Herzberg; etc.

I hope that students and those in the administration field will find it useful for academic and competitive examinations. I owe a deep sense of gratitude to my publisher for materialising my present endeavour.

ASHOK KUMAR

Contents

1

Introduction to Administrative Thought

In ancient India administration of the people was considered the foremost duty of the King. The whole thought revolved round one point namely the welfare of the people. An administrator was required to promote religion and develop ethical values and moral standards. Success of an administrator was measured in terms of promotion of religious values and morals of the people. Though King was supreme head of the state yet he could not ignore religion. Administration and administrative thinking was very much influenced by *rishies*, saints and religious priests. In administration more stress was laid on practice rather than on theory of state and government.

Administrative thought in ancient India was neither purely dogmatic nor idealistic but it tried to establish close relationship between theory and practice. In fact, it was ensured that the administrative theory was not devoid of practice. It was not an isolated and exclusive subject of study but was closely linked and associated with other subjects. It aimed at the welfare of the people. Since no distinction was maintained between state and society therefore, thought was of a nature in which stress was laid both on rights and duties. It was believed that each one in the society has certain obligations and unless those were discharged, rights could not be claimed.

In the Vedas. From the Vedas we learn that the pivot of the whole administrative system was the King. He was supreme head of the state. He had his Council of Ministers who aided and advised him on all state matters. While running his administration the King ensured that the people were morally uplifted. Since King was a highly respected therefore, his subjects willingly accepted his commands. The authority of the King was not challenged either by his subjects or by his Ministers. It appears that in those days two important institutions which helped in the development and framework of administrative activities, were Sabha and Simiti.

Administrative Thought in Mahabharta. Mahabharta gives considerably good idea about administrative system of ancient India. According to Altekar, it is an important source of science of polity. In those days polity and administration were inseparable. Shanti Parva of Mahabharta throws flood light about administrative thoughts and systems of those days. It discusses several theories about the origin of the state and duties of the King and his Ministers, who were responsible for running state administration. It appears that in those days whereas control of the King over state administration was increasing that of his Council of Ministers was weakening. There was regular set of officers to collect taxes which were levied by the King from time to time.

Administrative Thought in Kautilya's Arthasastra. Kautilya's Arthasastra is the most important treatise about administrative thought of ancient India. In fact, today it has become possession of the world. It is based on the practical experience of the author. It also touches every aspect of administration and deals with duties and responsibilities of the King towards his subjects on the one hand and those of the subjects towards the King on the other. It has also dealt at length the duties of all officers of the state, the kind of taxes which the state should levy and what should be administrative relationship of the King with his Ministers, Kautilya has also dealt with the administration of army, Central and State governments and also with the administration of local self-government institutions. Arthasastra has been called as a treatise on state administration. It aims at describing administrative machinery of a normal state and has gone into its deep details. It even deals with the methods of war and treatment to be meted out to war captives and role of administrators in suppressing internal revolts. It also discusses how state administration should run economic administration so that there is no unwanted price fluctuation.

Administrative Thought in Smritis. Smritis, particularly Manu Smriti, gives sufficiently good ideas about administrative system being followed after Kautilya. From these it also appears that though the King was still the head of the state, yet even now his foremost duty was to look after the welfare of the people. A tyrant ruler could even be killed. The people, under certain circumstances, could stop payment of taxes to him. He was supposed to be virtuous and kind hearted. He was to ensure that the whole administration ran smoothly and that the interests of the common man were fully protected.

Administrative Thought From Some Other Sources. Sufficient information about administrative thought in ancient India becomes available from some other sources as well. From Karnandakiya's Nitisastra written in 500 A.D. It is learnt that in administrative set up of the country, the King was still very popular and powerful. In fact, by now he had become real head of state and administration. Monarchy had come in the fore front. From Sukranitisar it appears that sufficient attention was paid to proper working of administration. Detailed description has been given about administrative set up of the state and duties and responsibilities of all high state officials. References have been made about administrative set up of the state. It also appears that whereas monarchy had strengthened itself, republics were practically disappearing from the scene.

Mannsollesa provides sufficient information about qualifications and duties of the King and his Ministers in so far as smooth running of state administration is concerned. It also gives information about military arrangements of a normal state both under normal and emergency circumstances. About administrative thoughts of ancient India sufficient information becomes available to us from Mudaraksha, Puranas and such other treatises as Raja Niti Ratnakara and Nibandhkaras. Foreign travellers like Fahien and Magesthenese also throw much light about the administrative system and rulers of the days when they were in India.

On the whole in ancient India it was administratively thought that an administrator should be at the service of the people. The King should see that his subjects were satisfied with the type of administration which they were getting. An administrator should not only be loyal to the King but he should be honest and kind hearted. Taxes should be collected by the administrator at a time convenient to the tax payer.

ADMINISTRATIVE THOUGHT IN THE WEST

Socrates believed that administration was an art which could be practised by few alone. For him to govern was the privilege of the few and they alone should administer while the others should engage themselves in the defence of the state. According to Maxey, Socrates believed that, "only those possessing the deepest wisdom and the highest virtue should be entrusted with the administration of government". He did not favour administration based on the system of equality of votes. He said that the politicians could differ in theories of politics but not in running state administration. Administrative powers should be in the hands of few wise persons. He believed that it was foremost duty of the citizens to obey the laws and their breach was a punishable offence.

Plato and Administrative Thought. Plato was a Greek Political thinker. He also believed that only few could be good administrators and possess the right and capability to govern. He developed the idea of philosopher King, who according to his view was most suited to administer the state. He alone had wisdom, ability and power of understanding. He stood for a separate ruling class, on which rested the responsibility of ruling and administrating the nation. For him the best administered state was one which was governed by a philosopher King. A good administrator should try to make all efforts to build character of both men and women. He favoured system of functional specialisation and laid particular stress on administration of justice.

He also believed that the individuals should have no say in the running of administration. He favours sacrificing individual at the altar of the state. The individual should not claim any rights against the state. He stood for the inequality of human beings on the one hand and one man rule on the other. In administrative matters he had faith in intellectual aristocracy. He strongly opposed organised expression against the authority of the state. He laid more stress on the performance of duties rather than on demanding of rights by the citizens.

Aristotle and Administrative Thought. Like Plato, his able disciple Aristotle also paid attention to administration. He also believed that all could not be competent administrators and possess the art of ruling. Only few noble citizens possess this art. Accordingly he did not believe that democracy was an ideal form of government. Administrator and individual could not be opposed to each other and that the former could not keep away ethical values in acual administration. Aristotle laid too much stress on observance of laws and pleaded that every administrator must obey the laws. He favoured common use of property so that no administrator was attracted by the desire of owning private property. To ensure that an administrator had sufficient time to administer, he favoured the institution of slavery and pleaded that only leisured class people should become administrators. He was firm believer of supremacy of law and that the law was even above the administrator. He was also in favour of a separate class of administrators and that of the theory of checks and balances.

Confucius on Administrative Thought. During 5th century B.C. Confucius laid stress on ethics and believed that administrators should strictly follow and enforce ethical values and uphold these. He stood for benevolent rule. In his opinion an administrator in the first instance should know his country well. He should try to identify his country's troubles and make efforts to remove these at the earliest. He should be very prompt in taking decisions and should not delay these. While doing so he should see that he is not at all harsh but moderate. His decisions should such which can be put into practice.

In delivering his judgement he should avoid both favouritism and nepotism. He should not become a party to the dispute. In other words he should avoid partisanship attitude and always keep public interest in mind. An administrator should see that he is honest and not selfish. He should be both a competent and qualified person and should go on improving his qualities of head and heart. He should also keep himself busy in the conduct of state affairs.

Administrative Thought Under the Romans. So far it was believed by all that the individual should completely merge himself in the state and as such the authority of the administrators should not be challenged. Thus individual and state were not separate from each other. According to Maxey, "The Romans separated state and individuals, each having rights and duties." They believed that protection of the rights of the individuals was the main purpose of the administrator. They loved laws and as such believed that no administrator was above laws. They believed that the people were ultimately the sovereign and administrators were responsible to them. They also believed in the concept of secularisation of law, which was quite separate from ethics and religion. The state was viewed by them as legal person and as such an administrator was not vested with absolute powers. But on the whole administrative system was part of any other system.

During Middle Ages. During Middle Ages each ruler wanted to territorially expand and also had keen desire to amass wealth. He also wanted to have efficient tax collection system. He therefore, wanted to have a team of both faithful and efficient administrators. Thus the rulers gradually began to feel the need and necessity of efficient administrative system. This need still more increased when the kings began to establish small industries and encouraged iron and coal mining to earn more wealth. But both need and desire for efficient administrators was badly felt when the system of colonialism and imperialism started. Need was then felt of efficient and honest public administrators who could be sent to colonies for administering the people and protecting the interests of mother country.

Parliamentary System and Administrative Thought. Before the beginning of Parliamentary system of government and introduction of parliamentary institutions there was no specialisation of functions. With the start of the system however, stress began to be laid on functional specialisation. Hitherto existing system of combination of administration with adjudication began to be replaced by the separation of two systems in government departments, thus giving a free hand to administrators. Political party system also began to emerge and political leaders began to associate themselves in administrative matters.

Rise of Economic Class. During 18th century all over world trade became brisk and a powerful trading community began to appear in every society. This community hitherto had no role in administrative matters. On the other hand, it closely followed the toes of administrators and ensured that they were not annoyed. This community began to organise itself by creating business corporations, which had commercial activities not only in its own country abroad. In many states this community became economically so powerful that it began to challenge the very authority of the King. It manipulated to send its supporters to Parliaments which enacted such laws which protected their interests and ensured that these were administered to their advantage.

After Industrial Revolution power of economically strong persons very much increased. The industrialists became pivot of power and effective employers. There wealth and power increased beyond any proportions. But with the emergence of this new class basic changes came in socio-economic structures of societies.

18th Century Developments. In the field of administration some important developments took place during 18th century. During this period Hamilton contributed a paper in 'Federalist' compiled in the U.S.A in which he defined the meaning and scope of Public Administration. In 1812 in France Charles Jean Bounin brought out a publication entitled "Principles Administration Publique". It was after Industrial Revolution that theoretical and academic discussions about public administration began to take place. These took place mostly in the U.S.A., where because of spoil system public administrators had become corrupt and inefficient. By the second half of 19th century in that country business had become a national activity and in effect had become a rival government. Government in that country began to show concern for the economy and the policy of laissez faire which was hitherto being followed, began to be reversed. But no effective checks could be introduced and as the power of the business increased with that their share in the governing process of the nation also began to increase. Not only in the U.S.A. but in many European states by the end of 19th century differentiation of functions became clear and independent civil service for public administration emerged. This was corrupt and inefficient system which draw the attention of Woodrow Wilson, who wrote his famous paper on the 'Study of Administration' in *Political Science Quarterly*. He has been called as founding father of Public Administration. It was this paper which laid foundations for systematic study of the subject. He made the subject as a separate subject of study. He brought together history, philosophy and concept of good society and also laid stress on the need of study and research of the subject on a continuous basis.

He wanted that the present status of the subject should be raised and its scientfic aspect brought to the fore. He stressed that its relation with politics should be studied on the one hand and the way how the administration actually functions on the other. In the study of Public Administration he laid stress on comparative method. Credit goes to him for providing an ideological base for administrative reforms in the U.S.A. during 19th century.

In 1926 in the U.S.A. Leonard White wrote his 'Introduction to the Study of Public Administration'. A year later in 1927 Willoughby wrote 'Principles of Public Administration.' Both occupy, even today, an important position in the study of the subject. These deal with common techniques of administration rather than a particular subject related to administrative study. They made an effort that Political Science and Public Administration should be separated from each other.

Thus administrative thought has been evolving and gradually creating interest of the scholars, politicians, economists, research scholars and common man in the subject. As already said with the political philosophy of Karl Marx becoming popular all over the world on the one hand and concepts of welfare state and popular sovereign on the other, public administrators were compelled to think in terms of public welfare. The gap which was existing between the administered and administrator began to narrow down and new trends in administration began to get roots.

SCIENTIFIC ADMINISTRATION

Administrative activity in social life has been in existence from time immemorials. In the words of A.E. Gorwala: "In a democracy there can be no successful planning without a clear, efficient and impartial administration". According to Nigro, 'Administration is the organisation and use of men and material to accomplish a purpose'. Another eminent scholar L.D. White in his 'Introduction to the Study of Public Administration' has said that administration is 'The art of administration of the direction, coordination and control of many persons to achieve some purpose or objective'. Administration to him thus is characteristic of all human enterprises to achieve a purpose or object in view. In the words of Simon: "In its broadest sense, administration can be defined as the activities of groups, cooperating to accomplish common goals. Managerial view of administration is doing of work or getting the work done by others. An administrator is consequently one who directs, coordinates and controls the activities of others." Administrative management is the process of directing and facilitating the work of the people organised in formal groups to achieve a desired end.

Now a question arises whether administration can or cannot be scientifically studied. In other words whether administration is science or art. Science has certain characterstics or features which can be uniformally applied. Science means exactness, precision and predictability. The laws of science can be objectively verified and have certain principles which operate almost in a sequence. Methods applied in its study are observation, investigation and experimentation. Scientific study needs developing some hypothesis, its verification by facts, correlation of facts with the help of data and some generalisation of facts after rigorous investigations and verifications.

Is Administration a Science? After having defined as to what is Science, a question that arises is whether administration is science or not. The laws of administration cannot be exact because these deal with human beings who are more complex to be dealt with than the objects of natural sciences. With the help of these imperfect laws no exact predictions can be made. Thus the laws of administration cannot be as perfect as those of the laws of natural sciences. In the laws of administration there cannot be exactness, precision and predictability.

But inspite of these difficulties efforts are being made to develop in administration principles which to a large exact possess universal validity and applicability. These are based on practical experience of administrators. Many administrators on many occasions on many issues think in similar terms e.g. delegation of authority, span of control, role of bureaucracy in administration, formal and informal organisation etc.

It is also said that administration is science because scientific method of study is applicable to it and facts of administration can be scientifically studied. In administrative studies it is possible to develop hypothesis and collect facts for its verification and refutation. The facts can also be observed, analysed and coordinated.

But values which are so closely involved in administrative facts cannot be scientifically studied and as such scientific methods of study are inapplicable to the study of administrative phenomenon. According to Robert A Dahl, as long as the study of administration is not comparative claims for a science of administration should rather hollow, Generalisation derived from the operation of administration in the environment of one nation still cannot be universalised and applied to administration in a different environment. L.Urwick has said that the principles of administration are approximate or probable anticipations.

Politics-Administration Dichotomy

For quite some time scholars believed that both have separate scope of study. According to Woodrow Wilson, 'Administration is outside the proper sphere of politics. Administrative questions are not political questions. Although politics sets the task for administration, it should not be allowed to manipulate its offices'. Similarly Blunchelli has said that, "Politics is state activity in things great and universal while administration is activity of state in individual and small things. Politics is thus a special province of statesman, administration of the technical official." In the early stages it was said that the areas or activities of both should be kept separate.

The Distinction Between the Two. There are scholars who have made a distinction between the two subjects i.e., politics and administration. They make a distinction between policy making and policy implementation. The first is the function of legislatures whereas the second is that of technical experts and civil servants. Whereas administration means how to do things, politics decides what is to be done. Politics is based on election process whereas the composition of administrative system is based on appointments made on the basis of technical knowledge.

Similarly whereas politics is concerned with policy decisions, administration has concern with matters relating to policy implementation. A politician is usually a non-technical person whereas an administrator is essentially a technical person. Then whereas a politician has no fixed tenure in office, an administrator has fixed tenure and once selected for a job, he continues on that till he reaches retirement age. A politician is very much affected and influenced by public opinion whereas an administrator is influenced in his decision-making process by datas, facts and figures.

A politician ensures that all departments work in close cooperation with each other, administrators do the actual work. They implement policies and programmes and thus infuse blood in the skeleton frame-work developed by politicians. A politician remains in close contact with the public, whereas there is no direct contact between an administrator and public at large. The politicians always have partisan attitude and always think in terms of party interests and party policies and programmes.

Whereas politics is concerned with values, administration is concerned with procedures and technicalities. Whereas administration is considered to be field of activity of public servants but that of politics is quite wide and comprehensive. Politicians ensure that promises made at the time of election and given in the manifestoes are kept and implemented at the earliest. The administrator see that the decisions taken by them are being properly implemented. Politics is concerned with principles of state and its theories like origin and growth of the state, forms of government, composition of legislature, methods of formulation of public opinion etc. On the other hand origin of administration lies in the implementation of policies impartially.

Criticism. Politics administration dichotomy has now come under much criticism. It is said that these days administration is very much involved in policy making process. No policy can be formulated without the assistance of administrators. Every Minister directly or indirectly is influenced by the views of senior administrators working under him. Administrators are behind the introduction of many Bills which are introduced by the Ministers in the legislature. Details of all laws which are passed by the legislatures are filled by the administrators.

Not only this but no successful policy can be formulated without proper knowledge of facts and figures which are to be supplied by administrators to politicians who are forced to amend or withdraw certain Bills after the administrators have come out with their difficulties. A policy which is divorced from official experience is very likely to have serious adverse consequences in the long run.

Present Concept. Today it is believed that politics and administration are very closely linked with each other. In 1948 Waldo in his work 'Administrative State' badly criticised the concept of dichotomy. Paul Appleby in his book entitled 'Policy and Administration' has said that every governmental activity has close link with administration. Policy is not formulated at the highest level only but in it administrators at all levels are bound to get involved. Since policies formulated by politicians are to be implemented by administrators, therefore, politics and administration cannot be separated from each other.

Success or failure of laws enacted by the politicians depends on the way in which these are implemented by the administrators. In our own times even politicians are more and more involving civil servants in policy formulation processes. Not only this but these days Ministers, who are political executive heads of the department, are very busy persons. Most of their time is spent in political activities and party politics and as such they do not find much time to think about administrative matters. Not only this but legislators also do not take much interest in legislative activities. Politicians are increasingly depending on administrators in legislative sphere. They prepare outlines of the Bills and ensure that the legislature enacts on the lines suggested by them.

Relationship between administration and politics becomes very close at the local self-government level. A head of village panchayat represents both the wishes of the people and he also functions as an administrator. Similarly whereas administrators help in policy formulation they are also responsible for policy implementation and execution. L. Gullick has rather rightly said that politics cannot be separated from administration and in the same way administration cannot be separated from politics. Both must go hand in hand.

❒

2

Kautilya

The science of Public Administration mainly studies three problems: the principles of Public Administration, the machinery of government and the personnel. The principles of Public Administration are not explicitly dealt with in Arthasastra. They are implied in the portions which elaborate the qualities of the King, of the ministers and various cadres of officers, the relations of the King with the highest executive and the lower rungs of government servants. Out of the fifteen books in which Arthasastra is divided, the books relevant to the study of the pattern of public administration as such are four; the first, the second, the fifth and the sixth. Half of Arthasastra is devoted to the tacties of foreign policy and defence which is no way concern the pattern of Public Administration. The second book entitled 'The Duties of Government Superintendents' depicts almost all the departments. But a consideration of the machinery of government would be incomplete if the portions in the first book regarding the relations of the King with the ministers, spies, envoys, and princes are not taken into account. The problem of personnel is attended to in Arthasastra, but here the higher personnels has engaged more attention than the lower personnel. The qualities of the higher personnel including the superintendents of various departments are satisfactorily dealt with. The position of the King vis-a-vis the ministers is also gone into in detail. The lower personnel is almost neglected. No reference, except a slight one in Chapter III of Book V, is made to the methods and ways of recruitment, training, grades of salaries including stages and quanta of promotions for each category of the personnel, transfer, and superannuation of the lower personnel. These matters (except recruitment) are neglected also in the case of the higher personnel. The focus of attention is the King. Every member of the personnel is considered not in isolation but as far as his behaviour affects the King and his domain. The qualitative aspect of the personnel is treated in minutest detail.

The most interesting and the most instructive part of Arthasastra from the point of view of the present-day student of public administration is that he gets a glimpse into the display of the sharp acumen of Kautilya. The principles of public administration implied in Arthasastra do not command as much attention as the machinery of government does. Firstly, they are indirectly stated. And secondly—and this is the proper reason—the principles governing the democratic public administration are in many respects different from the principles underlying a monarchical public administration as described in Arthasastra, as the source and the configuration of authority in the two systems are different. The qualitative aspect of the personnel so stressed in Arthasastra loses the accent of emphasis on account of the change in the source and the configuration of authority.

Kautilya does not give a definition of the science of Public Administration as such. In fact, the term 'the science of Public Administration' has recently arisen. As shown by the scholars on the Ancient Society and Polity in different parts of the world, the executive, that is the administrative branch of the government evolved earlier than the judicial branch and the legislative branch. The science of polity, which according to Kautilya is Arthasastra, mainly treats Public Administration. We understand Arthasastra as the equivalent of Economics. But the science of polity, according to Kautilya, is the combination of the science of wealth and the science of government. The contents of Arthasastra substantiate this definition. The finance department and the other departments dealing with business and various economic activities from a vital part of the machinery of government. The contents of the second book of Arthasastra would illustrate this. Moreover, finances are the nerves of the government. Financial considerations govern, control and guides all the activities of the government. And hence the importance of the science of Wealth, one of the two constituents of Arthasastra. "It is by means of the treasury and the army obtained solely through Varta," says Kautilya, "that the king can hold under his control both his and his enemy's party." In more than one place Kautilya refers to the finances as a very important factor influencing the activities and the status of the government. Kautilya rightly subsumes the science of Public Administration under the science of government. "That sceptre on which the well-being and progress of the sciences of Anvikshiki, the triple Vedas, and Varta depend is known as *Danda* (punishment). That which treats of *Danda* is the law of punishment or science of government (*dandaniti*). It is a means to make acquisitions, to keep them secure, to improve them and to distribute among the deserved the profits of improvement." "It is on the science of Government," maintains Kautilya, "that the course of the progress of the world depends." The science of Public Administration is also connected with the triple Vedas and Anvikshiki according to Arthasastra. The triple Vedas enjoin certain duties to be observed by belonging to the different stages of life. And according to Arthasastra the King should never allow people to swerve from their duties. Anvikshiki is the light to all kinds of knowledge including the science of Public Administration. The outline in Arthasastra of the relationship between the science of Public Administration and the sciences of Economics and of government is correct even today. But the relationship of the science of Public Administration with the triple Vedas as described in Arthasastra is not applicable today on account of the predominance of secular authority over religious authority today. The relationship of Anvikshiki with the science of Public Administration as with other sciences is taken for granted. The relationship which, according to Arthasastra, the science of Public Administration, holds with History is rather confusing. The science of Public Administration like the science of government is 'the fruit of History', but it is also analytical. Arthasastra along with Purana, Itivritta (history), Akhayayika (tales), Udaharana (illustrative stories), Dharmashastra, is included in Itihasa. The repetition of Itivritta and Itihasa causes confusion.

Arthasastra unmistakably emphasises every now and then the close connection between the art of Public Administration and the science of Public Administration. Arthasastra brings out that an administrator must possess the knowledge of the science of Public Administration. According to Kautilya, an administrator can be adept in the art of Public Administration only if he is conversant with the science of Public Administration. The proficiency in the science of Public Administration is enjoined on almost all the important dignitaries in the government such as the King, the crown-prince, the priest, the ministers etc. The high priest, according to Kautilya, should be well versed in the science of government. About the ministers it is told by Kautilya that whoever is not well versed in science should be unfit to hear of council deliberations. And regarding the King he insists that an erring King who is bent upon doing that in against the science, brings about destruction to himself and his kingdom by maladministration. Kautilya also unravels the connections between the art and the science of Public Administration in the opposite direction. Just as the proficiency in the art of Public Administration depends on the knowledge of the science of Public Administration, so also those alone who are adept in the art of Public Administration on account of their close association with it are able to possess and impart a sound knowledge of the science of Public Administration. Thus Kautilya exhorts a prince to study the science of Varta (i.e. Economics) under government superintendents and the science of *dandaniti* under theoretical and practical politicians. For the same purpose again he advises that when a prince is possessed of good and amiable qualities, he might be made the commander-in-chief or installed as heir apparent. The crown prince is bestowed by some scholars with the membership of the inner cabinet of the King. With regard to the art of Public Administration two things are worth being noted. Kautilya does not say anything about the proficiency in the art of Public Administration in the case of lower personnel below superintendents of departments.

The principles of public administration regulate the working of the machinery of public administration. These principles can be conveniently grouped in two sets: (*i*) the principles of authority, obedience and discipline, of duty and interest, and of responsibility; (*ii*) the principles of division of labour, of coordination, of separation, of speciality, of hierarchy, and of equity. The first set of principles embodies of essential attribute of the State, namely sovereignty. The second set of principles governs the actual method of work of the administration. Both these sets of principles are found in Arthasastra. The former set is more explicitly stated than the latter.

The principle of authority and of obedience and discipline sum up the essence of the State according to the legalistic theory of the State. The importance of these twin principles is expressed very graphically in Arthasastra. The passage runs as follows. "But when the law of punishment is kept in abeyance, it gives rise to such disorder as is implied in the proverb of fishes; for in the absence of magistrate, the strong will swallow the weak; but under his protection the weak resist the strong. Thus people consisting of four castes and four orders of religious life, when governed by the king with his sceptre, will keep to their respective paths, ever devotedly adhering to their respective duties and occupations." From another passage preceding the above one, it also would be clear that Arthasastra does not believe in the efficacy of the principles of authority and of obedience and discipline alone. Kautilya mellows these principles by laying stress on the principles of duty and interest and of responsibility. He abhors both severe and mild punishments. "But whoever imposes punishment as deserved becomes respectable. For punishment, when awarded with due consideration, makes the people devoted to righteousness and to works productive of wealth and enjoyment, while punishments, when ill-awarded under the influence of greed and anger or owing to ignorance," avers Kautilya, "excites fury even among hermits and ascetics dwelling in forests, not to speak of householders."

The first concern of the King is his own personal safety, because on that depends the exercise of authority and the obedience of that authority on the part of the people. "Just as he attends to the personal safety of others through the agency of spies", states Kautilya, "so a wise King shall also take care to secure his person from external dangers." And hence the wide prevalence of the system of espionage, not merely for the purpose of security of the King's person, but also for the purpose of maintaining security, integrity and stability of administration against the dangers of internal dissension and corruption and external aggression. That the unity, stability, and independence of command are ensured in the kingdom is evident from many precautions prescribed in Arthasastra. The unity of command and direction is maintained because of the King's authority. All the members of bureaucracy derive their authority from the King, stand before the people as representative of royal authority, and are ultimately responsible to the King. This is evident from the reference in

Arthasastra to the enforcement, of orders, the sending of writs and the procedure of forming royal writes. As for the stability of command, Kautilya writes: "A royal father who is the only prop for many shall be favourably disposed towards his son. Except in dangers sovereignty may be the property of a clan; for the corporation of clans is invincible in its nature, and being free from the calamities of anarchy, can have a permanent existence on earth." On the King's demise, Kautilya does not favour usurpation of royal power by the ministers, so much importance he attaches to the stability of royal command. The sub-principle of independence of command is illustrated in Arthasastra with reference to the business of council meeting. In deliberating with two ministers Kautilya is afraid that the King might be overpowered by their combined action. Fear, duty and interest; these three among a number of motives behind the act of obedience of the orders of administration can be traced to Arthasastra. To emphasise the motive of duty Kautilya refers to the injunctions of the triple Vedas, which is observed by the world, world bring about progress. Kautilya brings out how, for carrying out orders or administration, cooperation of the people as well as of the bureaucracy is required. He points out many ways to make people and bureaucracy interested in carrying out orders of administration. The purpose of *danda*, the symbol of authority, is to make the people devoted to righteousness and to works productive of wealth and enjoyments. This, the government of Kautilya's conception tries to achieve, by giving positive financial help to the needy and the distressed, so also by ensuring just treatment to the people in financial, economic, judicial, and other administrative matters by actively participating in or regulating activities in economic and other spheres. Government servants are to be enthused, according to Kautilya, to actively help the administration in carrying out orders by granting them promotion in salary, pension, financial and other kinds of help when needed, agricultural lands, and also by making them permanent in service. Authority is obeyed by the people on account of sanctions behind orders, position of the officer concerned who issues authority, and qualities possessed by the officer concerned. Qualities of the personnel are stressed in a number of places by Kautilya. He lays down a series of qualities, differing in number and order, for officers holding different positions of responsibility, Kautilya mentions the principle of responsibility not only in the case of the King but also of the government officers.

The full import of this group of principles is not clear in Arthasastra in so far as some of the links between the different parts of government machinery are not joined. This is illustrated in a subsequent paragraph dealing with the machinery of government in Arthasastra. The principle of division of labour is basic for the proper and efficient working of the machinery of government. This is clearly brought out in Arthasastra at the outset of the elaboration of the scheme of government. "Sovereignty is possible only with assistance. A single wheel can never move. Hence," tells Kautilya, "he shall employ ministers, and hear their opinion." The principle of coordination automatically evolves out of the principle of division of labour. Unless coordination is effected between the parts divided for the sake of efficiency and smooth working, division of labour would be futile. The application of these twin principles starts in Arthasastra obviously at the level of the council of ministers. Discussing the appropriate number of ministers is expounds the principle of coordination thus: "With minister more than four in number, he will have to come to a decision after a good deal of trouble; nor will secrecy of counsel be maintained without much trouble. In accordance with the requirements of place, time and nature of the work in view, he may as he deems it proper, deliberate with one or two ministers or by himself." The principles of division of labour and coordination are effected at several levels of the hierarchy of government. The principle of hierarchy is followed to make coordination and execution possible.

According to Arthasastra the more responsible the office is, the more numerous and the higher are the qualities required of the officer. According to remuneration there are more than seven rungs of officers one below another, the highest officer, drawing 4800 panas per annum, and the lowest, below 1000 panas per annum. Arthasastra is not clear about inter-relationships between different officers. The principle of equity also suffers from clarity on the same score. That Kautilya does pay attention to the department of finance from that of treasury and of the department of accounts from other departments, is treated in the following section.

To us, the most important and instructive part of Arthasastra is the portion or the machinery of government. This portion reveals a perfect mastery of details of administration on the part of the author, which could have developed only as a result of actual experience of administration. Not that the machinery of administration designed in Arthasastra closely resembles the present-day machinery of government. The machinery of government, like other institutions, grows out of conditions peculiar to the time to which the government belongs. It of course bears the imprint of human ingenuity, such as that exemplified in Arthasastra.

The first characteristic of the machinery of government in Arthasastra worth noting is that we do not come across well-defined departments of administration as such. The division of the functions of government in different departments is a comparatively recent process. Officers there are in Arthasastra; some of them are directly under the King, while others are controlled by the King indirectly through biggest officers. The King is the supreme executive of the land. The ministers are selected, not elected, by the King on the basis of their qualities. The so-called minister, in reality the highest officers directly under the King, are individually and collectively responsible to the King. The ministerial officer pertaining to a subject deals with the administration of the subject, and as such is more competent than other ministerial officers, to contribute to the deliberation on his subject in the council of ministers. But Kautilya says, "These ministers shall have to consider all that concerns the parties of both the King and his enemy. The Prime Minister and the High Priest are the most important ministers. With one or two additions they might form an inner cabinet. It is they who assist the King to examine the character of ministers appointed in government departments of ordinary nature. The qualities of the High Priest are described thus: "Him whose family and character are highly spoken of, who is well educated in the Vedas and the six Angas, is skilful in reading portents, providential or accidental, is well versed in the science of government, and who is obedient and who can prevent calamities, providential or human, by performing such expiatory rites as are prescribed in the Arthasastra, the King shall employ as high priest. As a student his teacher, a son his father, and a servant his master, the King shall follow him."

Among the important ministers in Arthasastra might be counted the sacrificial priest, the teacher, the prime minister, the high priest, the commander of the Army, Chamberlain or Treasurer-General, and the Collector-General. Arthasastra catalogues a phalanx of officers, called superintendents, lower in importance than the ministerial officer and much below them, belonging to the sixth order, according to remuneration. They are not heads of departments again. The superintendents might be regarded as chiefs of sections dealing with various economic and other activities of the government. Most of these sections are the modern business departments. A dual control is exercised over the superintendents. As far as control of the service of the personnel and collection of revenue are concerned, they are under the Collector-General. But in the matter of supply of produced and collected commodities and articles, they are responsible to the Treasurer-General. And there is the third control, that of the King, to which all officers are ultimately subject. The superintendents are helped by 'experts' in technical matters in which different sections deal.

Kautilya to Administrative Thought

Kautilya was a practical thinker and a far sighted person. It was because of his wisdom that an empire was not only created but was very ably administered. His real contribution to administrative thought and system is his originality in approach to every problem. In many ways Arthasastra can claim originality. He has not tried to follow rigidity of caste system in many matters which was then the order of the day. It was for the first time the Katuilya stressed on merit and not on the caste for making appointments to public services. His ideas that merit alone should be the basis for recruitment have now been accepted by all advanced states of the world. He went to the extent of suggesting that there should be a Sudra army because their numerical strength justified the creation of such army and that will keep the so called Sudras satisfied and loyal to the state.

Then comes his originality in the organisation of state craftship. As said earlier he suggested the creation of different departments and discussed with minute detail the function of each. For the first time he drew the attention of the state to possible chances of problems which each department was likely to face. Then credit goes to him for discussing in minute details and with sufficient far-sightedness, the duties of a King towards his subjects and also towards neighbouring state, which if followed by the rulers of today can remove many causes of dissatisfaction of their peoples. Then his another contribution is the way in which he dealt with interstate relations including those of war and peace. It bears ample testimony to the originality of his ideas and maturity of his thinking. He has not only discussed such ticklish issues as position of army, marching of armies, positions which the moving armies should take on the battle field but also dresses and equipments of soldiers and fortification of forts.

Then comes his views about organisation of spy system. In fact, for the first time he has made the whole system an integral part of state-craftship and has tried to ensure that spies were watched by the spies. By his shrewdness he successfully created such an atmosphere that every spy considered every other citizen as a spy and thus could not afford to relax. Needless to say that only a master-mind of his calibre could afford to manage the whole system both tactfully and successfully. If his ideas about liberty of citizen and authority of state are taken into consideration, then these also convince one about originality in his thinking. His predecessors had virtually failed to give any satisfactory solution of the problem and swing to the extremes and it appeared as if there was no link between the two. But Kautilya proposed a healthy combination and suggested that the individuals should enjoy liberty as long as they were patriots. For him the King had a right to claim subordination of his subjects only so long as he promoted Dharma or righteousness and did not try to go beyond legal established limits of law. Thus there was no antithesis between the individual and state. In fact his ideas are very much relevant for modern thinkers who are grappling with the problem of state vs. citizen for which many theories have been expounded.

Then it was for the first time that he placed Hindus polity on Scientific footings and made that really practical. He broadened the scope of state activity and placed that on a very sound footing. Coverage of his subject was wide. It included army, individual, finances, peace, war and even settlement of disputes between a husband and his wife. They find in it an answer to many of their questions and doubts. He studied problems analytically and in that age to the extent possible he separated politics from religion. He made a politics a pure science by giving in a distinct character distinct from religion.

Hindu political thinkers earlier to him also discussed and tried to tackle the subject of *dandaniti* but Kautilya made that more comprehensive. By prescribing punishment for every likely offence he left very little scope for the executive officers and also the judges to use their discreation. For the time, there was a realisation that power could be misused without effective checks and that there was need to prescribe necessary checks. His idea was that no one should transgress limits put on his authority.

His Saptanga theory, is his another original contribution. For the first time he vividly discusssed the problem of elements of state. Last but not least his contribution lies in his secular outlook. He was living in an age in which there was blending of religion with politics. The Brahmins were the favourite sons of the state and also economically least burdened. They enjoyed comparatively many more privileges than those enjoyed even by the taxpayers who were non-Brahmins Kautilya, followed the policy of least exemption and placed all on almost equal footing in so for as payment of taxes was concerned. He tried to end the influence of priestly class and developed a secular outlook. It is this approach which is being vigorously followed in India and the country takes pride in being a secular state.

Administrative Organisation by Kautilya

Kautilya favours division of labour in administration. He has said that the King should carefully listen to the view point of his Ministers. At the same time he has laid stress on the need of coordination in administration. According to him unless there is coordination between different divided parts, the purpose of division of labour will not be achieved. He has applied this twin principle of division of labour and coordination very appropriately in the case of relationship of King with his Council of Ministers.

In order to make the concept of coordination effective he has developed the principle of hierarchy. According to him authority would be fritted away if that is not channelised through hierarchical organisation and remains centralised. Arthasastra on the basis of remunerations makes us believe that there are seven levels of officers one below the other. Much is however, not known about inter-relationship of officers.

Arthasastra's views about government machinery have much resemblance with present day system of administration.

Characteristics of Machinery of Government

One of the characteristics of administration, as depicted in Arthasastra is that in it departments as such have not been mentioned. But all officers of the state are directly or indirectly under the control of the King. He is supreme executive head of the state and Ministers are selected by him on the basis of their qualifications. They are individually and collectively responsible to him.

Then another characteristics of government machinery is that the division of departments is made according to services required by the people and discharged by the government. Different functions of government seem of have been arranged horizontally. Under the Collector General are the Commissioner, the District Officer and the Circle Officer etc. It is not clear whether district officer and circle officer were officers who mainly represented local government or had several other functions to perform.

Then another characteristic of government machinery, as indicated in Arthasastra, is that in it more attention has been paid to the higher personnel and to the lower personnel. It was so primarily because the higher personnel are vested with more authority and responsibility than the lower personnel.

Then another feature is that in Arthasastra there are no definite rules out promotion though it is suggested that those government servants who increase revenue and serve loyally should be made permanent. The salaries of the employees should be increased according to their learning and work. In the Arthasastra transfer of personnel is suggested as a precaution and a remedy against misappropriation of government money. Every government servant is subject to punishment, if he is found to be corrupt. There is also no provision for leave for a government servant.

Arthasastra does not metion anything about the age of supernuation. It however, appears that some pensions were given to the wives of those servants who died in harness and also to the infant, aged and diseased persons related to deceased servants. Kautilya however, does not mention about payment of pension of those public servants who retire otherwise.

Then anothers feature is that in Arthasastra stress is laid on duties rather than or rights. In fact no rights as such have been given to the people. He has however, prepared a Code of Conduct for public servants. For breach of law even in private life conduct a public servant could also be tried by the courts of law. The members of administration had no right as such against the executive which could treat them in the way it liked.

Some thinkers have tried to establish that Kautilya's system of administration was authoritarian and corrupt, but this does not appear to be a correct charge. No doubt he has suggested harsh punishments for the criminals but for that he was helpless. He was living in an age and working under circumstances in which need of the hour was to check crimes with rough hands. The demand of the time was to maintain law and order at all costs. Without that hard task of unity of the country would not have been completed. On the other hand credit goes to him for checking authoritarian rule of the King, when he suggested his King to always consult his Ministers before taking any final decision. In order to check corruption at every level he developed a network of spies, who informed the King about corrupt practices of his officers. He clearly said that a corrupt administrator should be very severely punished.

Kautilya and Sources of Law

As we know in ancient India there was no legislative body or organisation of the modern type for enacting law necessary for administering justice. Whatsoever had been socially accepted and had come to stay and was good as law and all were obliged to accept and respect such types of laws. Function of state institutions and organisations was only to interpret these in an impersonal manner. As the society grew complex proportionately the need and necessity for giving prompt justice and codification was kneely felt. According to Kautilya there were four sources of law namely dharma, vyavahara, charitra and rajassana. According to Kautilya dharma did not mean religion of the King or of a particular community but it was reason and righteousness. A custom which promoted dharma was sound and scientific and as such dependable. From Vyavahara he meant 'evidence'. He has, therefore, separately discussed the category of persons to be accepted as witness, the circumstances under which a witness should be called and the punishment for not giving true evidence or refusing to appear before a court of law. Charitra was another important source of law. In Kautilya's philosophy Charitra meant law of community or society as a whole which had been accepted and approved as such. Accordingly such a source was every important as it represented the will of the whole community. Still another source was rajassana which meant decrees of the King issued from time to time. Since it was presumed that King was representative of the community and supposed to act in an impersonal manner, therefore, his decrees or ordinances of the modern type were another source of law on which the judges of ancient India relied.

In ancient India there was rule of law which meant that justice was to be given in accordance with the provisions of law. Social status and material position of the criminal did not influence the course of justice. It also meant that same code of law applied to all the people in the state, both high and low. In ancient India justice was to be given in accordance with the rules as embodied in the Dharmasastra. According to Kautilya whenever charitra or vyavahara and sacred law were in disagreement with each other the provisions of sacred law should be taken into consideration while pronouncing the judgement. "But whenever sacred law is in conflict with Dharmanyaya then reason shall be held authoritative for there the original text is not available." Kautilya has given so much importance to the rule of law that he has said that a King, who ruled with justice was bound to conquer the whole world. On the other hand, one who uses *danda* in vain was bound to go to hell.

Qualities of a Judge

Since justice was assigned a very important place and position in administrative set-up it was, therefore, most essential that a judge should be a person of high quality and calibre. He should also be well versed in the basic principles of law. He should be a person with the qualities of head and heart and should be capable of distinguishing as to what type of questions should or should not be asked. Similarly he should be capable enough to see as to what type of questions should be asked so as to arrive at right conclusions. A judge should be a person who can control his passions and temptations and is not very much tempted about cherishing his personal ends and motives. He should also be in a position to hold the balance evenly while pronouncing his judgement. He has also said that a judge should try to get himself acquainted and be familiar with the people and their customs and should also be adjustable enough to pronounce judgements taking all these factors into consideration. A judge should also not be greedy and as far as possible, care should be taken to see that wealth does not corrupt him. He should also be kind hearted and should not take pleasure in merely punishing the people.

Categories of Criminals

Kautilya has tried to distinguish between two types of criminals. In the first category are those who committ offences with cruelty. He has suggested that death penalty with torture should be awarded for such type of criminals. Other type of criminals are those who commit crime without any cruelty. He has suggested that death penalty without any torture should be awarded in such cases. He has also suggested that treason was as good as a crime committed with torture and as such death penalty should also be awarded for treason.

Kinds of Courts

Kautilya has broadly divided courts into two categories namely Dharamasthiya (civil) and Kantakasodhana (criminal) courts. Not only this but Kautilya has discussed in detail the types of cases to be dealt within both types of courts. N.N. Law in his 'Studies in Ancient Hindu Polity' has thus enumerated the cases to be dealt within each type of court. In his opinion a Dharmasthiya court should deal with:

(1) Employers rights and obligations and also rights, obligations and privileges of the slaves.

(2) Problems originating and connected with presents, gifts assault, defamation, robbery and illegal sale or property.

(3) Cases dealing with marriage, dowry, debts, deposits and sale and purchase of goods.

(4) Contracts in general and contracts of service.

(5) Cases connected with damage of crops, roads, right of possession of property.

(6) Cases relating to inheritance, succession and co-operative undertakings.

(7) Boundary disputes, rights of possession of houses and sites for construction.

Similarly a Kantakasodhana court was required to discuss the following types of cases:

(i) Ravishment of immature girls and suppression of the undesirables.

(ii) Cases relating to post-mortem examination and connected with mutilation.

(iii) Misuse of authority or official position including those of misappropriation of government funds.

(iv) Case in which capital punishment was likely to be awarded.

(v) Cases which are likely to be detected with the aid and assistance of spies.

(vi) All other cases not to be discussed by Dharmasthiya.

Provincial and Local Administration

Kautilya's Arthasastra also provides sufficient information about provincial, municipal and rural administration. Since Chandra Gupta Maurya's administration was run on the lines suggested by Kauitlya, therefore, much can be inferred about Kautilya's views about provincial etc. administration, as was actually in practice.

It appears that each of the four provinces was headed by a Governor who was a prince of royal blood or one who was very close to the King. Provincial administration then was replica of central administration. It was the responsibility of provincial Governor to maintain law and order in the province under his charge. He used to collect taxes on behalf of his monarch and also kept the King informed about important happenings in his province. He enjoyed considerable autonomy and had a Mantri Parishad which assisted him in his work.

Local Administration. From Kautilya's Arthasastra it appears that in administration much scope was left for local self-government institutions. Every effort was made to keep the cities neat and clean. Kot Palla was the officer incharge of the city. Administrator was called Nagaradhyksha or Purmukh. He was responsible for city administration. Each city was divided into four parts and each one was headed by a Sathanik. He was assisted by a junior officer called Gopa. Each one was responsible for looking after about 20 houses.

The Nagrika was supposed to maintain peace in the city and watch the activities of all new-comers. He was also to spy the foreigners and also to have vigilant eyes over prostitute houses. In addition, he was to have an eye over income and expenditure of the residents and help the foreigners in distress. It was also his duty to take possession of unclaimed property and to ensure that the city was safe and secure. He was to take both preventive and precautionary measures to control the spread of diseases. Then it was his responsibility to maintain saintary conditions.

The Administration of Patliputra. The administration of Patliputra was run on very scientific lines. It also appears that administration of Taxila and Ujjain was also being carried on more or less on the pattern of Patliputra. From the accounts now made available to us it is certain that there was a wide tunnel around the whole city which was always kept full of water. There was a board of 30 members divided into six committees of 5 members each to look after the administration of this capital town. One of the committees was responsible for the development and encouragement of handicrafts and other for industries. This committee also looked after the sale and purchase of raw materials and finished goods as well as tried to create market for all the goods produced. In addition to this, this committee also regulated employer employee relations working in these industries. Another Board dealt with the supervision of all goods imported into the city. It also saw that goods imported were not sub-standard and that no sub-standard article was on sale in the market.

Then there was another committee which was mainly concerned with the keeping of records of deaths and births in the cities. Thus it was primarily concerned with the census of the city. Still another committee was concerned with the collection of revenues. It saw that the people paid all taxes payable by them and none escaped the payment of royal dues. In this connection it is worth while to remember that under Chandra Gupta Maurya, avoiding payment of taxes was very seriously viewed and severe punishments were accordingly imposed on those who avoided taxes.

One of the committees dealt with assessing the requirements of goods to be imported as well as exported and accorded prior approval for import and export of commodities. It was supposed to check both scarcity as well as fluctuations in the market. Sixth committee was supposed to supervise the market and saw that no sub-standard articles were sold. It also saw that there was no under-weighing or under-measuring and that counterfeit coins were not in circulation. In other words, it saw that high market standards were maintained.

Every care was taken to see that only desirable types of people stayed in the city. Accordingly in the city each family was to inform the Gopa about the guests staying with them. Similarly medical practitioners were supposed to inform city authorities about the type of the people they were treating.

Rural or Village Administration. Population of the village varied from 100-500 families. The boundaries of village were separated by some river, jungle, hillock or by similar other method. The affairs of the village were looked after by Sangrahana. Every 200 villages had a Kharvatika, 400 had a Dharmamukha and 800 had a Mahagrama. It was ensured that each village had sufficient arrangements for storage of water. The villages enjoyed sufficient freedom. During Chandra Gupta Maurya days villages continued to enjoy maximum autonomy. Whole village administration was run and managed by the Gramik and Gopa. Whereas the former was a villager of the same village and latter was a government official. Though it is not clear whether Gramik was nominated by the government or elected by the people, yet the possibilities of election are more than that of nomination. He was held responsible for initiating all proposals for the welfare of the people. He negotigated with the central government for getting development plans approved. Similarly is case of distress and difficulty or calamities he got revenue remission.

Gopa was a state employee posted in the village. He decided bound disputes as well as many inter-village disputes. There was also a system grouping of villages in units of five. Each unit was controlled by some state official.

In the villages there were trade as well as industrial guilds which were mostly devoted to the development, production, growth or improvement of trade or industry with which they were associated. Normally, however, state kept a strict watch on their activities and prior approval of state was necessary before their formation. On the whole from Arthasastra it appears that proper attention was paid to village administration. The state usually did not interfere in village administration but those incharge of administration at this level ensured that the whole administration ran smoothly.

❐

3

Victor H. Vroom

Vroom is good writer and has brought out several publications and contributed a good number of articles in well known journals. He is professor of Industrial Management and Psychology at the Carmegie Institute of Technology. Some of his important publication include 'Work and Motivation', which came out in 1964 and 'Leadership and Decision Making' which was pubished in 1973. His research papers included:

1. Relationship Between Age and Risk Taking Among Managers.
2. Ego Involvement, Job Satisfaction and Job Performance.

According to Vroom all views so far discussed about leadership can broadly be divided in two categories namely those views which can be placed under the categories of 'Descriptive Theories'. These theories try to explain how the managers take decisions. Then are the views which can be categorised as classical or traditional views about leadership. These try to explain how a leader should take decisions. It is also known as normative thinking Vroom is mainly associated with this type of thinking.

Vroom on Decision Making. According to Vroom when a leader or any one loaded with the responsibility of decision making is required to take a decision he is mainly influenced by three factors namely the quality of decision, time and acceptance of decision. From quality of decision he means that the leadership is to find out how far and to which extent decision shall be useful or helpful in achieving the objective and solving the problem under decision. Decision quality is linked with important subjects e.g. decisions about the aims and objects of the organisation, strategic planning, solution of technical problems etc. If the problems on which decisions are required to be taken are important then decision quality also becomes important.

As regards 'time' Vroom has said that the point to be taken account is what is available with the manager for taking decisions. He also means that the decisions should be timely taken. Untimely decisions even make very good decision meaningless.

Alternative Decision Style. Vroom has said there are five alternative decision styles. These indicate the extent of involvement of subrodinates in decision making. In first situation the manager, on the basis of information available takes his own decision, without involving his subordinates. Then is another situation in which the manager obtains information from his subordinates but on the basis of that he himself takes the decision. In no way he involves his subordinates in the process. Even for collecting information it is not essential that the manager should inform his subordinates about the problem involved or purpose for which information is to be collected.

Third alternative is that manager discusses a problem with his subordinates purely on commercial basis. He does not discuss the problem even then on group basis. It is not necessary that a manager may take a decision under the influence of his discussion with his subordinate. He is fully free to take decision on his own ignoring the views expressed by the subordinates.

Then another alternative is for the manager is that he discusses the problem with his subordinates in a group and takes decisions on the basis of unanimous views expressed by it. The manager does not impose himself on the group but he helps his subordinates to take a decision. Then another alternative is the manager discusses the problem under decision with his subordinates in a group, but takes the decision ultimately by himself without involving the group. Last alternative open to the manager is that he discusses the problem with his subordinates in a group and takes decisions on the basis of unanimous views expressed by it. The manager does not impose himself on the group but he helps his subordinates to take a decision.

Vroom on Need of Participation of Subordinates. Vroom has discussed situations in which it is good if the subordinates are encouraged to participate in the decision making. He has said that subordination can prove useful when the manager has not got sufficient information available with himself to take some decision and he has to collect that from his subrodinates. In this situation participation can help in the improvement of quality of decision. He has also said that the participation can be useful when the subordinates have strong will power and desire to participate in decision making process.

Still another situation according to Vroom is when the problem to be solved is ticklish. In that case also participation by others proves useful. Then Vroom has said that participation of subordination can be useful when the issue involved is important from their view point. Similarly it can be useful when the policies about subordinate organisations are involved.

Vroom has said that participation proves useful if there is no shortage of time i.e. sufficient time is available for consultation.

JOB ENLARGEMENT AND JOB ENRICHMENT

There are several methods of motivating the employees. These are both financial and non-financial. Job enlargement and job enrichment fall the latter category.

Job Enlargement. It is one of the motivating factors of the employees. It is the process of increasing the complexity of job so as to appeal to the higher order needs of the workers. What is intended is that the employees should perform varied types of jobs or tasks so that work becomes less boring and monotonous. While discussing job enlargement Strauss and Sayles have said, "It implies that instead of assigning one man to each job, a group of man can be assigned to a group of jobs and then allowed to decide for themselves how to organise the work." According to them such an arrangement will mean more social contacts and greater over work process.

Dimensions of Job Enlargement. Job can be enlarged both horizontally as well as vertically. The former refers to the number and variety of operations that an individual performs on the job. The latter refers to the extent to which the job holder controls the planning and execution of his job. It also means participation of employees in the formulation of the policies of the organisation. Job enlargement in brief motivates the employees because it reduces their monotony. It also means less fatigue of the workers and increase in their efficiency.

Techniques of Job Enlargement. The whole idea of job enlargement is to provide the workers opportunities to make greater use of talents and skills so that they are able to satisfy their needs for self-esteem and dignity. For this is essential that the workers are given more complete or whole job. For this efforts are made to develop an environment in which employees are involved in their jobs. They are also made to participate both in planning and also in the evaluation of their peformance. He is allowed to perform other than his specialised job.

Job Enrichment. It is also a method of motivating the employees. It is a form of changing or improving a job so that a worker feels more motivated. It affords an employee opportunities for greater recognition advancement, growth and responsibility. The job is made more interesting, challenging, less specialised but more enriched. The workers are given more opportunities to plan. It means deliberate upgrading of responsibility, scope and challenges.

The goal of job enrichment is not merely to make the work more varied but also to make every employee a manager. Herzberg is of the view that job enrichment would provide an opportunity to the employees for their psychological growth. It will help the employees knowing the targets to be achieved and standards of their performance. An employee will then be able to plan his activities within certain frame works. He will then also be responsible both for meeting the dead line and producing work of necessary quality.

It may not be out of place here to mention that job enrichment usually results in improving quality of work rather than its quantity. It also results in improving morale of the workers because it makes the job more challenging and appeals to employee's higher needs for achievements.

Effective Use of Job Enrichment. Job enrichment can be used as motivating technique when stress is on quality of work and when one is not trying to deal with an acute moral problem caused by some non-job factors. It can be useful also when a job requires a good deal of originality and lower needs have been considerably satisfied. Then its effectiveness is considerable when the workers themselves clearly prefer less structured and less routine job and it is clear that the employees have strong desire to achieve something. Still another effective use of job enrichment can be made when the organisation is pre-occupied with making creative entrepreneurial decisions.

Implementation of Job Enrichment Programmes. A person gets motivated if he feels that the activity is meaningful to him and that he knows that he is solely responsible for its completion and can very quickly know the resutls. There are five core job dimensions which determine whether a person will experience responsibility and knowledge of results. These being skill variety which means the extent to which a job requires a worker to perform activities that challenge his skill and ability. It also means task identity which means the extent to which job requires completion of a whole or part of the job. Then next comes task significance which means the extent to which job has considerable impact on the work on the whole being done in the organisation.

The first step in developing job enrichment programme is to find out the problem i.e. to find out whether the job is amenable to job enrichment. It also means finding out if motivation and satisfaction are key to the problem and also whether it can or cannot be source of motivation. It also means finding out which specific aspect of a job is causing difficulties and to which extent the employees are ready to accept the change.

After identification comes the next step namely that of implementation i.e. the action to be taken to enrich the job. It can be changed in such a way that each person owns it. It can also be done by combining the tasks and also by allowing the workers to have frequent contacts with the consumers of the product. Then another method what is called vertical loading. By this what is meant is that let the workers plan and control his own work and lastly comes open feedback channels which means finding out for a worker better ways to get quick feedback on his performance.

COMMON MOTIVATION METHODS

Each and every organisation, whether commercial or non-commercial desires that its workers should remain motivated.

Motivation has been variously defined by scholars. According to Stanford and Wrightman, "A motive is an inner state that energises, activates or moves or directs or channelises behaviour towards goals". Fillis is of the view that, "It is the stimulation of any emotion or desire operating upon one's will and promoting or driving it to action". The Encyclopaedia of Management has defined motivation by saying that: "Motivation refers to the degree of readiness of an organism to pursue some designated goals and implies the determination of the nature and load of forces, including the degree of readiness". Thus motivation is willingness to expand energy to achieve a goal or reward. It is a force that activates dormant energies and sets in motion the action of the people.

Motivated behaviour can be expressed through several ways. But the purpose of motivation is to create conditions in which people are willing to work with some feeling, take initiative, interest and work with enthusiasm with a high personal group and moral satisfaction and with a sense of responsibility. Motivational techniques are utilised to stimulate employee's growth.

Types of Motivation. Motivation can be positive or incentive motivation which is based on rewards. It includes praise and credit for work, interest in subrodinates as individuals, competition, participation pride, delegation of responsibility and appreciation for work. It can negative or fear motivation which is based on fear and force. In it a person works under the fear of consequences for not working. It has a serious limitation because an employee puts in minimum efforts to avoid punishment. Then is extrusion motivation. It is concerned with external motivators which employees enjoy like pay, promotion, status, health insurance scheme, pension, etc. Then comes intrinstic motivation which is concerned with the feeling of having accomplished something.

The motivation of group is as important as that of individual. A group can be motivated by improving human relations and dealing with people in a human way, by developing the will to do, by encouraging the people to feel involved in their work and by giving them an opprotunity to improve their performance and by complimenting or praising them.

Management Techniques of Motivation. Management can motivate the workers by providing financial incentives. It is concerned with money directly or indirectly. This motivation includes payment of better wages, salary, bonuses, profit sharing, leave with pay, medical re-imbursement etc.

Then come non-financial incentives or motivators. These are not concerned with money or rewards. These are psychic rewards or rewards for enhanced position. Some of the most commonly used non-financial motivations are:

1. Appraisal, Praise and Prestige
2. Status and Pride
3. Competition
4. Delegation of Authority
5. Participation
6. Job Security
7. Job Enlargement
8. Job Rotation
9. Job Loading
10. Job Enrichment
11. Job Re-inforcement
12. Quality of Life
13. Job Sharing
14. Flexible Working Hours.

Praise very much motivates the workers when it is given as a recognition of good work, particularly in the open and in the presence of others connected with same and similar type of work. Recognition satisfies human needs for esteem by others. It car. in the form of praise, a pat on the back and recommendation for higher pay. Individuals try hard to gain status symbols and there is desire to have more and higher status symbols. It is therefore, essential that persons working in similar positions and enjoying the same status in an organisation should be treated equally.

Competition as a form of motivation is widely used in an organisation. The individuals compete to win and satisfy their ego. Therefore, opportunities should provided for healthy competition. But sometimes competition generates jealously and hostility among the competiting members. A good organisation should remain on guard in this regards. The delegation of substantial amount of responsibility to execute a given task often proves to be a strong motivating force. One feels like giving results but those who lack confidence for them it is motivation. Participation means physical and mental involvement of the people in an activity, specially that of decision making. This satisfies one's ego and self-esteem.

For most of the employees job security is an important motivator. It implies continuation on the job in the same plant and continuance to enjoy economic and social security. It may be provided by ensuring that as far as possible catastrophies shall be avoided. There will be elaborate programme of fringe benefits and adjustment of surplus labour in the organisation.

Job enlargement is the process of increasing the complexity of job in order to appeal to the higher order needs of the workers. It also implies that the employees perform more varied tasks which are all at the same level. The idea is to provide the workers with greater opportunity to make greater use of their minds and skills so that they are more able to help satisfy their needs for self-esteem and dignity.

The aim of job loading is to make the job more interesting. Horizontal job loading assumes that if employees are given more work at the same level at which they are currently performing, they will be motivated to work harder and will also be more satisfied with their work. In job loading the worker is motivated because his job is challenging and more meaningful.

Job enrichment means improving a job so that a worker is likely to be more motivated. It provides an employee with the opportunity for greater recognition, advancement, growth and responsibility. The goal of job enrichment is not merely to make the work more varied but to make every employee a manager. Re-enforcement is a powerful motivation tool. It is built on two principles namely that behaviour which appears to lead to a positive consequence or rewards tends to be repeated; while the bahaviour that appears to lead to negative consequence tends not to be repeated therefore, by providing the properly scheduled rewards, it is possible to influence people's behaviour.

The term 'quality of work' life means different things to different people. According to Prof. Llyods it means, "the degree to which members of a work organisation are able to satisfy important personal needs through their experiences in the organisation." There are several factors which contribute to the quality of work life. These include adequate and fair compensation; safe and healthy environments; growth and security, sensible integration of job career; protection and respect of employee's right to privacy and use of employees skills and abilities.

Under flexible worker hour scheme the employees are given the freedom to choose, within certain limitations, what time they will begin and quit their job each day.

Guidelines for Motivating Employees and Managers. In order to motivate the employees it is essential that the management should ensure the employees that for them they are important and show them due respect. It should ensure that the workers have adequate tools to finish their work satisfactorily. The employees should be provided adequate feedback and also assigned the work which is most suited to them. The management should ensure that the workers are getting adequate salary under good working conditions.

The management should set such goals before the workers which can be easily achieved and communicate these to the employees. They should also be made known through feedback how they are doing.

If these methods are adopted it will be possible to motivate the workers and they can be expected to put in their maximum work.

❐

4

D. Waldo

D. Waldo has discussed at length both internal as well as external factors which influence public administration environment. He feels that the subject is drawing more and more attention of the scholars, students, administrators and business circles. He has also given his views and expressed his ideas about certain other problems and issues which fall in the area of public administration.

Public and Private Administration. According to Waldo today public administration is faced with many problems. There is everywhere serious social conflict. There are certain paradoxes in the system itself as well. There are conflicting ideas about the proper division between public and private areas. The conflict was already existing but in the present period it has assumed great intensity. It is creating new situations because of complexity of the problem. There is serious reaction of the people against governmental institutions and no easy solution is in sight. It is common belief that during recent years justice, honesty and efficiency of public officials and employees has declined. Inspite of this sickness of government, it is rapidly growing. The society still feels that government alone can solve complex and serious problems. The area of public problems is also expanding and the government is called upon to solve these problems, because there is no alternative in sight.

Waldo has said that there is a movement towards publicisation of private administration and vice versa. The result is that there is expansion of both the areas in a very intricate way. This has necessitated desire for a very simple and clear division between public and private administration.

Concept of Rising Expectations. This got focus during 1950's in the U.S.A. By now vast majority all over the world has become conscious enough to realise that poverty is not will of God but man made and as such it should be eradicated. The poor now desire to have some living standard and end their poverty. There is graudal revolution of rising expectations. Not only this but since World War II 'Development has become a World wide ideology and movement'. But what is 'development' there is no clear definition of the term. The scholars have given different interpretations. Whereas some have related it with productivity and industrialisation, the others with living standard. This desire for development has affected both domestic as well as international politics.

Waldo has said that industrialisation has so far been the focus of development but many now agree that the development with which the poor are concerned can be possible only in non-industrial terms. They believe that scientific and technical advances change socio-economic conditions of the people. Not only this but codified knowledge is becoming incresingly important as against conventional factors of production. This factor is being transformed into new techno-social patterns. Waldo has said that these technical and economic changes have profound implications for social organisation and life-style.

Impact on Public Administration. Very rapid changes are coming in society and these have their impact on public administration as well. It is because public administration is government's central instrument for dealing with general social problems. It is also affected by every disturbance in society and is responsible for either bringing or restoring changes. Public administration is also confronted with the problem of taking suitable and timely decisions within the constraints of law on the one hand and possibilities of realisation of objectives and goals of the organisation on the other.

Organisational Humanism. Waldo has given his concept of organisational humanism. By this he means a continuing movement to humanise and democratic organisations. By this he also means greater organisational productivity and happiness on the one hand and increased self-realisation on the other. Thus this concept is continuation of human relations movement which has its roots in the Hawthorne experiments.

Organisational humanism is associated with social psychology but as a complex of ideas it exerts significant influence on public administration in various ways. It tries to improve organisational output and performance and wishes to introduce changes in organisational system and set up.

Internal Environments of Public Administration

Waldo has not only discussed external but also internal environments of Public Administration. He has however made it clear that no very clear distinction between the two, can be maintained. In his opinion Public Administration interacts not only with the world of public affairs but also with the ever changing ideas and institutional arrangements of academic world.

Waldo's Views about Internal Environments of Public Administration:

1. Desire for Change. Waldo is of the view that though the academician should have brought about radical changes but on the whole universities in many ways are conservative. These do not readily agree to demand for change and try to uphold their own values and organisational systems. Not only this but in the systems which these follow even revolutionary ideas become traditional. He however, witnesses some ferment in the university system because of rapid changes which are coming in the society.

Waldo has further said that because of this the hold of some prevailing ideas on the society is getting weak and research for new ideas which can bring changes has started. He however, feels that interaction between the old and new ideas is not easy. It is both difficult and complex because one man's progressive ideas are menace for the other.

2. Shifts in Philosophical Orientation. Because of desire for change and cry for relevance Waldo sees a movement which aims at bringing far reaching changes in ideology in public administration. Philosophical orientation is shifting towards new ideas. Logical positivism is weakening and its place is being taken by such new ideologies as neo marxism and existentialism.

3. Cry for Relevance. Waldo feels that there is cry for relevance in Public Administration and dissatisfaction with mere theoretical propositions. Within the university system itself, there are pressures from different sources, social, economic and political, for a change and shifts in emphasis in research and instructions. He has said that to some extent belief in accepted theories has been shaken because of various reasons. Today many social scientists are inclined towards addressing themselves to applied administrative problems rather than confining themselves to abstract theoretical problems.

4. Public Administration and Political Science Relationship. Waldo has discussed at considerable length the relationship of Public Administration with Political Science. He agrees that Public Administration is the creation of such Professors of Political Science as Woodrow Willson, L.D. White and W.F. Willoughby. It was therefore, considered as part of Political Science till the beginning of the present century. But gradually many changes have since then come and today the questions being posed are:

(*a*) whether the relationship between the two shall be closer;

(*b*) whether the subject will become quite independent; and

(*c*) whether subject as such will disappear?

Waldo feels that on logical grounds case for regarding Public Administration as a part of Political Science is quite strong because Political Science concerns itself with state, government and public affairs with which Public Administration is equally concerned. Not only this but most Professors of Public Administration have regarded themselves first of all Political Scientists and have also found departments of Political Science suitable for the study of Public Administration.

But even then relationship between the two has not been satisfactory in some ways. Political scientists have regarded Public Administration as subject necessary only for providing training for career in government service and not a subject of scholarly value. Then he feels that another reason for this is the rise and increasing predominance of behaviouralism in Political Science. The result is that public administrators have become restless in an environment in which they feel that they are at best being tolerated by the Political Scientists.

A Difficult Problem. Even if it is accepted that Public Administrators are being tolerated by Political Scientists then the question that arises is as to what is the solution of the problem. It is really very ticklish. A separate identity means raising of additional resources in men, money and political support, which if not impossible, is at least a difficult problem. Then another way out can be to leave political science and to shift to business or management departments which again means exchanging one type of second class status to another and this is no solution to the problem.

But nevertheless restlessness prevails among public administrators because they feel that political science does not meet their needs because of several reasons. New management related technologies are coming to the fore which have little relations with Political Science. There is increasing penetration of inter-disciplinary approach in Public Administration which has created a feeling that Political Science is neglecting its intelectual as well as professional needs.

Public Administration has a desire to escape from Political Science but the task is not easy. It is becoming difficult also because Political Science is trying to make itself more relevant to public problems, more public oriented and more concerning itself with achievements and performances. Since the subject is showing more interest in public policy therefore, it is dramatising more interest of public administration day by day.

Growth of Programmes for Public Administration. Waldo views it as an important development in the area of Public Administration. Though attention to programming was paid earlier by business and management circles, but it was inadequate. Now however, attention to this area is being paid with considerable seriousness. One reason for this is social forment which has come during these years. There are now many who propose to have business as their long-term career and also wish to solve some problems of the society. Then another reason is growth in the public sector of national economy and a feeling that greater knowledge of governmental affairs is useful in business.

Movement Towards Political Economy. Waldo feels that movement towards political economy holds the possibility of making Political Science attractive for Public Administrators. He has pointed out that sometimes back Robert A. Dahl tried to develop the area of Political economy by joining Political Science and economics for better policy guidance but no coherent efforts were then made. But of late some interest is being shown and some economists have crossed into the area of Political Science. They have tried to experiment with the application of economic methods and models of Political problems. Similarly political scientists who are very familiar with Public Administration are familiarising themselves with economic theories and techniques. Thus now this movement is considerably picking up.

Not only this but public administration on its own, Waldo says, is trying to establish liasion with economics. The areas of this common interest are budgeting, fiscal accounting, planning, programming etc. Many public administrators regard economics as a more relevant and useful discipline than political science. They believe that public administration is route of economic policy. Waldo is of the opinion that to the extent to which political science moves towards political economy to that extent its attractiveness for public administration for nearer and closer to each other may increase.

Waldo has come to the conclusion that there is movement towards interdisciplinary approach with economics, sociology social psychology and management science playing a big role in that. He also feels that there is some stress on some sort of research components and focus on the study of some specialised problems.

Views about the External Environments

D. Waldo believes that Public Administration is trying to respond to conflicting forces of a complex society and is a very significant development in the field of Public Administration.

According to Waldo Public Administration has varied and wide area to cover. It deals with institutions and their activities but is influenced both by internal and external environments. He has tried to approach the study of the subject on the basis of self-conscious enquiry. It is concerned with public institutions and activities. He believes that the subject is passing through a period of stress and changes. In a very complex world of today it is responding to many conflicting forces. In order to properly study the subject, he has said that it can be studied first by paying attention to the total field of such social forces to which it is responding and then by narrowing down its scope. It can be usefully studied by finding out its interaction with external and internal environments.

The New Public Administration. Waldo believes that a significant development in the field of Public Administration during recent years is the emergence of New Public Administration. By few scholars it is considered a movement. He has said that new public administration is a reflection within public administration of the events and ideas of recent period. Its participants have been mainly the younger generation of public administration.

Criticism of Old Public Administration. Those who support new public administration agree that old public administration lacks respectable and consistent ideological frame work. It also lacks sophisticated methodology and becomes a tool of the system. It is efficient in wrong ways. Not only this but they allege that old public administration system is both unresponsive and unimaginative.

Approach of New Public Administration. Waldo believes that new Public Administration is linked with post behaviourlists in Political Science who are responsible for bringing a new approach in the study of the subject. It is also linked with certain radical movements in Public Services, which aim at reforming these. It stands for promoting social equality and is sensitive to social and human needs of the individuals. New Public Administration also stresses that it should not only be reactive but activist. It stands for the use of advanced methodologies and procedures for their own sake but in the context of reforms. It also pleads that calculations of public administration should be sensitive and humane. Waldo believes that the scope of Public Administration should be enlarged. It should study such problematic areas in greater detail as poverty, violence, inequality, racial discrimination etc. It should take more interest in organisational humanism.

Waldo has said that after the new public administration concept got some roots it helped in bringing some changes in Society in the existing system of Public Administration. Its literature is now widely read and its ideas get circulated in the public administration community.

The External Environments of Public Administration. Waldo believes that several environments are influencing Public Administration. Each area is discrete and each one is closely intermingled with the other.

1. Anti-Poverty Area. One such area which he has identified is anti-poverty area. In sixties poverty was rediscovered in the U.S.A. and researches brought to focus the depth and breadth of domestic poverty and low income groups in the society. The nation launched a war against poverty. During New Deal period major anti-poverty programmes were launched, mainly those dealing with income, agriculture and labour. The result of war against poverty has been in the form of special programmes which aimed at improving living conditions, raising income etc. on the one hand and increasing employment opportunities on the other. Waldo has said that in the process new administrative problems had to be faced which were quite difficult to be solved. He has come to the conclusion that by and large only limited success in achieving the objectives could be achieved.

2. Avoidance of Concentration of Powers in Central Government. Then is the movement which aims at not bringing more programmes under the control of states and under the jurisdictions of local government. This as well as the participation movement have resulted in various types of actions with the main aim of returning the power to the people or atleast in ensuring that there is no further concentration of powers in the hands of Central Government.

3. Participation in Public Administration. Waldo has drawn attention towards problem of participation in the context of public administration. He has said that it is an important theme of late sixties and early seventies. It has manifested itslef in two ways. Firstly its actions are directed both towards greater personal involvement in decision making in several important areas and secondly these aims at greater community participation in decision making in agency programmes and in the implementation of decisions.

4. Racial Ethnic Equality. It is an area which has been identified by him. The movement started in early sixties in the form of civil rights of the black and gradually became broad based. The blacks began to assert their identity and started pressing for more equality in education, housing, employment and income. There was also resurgence of ethnic self-identity among European populations. Much government reaction in the U.S.A., in the past, Waldo believes, been discriminatory, insensitive and coercive. In recent years however, the goal of equality has been taken up with more seriousness but its results have not been very effective even now. He has said that so far no legislatures and courts and no large government agencies have been established for achieving the task of racial ethnic equality. But issue remins still central and is very much involved in such areas as education, housing and employment. In administration of governmental personnel programmes, the issue of equal treatment is as such an increasingly important issue.

5. Urban Area Problems. Waldo has drawn attention to urban problems which are straining public administration of our times. He has said that the shift from an agricultural economy to an industrial economy, which accompany the growth of the city was reflected in American Public Administration well before the end of 19th century and in the civil service reform movement and shaping of formulas for structural organisation. After World War I due to technological advancement, population growth and because of several other reasons city population considerably increased in the urban areas at the cost of rural areas. The result was that by the sixties the city had become a problem centre of a new order for public administrators. The magnitude of the problem is increasing day by day. The implications of this migration for public administration are by now quite clear.

6. Growth of Public Employees Union. Another external factor which has shown its impact on public administration system is the growth of public employees union systems and collective bargaining at all levels. So far the membership of public employees union was not large and these had no bargaining capacity. These unions have now become strong due to various reasons including rise in the number of the working population in employment, relaxation of laws and regulations etc. Increasing Unionism together with new assertiveness, even militancy has resulted in the creation of many new ticklish problems which have serious implications for traditional public administration. Waldo has said that the traditional area of personnel administration is most adversely and immediately affected but its implications are felt by all public organisations and managements.

7. Experimental Jurisdictions. Waldo has linked all these problems with the creation of more or less experimental jurisdictions operating in unconventional ways. These include regional organisations created as a part of national programme to raise economic and social level of backward or depressed region of the country on the one hand and community action organisations, particularly in the city areas on the other. This has resulted in administrative problems.

8. New Management Techniques. Waldo has said that recent years have witnessed growth and spread of new management techniques and instrumentalities in public administration, which are being shared with business administration as well. Some of these techniques, especially project management, have been refined by public sector. Some techniques involve blending of both public and private sector in development and policy making. It has a new significance as a means of relating public jurisdictions one to another. He has also drawn attention to government by contract which he says has an important role in the areas of defence, economic development and space exploration.

9. Impact of Population on Society. Waldo has further said that ever increasing concern for pollution growth and its impact on environment on the one hand and an increasing more generalised interest in the quality of life on the other have significantly affected public administration and may be expected to affect it more with the passing of time. The administrations have been forced to set up Environmental Protection Agencies for pollution control.

10. Productivity Oriented Problems. Waldo has pointed out that productivity is another area which in influencing public sector administrative system because productivity oriented problems are coming to the fore front in evey society. With public sector of economic steadily enlarging, the problems of productivity are becoming more complicated and controvertial. The unions are demanding more economic benefits, reduced working hours and control over labour conditions. Then other problems are increase in taxes and ever increasing criticism that services are unresponsive, inefficint, unproductive and wasteful. There is demand on the government for subsidisation of corporate enterprises that have become closely government related and public funding of medical care etc. Waldo hopes that a sharpening of controversy over productivity issues will increase the importance of what is already important problem of present day public administration evaluation.

11. Impact of Citizens As Consumers. Some other areas which Waldo has identified and which in his opinion are straining administration; include public works, transportation, automobile exhaust emissions; recreation; government's concern for consumer, food and drug administration etc. The impact of citizen as consumer on public administration has direct effects.

12. Planning and Programming Systems. Waldo has said that still other external problem which is influencing public administration is attempt by many societies to instal planning, programming and budgeting systems. He points out that cost benefit and input and output studies these days are at the heart of every enterprise. These essentially deal with productivity.

13. Correctional Administration. In this he has made a mention about rising tide of domestic violence with its implications for such matters as police and correctional administration, socio-economic policies and judicial administration. He has included in this category economic and financial difficulties which came to the fore in sixties which had significant reprecussions in Public Administration.

Human Relations Theory of Organisation

The theories of organisation discussed in three preceding questions are termed as classical theories of organisation and management. The Human Relations Theory is described as Neo Classical (New Classical) theory of organisation. The theory is a modification nay an extension of the earlier theories. In the words of Hicks and Gullett, "The basic assumption of neo classical theory is that psychological and social aspects of the worker as an individual and his work group ought to be emphasised."

Though the theory can be traced from ancient literature yet its development took place in 1920' and 1930's as Harvard Business school under the leadership of Elton Mayo and his associates conducted research at the Hawthorne plant of the Western Electric Company. These studies reveal the ideological revolution in organisational theory. The revolution focussed on organisation as a social system.

The Hawthorne studies established the informal group as a major explanation of behaviour in organisations. The conceptual horizon of organisation was extended to include a large range of socio-psychological variables. Neo classical approach is discerned in Human Relations books—"Human Relations in Industry" by Gardner and Moorie and "Human Relations in Business" by Davis, to some extent work done in industrial psychology and industrial sociology also is a reflection of new classical point of view.

The Hawthorne experiments conducted between 1924 and 1932 established that social or human relationship among the workers played more important part in the determination of productivity than the changes in working conditions. The high morale of the Test group workers was deemed responsible for the productivity augmentation. Morale was considered as the consequence of individual, personal, emphatic attention paid to the individual worker and the social structure of work group. Sanctions, even trivial factors *viz.*, who sat next to which, played vital role. The Hawthorne researchers thus came to the conclusion that the workers' feeling about himself and his work group was no less important. These experiments reveal that organisations have social and emotional aspects besides economic ones. It was found that productivity of the workers increased where the sentiments of the informal group were in consonance with the objectives of the formal group/organisation.

Besides emphasis was laid on the development of the human relations skills which could enable the supervision to effectively bridge the gap between the informal and formal organisations.

Basic Conclusions

(*i*) A worker is a social being deriving satisfaction primarily by membership of stable work groups.

(*ii*) The management should work through small group rather than operate through 'atomised economic automations'.

(*iii*) Techniques like 'expressive supervision and workers' participation could promote a congenial climate of good human relations resulting unfruitful functioning of work groups.

This approach has been widely accepted both by Public and Private Administration. In the words of Stahl, "The core of the problem is in devising those working arrangements and relationship which contribute most of the employees sense of security achievement and belonging—the elements of job satisfaction. Efficiency and productivity normally flow therefrom automatically."

Elements of Theory

The writers of this theory have concentrated on three elements *viz.* individual social aspect of work groups and participative management. A brief explanation will not be out of place.

(*i*) **Individual.** The theory emphasies that each worker is unique and adapts to the job situation. Certain attitudes develop and also ways of life besides certain skills technical, social and logical. Each worker has certain, aspirations and expectations of job situation. The emotions and perceptions are recognised as important.

(*ii*) **Social aspects of Work Group.** This aspect focusses its attention on the social aspects of man whose main desire is seen in the sense of belongingness, ready acceptance and proper recognition by the Group. In the words of Mayo, "Main social situation in his work group ranked first and the work was incidental." William G. Scott also refers to importance of the informal organisation when he remarks, "....these associations are not specified in the blue print of the formal organisation. The informal organisation means national groupings of people in the work situations."

(*iii*) **Participative Management.** The increased exphasis on the individual and work groups led to the emergence of participative management. It involves participation of the workers in the decision-making

> about their work conditions. The workers discuss with supervisors and exercise influence on the decisions affecting them. Hawthorne researchers observed, "Before every change of programme the group is consulted. 'Their comments are listened to and discussed; sometimes their objections are allowed to negate a suggestion. The group unquestionably develops a sense of participation...the girls have ceased to regard to man incharge as boss..."

Chester & Barnard—a contemporary of Mayo—has elaborated his view in, "The functions of the Executive" published in 1938. He disapproves the theory of economic men and proposes the theory of contribution—satisfaction, equilibrium. He was of the view that formal organisations are artificial systems and have grown out of informal organisations the natural systems. The formal organisations sometimes cause the rise of informal organisations which perform three positive functions *viz.*, (*i*) They add to communication by providing viable alternatives to formal channels. (*ii*) They maintain the socio-psychological cohesiveness of the organisation by creating relationship among individuals that would not otherwise develop. (*iii*) Informal ties and activities allo members to develop feeling of personnel importance and effectiveness.

MODERN THEORY

Modern theory termed as system analysis of organisation emerged in 1950's. It is a unique theory as it takes into consideration all elements both of the whole organisation as well as its component parts. It portrays an organisation as an adaptive system. For its survival the organisation must adapt to changes in the environment. Modern Theory considers organisation and its environoment as interdependent, each dependent on the other for resources.

The theory laying emphasis on synthesis and design makes a provision for small view of organisation. Unlike certain theories the Modern Theory (System Analysis) deals integratively with the problems of fully describing and explaining organisational pehnomenon. In a way it casts look at the organisation in totality. 'Organisation' by March and Simon and 'Modern organisation' Theory by Haire are prominent writings on the subjects. Norbert Wiever gave a clear exposition of the organisation as a system composed of inputs process, outputs feedback and environment.

Hicks and Gullet enumerate characteristics of Modern Theory as dynamic multi-level and multi-dimensional, multimotivated probabilistic, multi-disciplinary, descriptive, multivariable and adaptive.

Nigro and Nigro also point out certian characteristics of all social organisation which are common and are as follows:

Characteristics of Organisation

(1) Organisation, "constantly seek and import resources (inputs) in both human and material form and transform these inputs into products and services using internal, social and technological processes (through points)."

(2) Organisations export their products to the external environment and these outputs usually become the inputs of other organisation.

(3) "Organisation structures develop around patterned activities that from stable and predictable input throughout and output cycles."

(4) "Feedback in the form of information about environmental responses to organisational activities (outputs) is used to keep the system of course with regard to its goals and to evaluate the performance of the organisation and its sub-units."

(5) 'Overtime structural differentiation and task specialisation are common system responses to the search for resources and adaptiveness and as the organisation becomes more complex managerial structures for co-ordination and control became more elaborate.

(6) Organisation as system seek equilibrium or a stable state both internally and in relation to external forces and they achieve equilibrium through a constant process of adaptation to their environment.

Organisation as a system banks upon the effective functioning of its parts and such systems. Each sub-system discharges a series of needed activities. In any large and complex organisation these activities are entrusted to specialised units but they are indispensable to organisation and may not necessarily be centralised. The sub-system of an organisation are as follows:

(*a*) Production or technical sub-systems are called operation or technical core. These are categorised as the human and mechanical processes. They transform inputs into the primary outputs of the organisation.

(*b*) **Managerial Sub-System.** Termed as the administrative structure "coordinate and interrelate the other sub-systems, resolve conflicts between units, allocates resources and relate external condition to internal garland requirement".

(*c*) **Adaptive Sub-System.** They assist the organisation anticipate and respond to changing environmental conditions and demand *e.g.*, Planning units, research and development units.

(*d*) **Supportive Sub-Systems.** The first type of supportive sub-systems procure raw materials and dispose of outputs like purchase sales etc. The second type specialise in the development of supportive relationship with external actors *e.g.*, search advertising and public relations.

(*e*) **Maintenance Sub-System.** They ensure the necessary inputs of human skills of personnel function of all kinds.

The Modern Theory goes to the extent of emphasising that organisational systems like social systems are construed to be 'cybernetic' in their behaviour towards the external environment, That clearly reflects that they are, "self-steering using feedback to guide and control their behaviour" (F.A. Nigro). They develop mechanisms to collect, interpret and apply feeback in their decision-making processes in order to acquire the capacity to adapt, correct flaws and evaluate performance.

❒

5

Henry Fayol

Henri Fayol was born in 1841 of a French middle class family. After his graduation in mining engineering, Fayol was appointed as an engineer in a mining company (S.A. Commentry-Fourchambault) in 1860. By 1888 he had risen to the position of Managing Director of the company. He retired from the position of Managing Director in 1918, though he remained Director of the company until his death in December 1925, at the age of eighty-four. During his tenure as the Managing Director of the mining firm, Fayol's efforts enabled the company to rise from a position of bankruptcy to that of great financial success. Fayol attributed his success not to his own personal attributes, but to the system of management which he evolved and applied with great care and imagination. Fayol was influenced by Cartesian philosophy and Adam Smith's writings. His conception of functionalism could be traced to Adam Smith's ideas on division of labour. The most outstanding of his writings in his book *General and Industrial Management* (1916). His reputation to a large extent rests on this single short publication which is still being frequently reprinted. A large number of his papers are concerned with the reform of the public services.

Basic Ideas

A widespread tendency in the English-speaking countries was to draw a distinction between management as an activity confined to conducting industrial or commercial undertakings, and Public Administration as the art of conducting governmental activities. According to Fayol, such a distinction between management and public administration is false and misleading. He observes:

> The meaning which I have given to word administration and which has been generally adopted, broadens considerably the field of administrative science. It embraces not only the public service but enterprises of every size and description, of every form and every purpose. All undertakings require planning, organisation, command, co-ordination and control, and in order to function properly, all must observe the same general principles.

To Fayol, the attempt to sub-divide the study of Management or Administration in accordance with the purpose of the activity is untenable. It is sometimes argued that this could simply mean that Fayol is concerned only with industrial management, whereas his claim to universality in categorical: "Management plays a very important part in the Government of undertakings; of all undertakings, large or small, industrial, commercial political, religious or other".

Indeed, in his later years he studied the problems of state public services and lectured at the Ecole Superieure de la guerre. So it can be accepted that his intention was to initiate a theoretical analysis appropriate to a wide range of organisations. Fayol's ideas about managerial activity are presented in the context of his writings on industrial undertakings. The totality of activities of an industrial undertaking are divided into the following six groups:

(1) Commercial activities (buying, selling, exchange): Knowledge of commercial activity is just as important as knowledge of efficient production. Commercial activity includes, together with acumen and decision, a thorough knowledge of the market and of the

strengths of the competitors, long-term foresight, the use of contracts and price regulation.

(2) Financial activities (search for and optimum use of capital): Capital is a pre-requisite for personnel, plant, raw material, expansion of the plant or machinery, reserves, etc. Proper financial management is necessary to obtain capital, to make optimum use of available funds for the success of the undertaking.

(3) Technical activities (production, manufacture, adaptation): These are sometimes more conducive to the progress and goal attainment than other activities.

(4) Security activities (protection of property and persons): It is necessary to safeguard the property and persons against theft, fire and flood and all social disturbances including strikes.

(5) Accounting activities (stock-taking, balance sheets, costs, statistics): An efficient accounting system, providing an accurate idea of the organisation's financial condition, is a powerful managerial instrument.

(6) Managerial activities (planning, organisation, command, coordination and control): Fayol describes management as a function, a kind of activity. He is quite indifferent whether those exercising this activity are described as 'Managing Directors', or 'Supervisors', or 'Clerks'. He is concerned with the function, not with the status of those who exercise it. However, he is sensitive to the fact that those holding positions at higher level in the hierarchy would devote a larger proportion of their time to this function than employees at the lower levels. Fayol classifies this

key function into five main elements : (*i*) Planning, (*ii*) Organisation, (*iii*) Command, (*iv*) Coordination and (*v*) Control

(*i*) **Planning.** Its chief manifestation and most effective instrument is the plan of action. Planning enables the separation of the short-run events from the long-range considerations. It endows forethought to the operations of an organisation. Fayol considers that experience is an asset in drawing a realistic plan. He also states that, unity, continuity, flexibility and precision are the broad features of a good plan of action.

(*ii*) **Organisation.** To organise an industrial firm or a Government agency is to provide it with everything required for its functioning: raw materials, tools, capitals personnel etc. Fayol classifies these activities into two categories: (1) the material organisation, and (2) the human organisation. The latter includes both personnel leadership and organisation structure. Every organisation has to perform the following managerial functions.

(*a*) Ensure that the plan is judiciously prepared and strictly carried out.

(*b*) Harmonise activities and coordinate efforts.

(*c*) Arrange for efficient selection and appropriate placement of the employees.

(*d*) Formulate clear, distinct, precise decisions.

(*e*) See that the human annd material organisation is consistent with the objectives, resources and requirements of the concern.

(*f*) Define duties clearly.

(*g*) Set up a single, competent, energetic guiding authority.

(*h*) Motivate employees to show initiative and demonstrate responsibility.

(*i*) Make use of sanctions against irregular and unethical conduct.

(*j*) Reward employees in a fair manner for services rendered.

(*k*) Provide for the maintenance of discipline.

(*l*) Pay special attention to unit of command.

(*m*) Ensure that individual interests are subordinate to the general interest.

(*n*) Supervise both material and human organisations.

(*iii*) **Command.** According to Fayol the art of command rests on certain personal qualities and knowledge of the general principles or management. Its degree of proficiency differs from unit to unit. Fayol claims that the manager who has to command should:

(*a*) have a through knowledge of his personnel;

(*b*) be well-versed in the arrangements binding the business and its employees;

(*c*) eliminate the incompetent;

(*d*) set a good example;

(*e*) bring together his chief assistants by means of conferences, at which unit of direction and focussing of effort are provided for;

(*f*) conduct periodic audit of the organisation and use summary charts;

(*g*) not become engrossed in detail.

(*iv*) **Coordination.** It consists of working together and 'harmonising' all activity and efforts so as to facilitate the working of the organisation. Essentially, the objective of coordination is to ensure that one department's efforts are coincident with the efforts of other departments, and keeping all activities in perspective with regard to the overall aims of the organisation.

(*v*) **Control.** Its objective is to obtain conformity with the plan adopted, the instructions issued and principles established. In the process, weaknesses and errors have to be rectified and their recurrance prevented. For control to be effective it must be done within a reasonable time and be followed up by sanctions. He uses the term control in the wider French sense of watch, monitor, check, audit and obtain feedback.

Need for Administrative Training

Fayol is also a pioneer in suggesting the need for systematic training in administration. He criticises civil engineering colleges in France for excluding administration from their syllabi. Fayol stresses the administrative training in the following words:

Everyone needs some concepts of administration; in the home, in affairs of the State, the need for administrative ability is in proportion to the importance of the undertaking and for individual people the need is everywhere greater in accordance with the position occupied. Hence, there should be some generalised teaching of administration; elementary in the primary schools, somewhat wider in the post primary schools, and quite advanced in higher social educational establishments.

Fayol suggests that training is a continuous process, starting from the school and covering inservice training of the employees within an organisation. He considers every superior officer in an organisation as a teacher to his immediate subordinates.

Although Fayol places emphasis on formal organisation, he is alive to the dangers of conformity to hierarchy and formalism. 'It is an error to depart needlessly from the line of authority, but it is even greater one to keep it when detriment to the business ensues', asserts Fayol. He illustrates the problem with reference to the following figures.

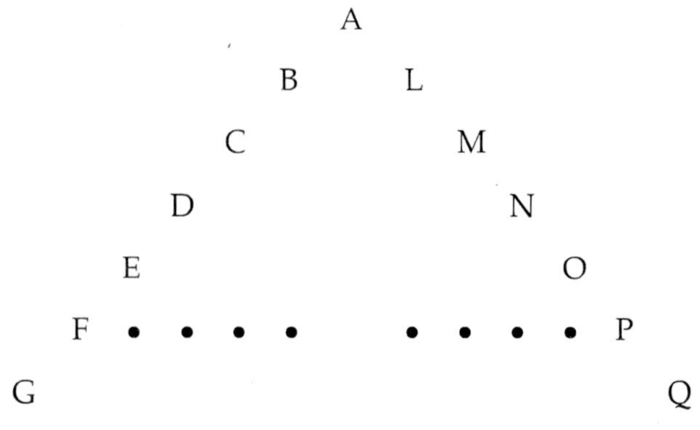

If 'F' follows the principles of proper channel of communication, he has to send his meassage or file to 'P'through 'E', 'D' and so on, covering nine levels. It is, however, possible for 'F' to use 'gangplank' and avoid going through 'A' and all the other intervening layers as intermediaries. Recourse to 'gangplank' is possible only when the immediate superious (in the case, 'E' and 'O') authorise such a relationship. Whenever a disagreement develops between 'F' and 'P', they must turn the matter to their superiors.

Evolution of Management Thought

Management, as a separatic discipline, has not developed overnight. It is not exactly a series of steps that has resulted in management dicipline. One primary reason for this line of argument is that management is extremely eclectic. Every manager deals with both technology and people. Added to this, advances in management theory have always depended on advances in supporting disciplines such as psychology, sociology, anthropology, mathematics. As a result, the management scholars and resarchers have tried to identify the factory contributing to organisational success and effectiveness.

Yet another reason for the fast development of management as a discipline is explained in terms of technological revolution, which forced the management thinkers to become increasingly aware of the forces lying outside the enterprise.

A simplified version of the evolution of management as a separate dicipline is presented in the above diagramme. There have been four major approaches that have made lasting contributions to management thought: *viz.*,

(*a*) *The schools approach*: This approach consists of scientific management school, administrative school, human relations school, behavioural school, management science school or quantitative school.

(*b*) *The process approach*: This approach considers management as a process of planning, organising, staffing, directing, and controlling.

(*c*) *The systems approach*: This approach stresses that managers should view an organisation as a set of interdependent parts, such as people, structure, tasks, and technology, that try to attain diverse objectives in turbulent environment.

(*d*) *the contingency approach*: This approach stresses that the appropriateness of various management techniques is determined by the situation.

The present-day contemporary thinking is that there are multifarious factors in both the organisation and environment that there is no single best way to manage the affairs of the organisational unit. The most effective technique in a particular situation depends on the situation itself.

(1) Scientific Management School. Early management history began with the development of scientific management movement. Industrial revolution paved way for translating the self-sufficient agrarian communities into urban and semi-urban societies. This has resulted in the escalated importance of management of organisations. The contributors to the scientific management school include Adam Smith, Charles Babbage, Fredrick Wilson Taylor, Henry Gantt, The Gilbreths, and Henry Ford.

Adam Simth is credited with the concept of 'division of labour and specialisation'. According to Smith, division of labour results in increased production because of three important reasons:

- increased dexterity on the part of each employee;
- avoidance of loss of time on the part of workers due to handling, and
- the invention of great number of machines which facilitate and abridge labour, and enable one man to do the work of many.

(2) Administrative Management School (Classical School). Henry Fayol, Mooney and Reiley, Urwick, Chester Barnard are famous for the development of the administrative management school.

Henry Fayol, the father of Modern Management, was the Europe's most distinguished contributor to the field of management theory and practice upto the middle of the present century. According to Fayol, management was a separate and distinct skill from other business functions. The activities of an industrial organisation could be divided into six categories *viz.*,

(*i*) technical : producing the manufacturing products

(*ii*) commercial : buying raw materials and selling products

(*iii*) financial : acquiring and employing capital

(*iv*) accounting : recording and taking stock of costs, profits, and losses.

(*v*) security : protecting employees and property, and

(*vi*) managerial : administering activities of an organisation by performing certain basic functions based on priciples.

Fayol's concentration was on the last activity *i.e.* managerial, because he strongly felt that managerial skills have been grossly neglected in business operation. He listed planning, organising, commanding, coordination, and control as the main elements of management. To forecast or plan, he pointed out, is to examine the future and evolve a plan of action to meet it. Organising means mobilising the material and human resources of the organisation to translate the plan into action. Commanding signifies providing direction for employees and getting things done. Coordination implies bringing together unifying and harmonising all activity and effort.

Max Weber, yet another scientist belonging to the classical school, has contributed to the management thinking in terms of advancing the ideal bureaucracy. Weber's bureaucracy is characterised by division of labour, a clearly defined hierarchy, detailed set of rules and regulations, promotion and selection based on technical competence, and impersonal relationships between members in the organisation.

Chester I. Barnard, a practicing management scholar, describes organisations as social systems that require human cooperation. He introduced the concepts of informal organisation, status, and communication. According to Barnard, formal organisation is a cooperative system in which there are persons able to communicate with each other, and who are willing to contribute toward a conscious common purpose. The ultimate success of organisation depends on the efficiency of manager in obtaining cooperation from members.

(3) Human Relations School. The human relations approach had its beginning during 1930 and the twin contributors to this school and Elton Mayo and Mary Parker Follett. Elton Mayo and his Harvard associates conducted some experiments from 1924 to 1932 under three phases: *(i)* test room studies, *(ii)* interviewing programme, and *(iii)* observational studies. These studies revealed that work groups, norms, beliefs, sentiments had a tremendous impact in influencing individual behaviour than did the economic incentives offered by the management. Elton Mayo's experiments at Western Electric's Hawthorne plant opened a new dimension to management thought. Mayo concluded that an efficiently designed job and adequate pay would not always lead to increased productivity. Most importantly, forces arising from interaction between people could and often did override managerial efforts. People have inherent tendency to react to the pressures from the workgroups.

(4) Behavioural Sciences School. The post-Hawthorne experiments revealed the fact that a rigorous examination of psychological and social aspects of organisation is indispensable for further study of management.

This has resulted in behavioural sciences era contributed mostly by the scholars like Abraham Maslow, Douglas McGregor, Henry Mintzberg, Chris Argyris, Rensis Likert.

The Human Resources Approach assumes that the job or task itself is the primary source of satisfaction and motivation to employees. The emphasis here is on individual involvement in the decision-making in the organisation. The focus is on people, the emphasis is on creating a work force with high morale.

Contributions of Behavioural Sciences School

The behavioural sciences school has pointed out that:

- People do not inherently dislike work if they establish goals that they wish to achieve.
- Most people can exercise a great deal of more self-direction, self-control and creativity than are required in their current jobs.
- The primary job of a manager is to tab the latent human potential in the organisation.
- The manager is entrusted with the task of creating a healthy environment wherein all subordinates can contribute to the best of their capacities. The environment should provide a healthy, comfortable, and convenient place of work.
- Expanding subordinate influence, self-direction and self-control would automatically lead to increase in the operational efficiency.

The behavioural sciences school has contributed to the management thought by providing new insights than just introducing new techniques. This school has provided a new fund of knowledge by prescribing new thinking about the role of manager, the nature of organisations and behaviour of individuals within the organisation.

(5) Quantitative School of Management. Also known as management science approach, the quantitative school owes its origin to the Second World War. During the war, scientists belonging to various disciplines pooled their knowledge and applied scientific research into strategic and military operations. The present-day term for the quantitative school is the 'operations research'. The quantitative school is aimed at applying the mathematical principles, simulation and model building, linear and non-linear programming techniques to business problems. The quantitative school follows a scientic approach. It starts with the statement of objectives, definition of problem and goes to formulation of hypotheses. Further, after collecting data the results are evaluated and the hypotheses are tested. The quantitative school makes the following assumptions:

- Business units are predominantly socio-technical-economic systems.
- The organisational activities are primarily directed at the attainment of these objectives.
- Organisations are constructed and reconstructed to achieve specified goals.
- Management is concerned with the decision-making which is carried out logically and systematically.
- The organisational decision-making employees quantitative techniques wherever possible.

Thus, the quantitative school is an improvement over the scientific management thought. Scientific management and management science are not one and the same thing. Scientific management is a classical theory propagated by F.W. Taylor and his associates whereas the management science is of recent development. Management science represents the development of general scientific knowledge and philosophy on a broad theoretical base. The basic aim of management science is to reduce uncertainty in decision-making.

The quantitative school of management draws heavily from other disciplines such as mathematics, statistics, accounting, computer science, systems science, industrial engineering, and econometrics. The basic techniques employed by the quantitative school are linear programming, network analysis, simulation and model building, queueing theory, game theory etc.

(6) Systems Approach. The systems approach is the outcome of continuous research on management. This represents a new thinking on management altogether. The systems approach owes its origin to the General Systems Theory (GST), developed by Ludwig von Bertalanffy. Further, scholars like Fremont E. Kast and James E. Rosenzweig, Daniel Katz and Robert L. Trist, John Kotter and several others have made lasting contributions to the systems school.

A system is a set of interrelated parts. It is a group of interrelated but separate elements working toward a comman goal. Every organisation is a deliberately created system consisting of a set of parts, functions, processes, or subsystems. The arrangement of elements must be orderly; and there must be proper communication between the elements.

Under the systems approach, the organisation transforms inputs into a variety of outputs and offers the same to the external environment. These outputs can be seen in terms of goods produced and services rendered by the organisation. Organisations are open systems in the sense they constantly interact and get interacted with the environment. On the other hand, a closed system is one which does not have any interaction with the outside world. Every organisational system comprises of inputs, process, output, feedback, and the environment.

Nature of Management

In a large-scale organisation hierarchical pattern is adopted. At the top management is run by elite termed as managers or directors. Hence it is called top-management. Middle management and rank and file constitute the next rungs of the hierarchical ladder.

Some of the main features of management reflecting its nature are:

(1) It is a Technique. Management is a technique or a distinct skill for getting the work done. As it is a skill, it is universal in nature. Whatever the type of organisation it may be, the skill of management has to be applied for achieving the desired objectives. It is on account of this fact that even technical departments are headed and controlled by generalist-administrators. The growing trend towards the transfer of personnel at the top managerial level from public administration to private or business administration indicates that management is a growing science.

(2) Management is a Collective Activity. Management is more than a single manager or administrator. It is a group of persons who exercise jointly the authority and the responsibility for group activity. In the words of Millett: "Formal authority and responsibility may be vested in a single person, but effective performance of the work of management requires a number of competent, specialised assistants. In these situations management is not just a single individual with the title of superintendent, or chief engineer, or director, or Secretary: management is a whole group of persons." It is thus a team work. In the words of Fayol, management "is neither an exclusive privilege nor a particular responsibility of the head or senior members of the business;

it is an activity spread, like all other activities, between head and members of the body corporate."

(3) Authority as the Basis of Management. Authority is the basis of management. It is the foundation upon which management constructs its efforts to influence the action of the subordinates of organisational hierarchy. Authority, in the words of Millett, involves three different steps: "(*i*) The making of a decision, including all the legal, organisational, and personal considerations which permit a person or group of persons to decide the issue in question; (*ii*) the communication of a decision by various media and in various terms to those whose action is to be affected thereby; and (*iii*) the execution of a *decision* in varying degrees of conformance with the original intent."

(4) Management as Profession. Management is professionalised in so far as it is specialised in knowledge which is used in instructing, guiding and advising others. However, it is becoming more a staff function rather than a line function. This is because of the fact that modern organisation are multi-purpose and the head of the organisation has to rely on the advice and assistance of qualified technical personnel.

(5) Accountability of Management. A public management must be responsible and accountable. If authority is the foundation of the management, responsibility is the justification for the exercise of that authority. According to Millett: "In essence responsibility means that management is held accountable for the results arising from its exercise of authority. Management must have, authority in order to achieve its purpose in giving direction to group effort. But this authority is accompanied by responsibility for the results of its exercise." Such a responsibility can be of three types: (*a*) Political Responsibility which is other words means Ministerial Responsibility to Parliament for the management of administrative agencies; *(b)* Institutional Responsibility which means the responsibility of an administrative agency "for the good name and continued existence of the agency itself"; *(c)* Professional responsibility which means the acceptance of standard of ethical conduct to guide the utilisation of knowledge and technical skill by the employees.

Values of Management

To a few persons, the principal concern of management is effectiveness, or efficiency, in the operation of an enterprise. Luther Gulick has spoken of efficiency as "the single ultimate value is administration". Herbert Simon has been much concerned to demonstrate that rational behaviour in administration is primarily a calculation of means reasonably expected to realise a given end. Waldo has pointed out that economy and efficiency have been the twin beacons which have guided administrative reformers and writers in America. But what is this term 'efficiency' Herein, again it is very difficult to define the term except that in scientific analysis, efficiency is measured in terms of output in proportion to input. But what is input in management? In brief, we can say that input in management is the quantity of men, money and material applied in the working of an organisation.

But can we regard 'efficiency' in its most wooden form as the basic value of management? Should we agree with Simon that "knowledge of administration, like all knowledge, is amoral?" Waldo has been critical of this trend. He has put his objection: "We hold that efficiency cannot itself be a value." He has pointed out that efficiency is concerned only with relationships, and that it must therefore be defined in terms of some purpose or end. Robert Dahl has argued that the "student of public administration cannot avoid a concern with ends." He has asserted that no science of administration would be possible until the place of normative values was made clear. Emmette Redford has written that a "sense of the importance of values needs to pervade the study of administration," especially because of the growing importance of administrative agencies in defining the public interest. It is, therefore, essential that management, instead of being "goal-oriented", should be "value-oriented". Of course, we cannot speak exactly as to what these values are for they will differ from country to country and from organisation to organisation. But what we can speak definitely is that the justification of a management lies in public service and within this broad end, values should be determined. In the words of Millett: "Unless an organisation contributes continually to fulfilling some basic public service deganization has no justification for its existence."

Tests of Good Management

Millett postulates three values as tests of good management :

(*a*) **Satisfactory Service.** By satisfactory service he means firstly, equitable service, *i.e.*, equal treatment of all the citizens. "No discrimination in the service provided by government can be tolerated because of the citizen's "race, colour, or previous condition of servitude", because of the citizen's economic and social status, his party affiliation, his personal acquaintanceships, or his ability to reward the administrator."

Secondly, it means timely service, *i.e.*, service performed in time. "If the fire-fighting equipment arrives after the fire has wrecked its havoc, the service has not been satisfactory, the rubbish must be collected and disposed of on schedule.

Thirdly, it means ample service, *i.e.*, suffcient service for all citizens. It means the supply of right quantity at the right time. "Equity or timeliness cannot be realised unless the required amount of service is also available."

Fourthly, it means a continuous service, *i.e.*, always available to the citizens who need its assistance.

Fifthly, it means progressive service, *i.e.*, a service which improves in equality and performance.

(*b*) **Responsible Performance.** Woodrow Wilson proclaimed a fundamental values of the administrative process, the value of responsible performance when he said that one of the purposes in the study and development of a "science of administration" should be to "crown its duties with dutifulness." "Responsible performance of the public service", according to Millett, "means that management provides direction for administrative effort by working with and through those institutional devices which exist to express the will of a democratic society."

(*c*) **Good Government.** By good government, Millett means a limited or constitutional government, a government which believes in the dignity of the individual and allows the existence and preservation of circumstances which perpetuate a "multiplicity of social units performing many of the complicated tasks of modern society." The concept of good government has a very real meaning for management. In the words of Millett: "This value places certain responsibilities and obligations upon management. The purposes which management pursues the methods which it uses, the use made of the results it accomplishes—in all these respects management in our society is expected to promote and preserve the conditions of good government.

Types of Management

The organisation of a large-scale body falls in three well defined zones, *viz.*, top management, middle management and the rank and file. In fact, no hard and fast line of demarcation can be drawn between them. However their levels of work and responsibility are well marked at least in Great Britain and India. In Great Britain, for instance, Administrative Service constitutes the top management, the executive service comprises the middle management and the clerical service forms the rank and file. In India the demarcation is not so well defined yet it many be said that the Indian Administrative and class I services constitute the top and the class II and other field officers comprise the middle management.

(1) Top Management. Top management comprises political and administrative personnel. In India, for example, political top management is represented by cabinet ministers, ministers of state and deputy ministers. Administrative top management is composed of secretaries, joint secretaries and deputy secretaries.

Functions of Top Management

Top management is mainly concerned with direction and control. Direction means providing for right kind of action. Control means looking towards the attainment of accountability for the execution of a policy. These two simple words, are, in fact, meaningful Direction includes planning, co-ordinating, and programming. Control involves organisation, supervision, documentation, and reporting. Certain functions entrusted to top management involve both direction and control. Budgeting for instance is a tool of planning and method of accountability. Likewise personnel administration serves both-direction and control. Following are some of the important functions of the top management:

(*a*) It performs managerial functions of direction and control.

(*b*) It furnishes the minister all sorts of information require or likely to be required by him.

(*c*) It provides the legislature information asked by it through interpellations, short notice questions and its committees.

(*d*) It prepares notes, reports and information required for the press, the public and the legislature.

(*e*) It has to supply information regarding legal matters pending in the law courts. Dr. White has explained this function of the Top management in the words: "On the normal management job it piled the urgent necessity of dealing with legislators and their communities party leaders high and low, the press and important organized often highly, vocal groups affected by the work of the agency.

(*f*) It is to gather information which minister is required to supply to the legislature, the pressure groups, his partymen and the constituency. Such information appears in the forms of press communiques, reports and circulars.

(*g*) It serves as a co-ordinating body for inter or intra-departmental agencies.

(*h*) It serves as a link between the cabinet and the civil services.

(*i*) It coordinates the activites of the various departments, commissions, boards and divisions.

(*j*) It has to assimilate the activities and energies of various technical agencies into general administrative business of the state.

Government Work As A Team Work

Government work is as a matter of fact a team work. Though formulation of policy is theoretically the function of a political head. Yet in actual practice top administration plays a vital role. Policy execution also involves team work. Rank and file collect the data, the middle management arranges it systematically and the top administrative management on the basis of systematised, material formulates the policy. Final word of consent or dissent is left to the political head. Things may happen otherway round. Broad basis of policy may emanate from an enthusiastic minister. However such a policy is apt to remain vague and a mere utopian dream unless it is accorded a practical shape by the administrative top management. In fact, modern administration is a highly technical and fairly vexing affair. It is in many cases far beyond the comprehension of a lay politician.

(2) Middle Management. As already said there are no sharp lines between these levels of work and responsibility but in some public services as in Great Britain, they are separate establishments. In the U.S.A., formal differentials or barriers do not exist though three zones of work can be easily demarcated.

Middle management, with a few exceptions covers bureau chiefs, division and section heads and other intermediate grades and the departmental auxiliary agencies. Thus budget and accounting officers, purchasing officers, personnel officers, procedures experts, public relation officers, liaison officers, the managers of public institutions and their subordinate staff, etc., etc., comprise middle management. Each ministry is manned by its own service recruited on different principles and under different conditions. Despite such a diversity, there is one common factor to be traced in all such services, *i.e.*, they are recruited by the Civil Service Commissions under specific rules and set standards. Branch officers commonly known as under secretaries, section officers, heads of attached and subordinate officers, officers of field establishments, heads of departmental auxiliary agencies constitute middle management in India.

Functions. Dr. White has well described the main functions of middle management in the words, "The normal task of middle management is to supervise, direct and control the performance of business within the scope of law, policy and regulations already established".

(*i*) **Programme and Operational Planning.** Though middle management is not responsible for the formulation of administrative policy—the task of top management—yet it is directly concerned with the programme and operational planning. In the process it does modify the details to make the policy formulated workable. Hence F.M. Marx remarks: "The middle manager is always a policy maker". In his words "Not only does he take part in policy formulation by translating strategy into tactics, by tracing out top determination into line activities by framing operating policies under his own responsibility. He is also a policy maker indirectly—by implicit or explicit reference in his reporting functions to existing weaknesses in the administrative approach, inadequacies in current policies and emerging problems and issues that warrant top level consideration."

(*ii*) **Skilful Supervision.** Supervision runs through entire organisation. Each superior supervisor supervises his immediate subordinates. The middle managers have to be skilful supervisors. The lower levels supervise the rank and file, the higher supervise the lower and assist them in their supervisory duties.

(*iii*) **Control and Direction of Operations.** The most important function of middle management lies in control and direction of operations, in order to get the job done. Such a task involves, matters like production standards, provision of personnel supply and equipment, the spelling out of particular assignment, the definition of standards of performance, the establishment of recording and reporting requirements, the designation of appropriate methods and techniques, the determination of the most expenditures flow of work, the review of the end products, co-ordination of operations, maintenance of morale with constant regard to improvement of operations and good working conditions Dr. White describes such functions "vital to good administration."

Qualities of Middle Managers. Keeping in view the complex task of the middle managers it is imperative to state who should constitute the middle management.

(*i*) **Vocation Specialists.** If they have to be successful middle managers they should be vocational experts, *i.e.*, they should be equipped with professional education required in the field in which they are working.

(*ii*) **Knowledge of Rules.** They should be fully aware of law, rules and regulations, court decisions governing their organisations, laws and regulations affecting government operations generally.

(*iii*) **Long Experience.** The longer the experience the better the functioning of middle managers. The longer a middle management official remains in his group, the more he becomes a specialist.

(*iv*) **Skilful Supervisors.** They should be perfect in the art of supervision. They must be imbued with team in spirit. As such, they must work in collaboration with supervisors and subordinates. In other words they should have capacity for leadership.

Importance of Middle Management. The tasks assigned to the middle management make the importance of the middle management evident. It is here that the "substantive action of government on behalf of citizens comes to fruition; here it is that citizens deal with government when they pass beyond their first contacts; here it is that the spirit and temper of the public service and its reputation are largely made."

Moreover, it is in itself a career.

Besides, it is a training ground from which a considerable part of top management emerges. In fact middle manager represents most of the length of the 'chain of command' and enjoys an envious position. He is equipped with the arts of giving orders and of obeying them.

Principles of Management by Henri Fayol

Henri Fayol has enunciated several principles of management, which according to him are basic to all types of management. He has discussed these at some length in his publication entitled, "General and Industrial Management." The principles are:

(1) Authority and Responsibility. By this he means that authority and responsibility must go hand in hand. Since each position holder in an organisation is given some responsibilities to discharge, it is very essential that for discharging these he should also have sufficient authority. He has said that vice-versa is equally true. In other words if he has some authority, he should also be given certain responsibilities.

(2) Division of Work. Henri Fayol favours division of work. According to him it means specialisation and a specialised labour produces more and does better work with the same amount of labour as compared with others. He has said that division of work principle should be applied both in the case of technical and non-technical organisations. He has said that in order to have maximum use of available specialisation in the organisation, as far as possible there should be division of work. He has pointed out that every individual is not competent to do each and every type of work and that each one should be allotted only that type of work which he can perform efficiently and competently.

(3) Unity of Direction. By this he means that in an organisation these should be one head and one plan. He has made a distinction between unity of command and unity of direction. He has said that whereas the former in concerned with group, the latter with the individual.

(4) Stability of Tenure of Personnel. By this he means that in an organisation such an atmosphere should be created that the employees feel secure and that they do not feel tempted to leave it. According to him such a stability is essential not because that the employees should identify themselves with the organisation but also that they can easily pick up new assignments and perform their duties efficiently. Instability in any organisation is an indication of poor management. Fayol has drawn the attention of the management towards the serious consequences of labour turn over on the one hand and increased labour cost on the other. He has very strongly stressed the need of stability of tenure of personnel in the organisation so that they can efficiency and devotedly discharge their obligations.

(5) Unity of Command. It is very essential for an organisation which is based on hierarchical basis. By this Fayol means that every employee should have only one boss to whom he should be accountable. In case he receives commands from more than one person then there will not only be doubts and confusions but also there will not be proper accountability.

(6) Discipline. It is his another principle of management. By this Fayol means that all workers in the organisation should obey the orders of the superiors in accordance with the standing agreements between the firm and its employees.

Fayol has said that discipline alone can help in achieving the targets. It includes obedience to orders, his behaviour and way of functioning.

(7) Initiative. It is essential that in an organisation not only Manager but every employee should be provided an opportunity to take initiative. By this he means ability to think afresh in a positive manner which can prove a powerful motivator of human behaviour. It means that an employee should be encouraged to come forward with his positive suggestions for the improvement of work and enthuse him to do more work. He has, therefore, suggested the seniors and superiors that they should give us false prestige and provide full opportunities to their subordinates to work on the basis of their experience and knowledge. Fayol has said that it should not be forgotten that every employee has desire to take initiative and this desire should be met in the over all interest of the organisation.

(8) Centralisation. Fayol has not used the word centralisation of powers and authority but even then he believed that in order to efficiently run management, a manager should have some powers, this will enable him to properly plan, organise, coordinate and control the work of the organisation. The powers to be vested however, very depending on top managers, number of subordinates and on the business conditions. He has therefore, laid down no hard and fast rules about the extent of centralisation leaving it to the conditions and circumstances in which organisation in functioning.

(9) Scalar Chain (Hierarchy). Briefly speaking hierarchy of scalar chain is a system in which there is a chain of officers from above to down below. In other words, at the top is the superior whereas at the bottom is the lowest placed employee. In between there are severl other officers. He has however, said that direct contact out of this straight line should be allowed only in exceptional circumstances. In other words, one should establish direct contact with a superior, with whom he is not supposed to ordinarily establish his contacts but only in exceptional circumstances. He has also said that if need be two officers may directly establish their contacts with each other.

(10) Remuneration. From the remuneration of personnel he means that each employer should be adequately paid for the services rendered by him. The wages and salaries paid should be such that these provide satisfaction both to the employees as well as the firm. Not only this but the method of payment should also be satisfying. In case an employee is not paid adequately there is every likelihood that he may not his work satisfactorily and to the best of his capacity. This is bound to prove to the disadvantage of the organisation. In order to attract the workers to do the work with devotion and interest, it is essential that he should be paid in accordance with well establish norms of payment.

(11) Subordination of Individual to General Interests. By this Fayol means that in an organisation over all interests of the organisation should get top priority. The interests of one employee or group of employees should not prevail over that of the total organisation. He has said that in order to achieve the objectives of the organisation and for its progress, if necessary the managers should sacrifice their personal interests for collective interests. If however, there is any clash at any point of time individual interests should be surrendered so that collective interests do not receive any set back.

(12) Equity. It is one more principle of management which Fayol has put forth. According to him in order to encourage the personnel to perform their duties with devotion and loyalty there must be equity based on kindness and justice in employer-employees relations. By this he also means that an employer should behave with his employees on just basis and his approach should be liberal and broad based.

(13) Esprit-de-Corps. By this Fayol means that harmony and unity among the personnel of an organisation is a source of strength for the organisation. This principle believes that strength lies in unity. He has said that when number of persons work in an organisations differences are bound to arise but this principle stresses that frictions and differences should be replaced by cooperation and unity. Disunity and disharmony among the employees is bound to result in the disadvantage of the organisation. He has said that in order to maintain unity among the workers it is essential that unity of command should be strictly enforced. It is equally essential that personal loyalties, unnecessary correspondence and politics in the organisation should be avoided because these are the causes which create disunity in the organisation

(14) Order. By order Fayol means proper placement of the employees. Fayol has said that once the basic job structure has been decided and job requirements finalised and personnel to fill various positions selected, it is essential that each employee should be placed in such a position and assigned such duties and responsibilities which are most suited to his tastes. He will then be in a position to provide most effective service. Fayol has laid stress on proper placement of every thing and every one in the organisation. It is very essential for every organisation that everything and every person should be placed at proper place. This will mean maximum production with minimum cost. Not only this but hurdles which come on the way can be easily removed and fully well appreciated.

❑

6

Woodrow Wilson

Woodrow Wilson was born on December, 28 1856 in Virginia in the U.S.A. and in 1886 when was about 30 years of age he got his Ph.D. degree. But before that when he was in his graduation at St. Hopkins University, he wrote his first book entitled 'Congressional Government', which had no concern with his studies. In 1886 he started his career as Professor of Political Science, on which position he continued till 1902 when he took over as the President of the Princeton University. In 1910 he left that when he was elected as Governor of New Jerrsey. In 1913 he took over as the President of the U.S.A. at a time when the clouds of war were hovering over Europe.

Woodrow Wilson came to prominence when he contributed his essay on the 'Study of Administration' in 1887. Earlier to this in 1885 he started serious work on Comparative System of Administration. The essay before it was published in Political Science. Quarterly was presented before historical and Political Science Association at its meeting held in Ithaca, New York. It was considered and evaluated as one of the best essays written on administration, though Wilson himself considered it as not worthy of publication. It began to be seriously studied by scholar of administration. Henry W. Bragden, a scholar in his own right, considered it a mine of knowledge.

Woodrow Wilson was significantly influenced by contemporary events. It was a time when in the U.S.A. spoils system had degenerated itself and its abuse at political level was an open secret. He was very much concerned with it and wanted to reform the system. He felt that the system could be reformed only with the help of study of administration. In his philosophy he was very much influenced by Edmund Burke and Walter Bagehot. Wilson's ideas were stimulated by Professor Richard T. Ely of Johns Hopkins University.

Wilson is not much clear about his views on the subject. He has said at some places, that both are not only closely linked with each other, but are inter-dependent as well. It was not possible to draw a line of demarcation between the two. He also said that no topic in the study of government can stand by itself, much less administration, without studying the principles of government in operation.

Whereas at one state he laid stress on the relationship of administration with politics, at another place he has said that both these subjects are quite separate from each other. He then said that administration was outside the sphere of politics and that administrative questions were not political questions. While elaborating his view point at this stage he said that whereas politics falls within the purview of statesmen, administration falls in the domain of technical officers. He now does not stress on the close relationship of politics and administration but considers the two separate from each other. He thus was not very clear whether the two were separate or not. That is one reason that later scholars found themselves is difficult situation when they began to study Wilson's views about the relationship of administration with politics.

Administration as Business. As said above Wilson's ideas about the relationship of politics with administration are not very clear. Whereas Riggs is convinced that Wilson believes that the two subjects are closely interwoven. He has gone to the extent of saying that Wilson believes that administrative actions can hardly be thought except implementation of general policies formulated by political bosses. He has come to the conclusion that Wilson believes that no administrative development can be possible when there is political vacuum. There are however, several other thinkers who have tried to stress that Wilson believed that field of administration was field of business and that like any other business it has no concern with politics. When divorced from politics it goes no uninterrupted.

Civil Service and Administration. Wilson was of the view that civil servants impartially selected purely on the basis of merit were essential for successful working of democracy. He was opposed to the very idea of bureaucratic elite and as such he believed that the bureaucrats should subject themselves to political control. He favoured reforms which were then going on in the U.S.A. A non-partisan civil service could make administration run on business lines. For him administrative reforms will mean over all reform in the administrative set up.

Public Opinion and Administration. While expressing his opinion about the relationship between public opinion and administration Wilson has said that public opinion takes the place of an authoritative critic and has laid stress on the need of an efficient public opinion. He believes that public criticism of administration is both useful and necessary, though at times it becomes nuisance when it begins to go deep into administrative details.

Wilson on Public Administration. He believed that public administration is implementation of laws and provisions of Constitution. It has two important objectives to achieve namely political insulation and sophisticated managerial competence. He has further said that it is the responsibility of the scholars and politicians to find out the central point of political powers and also that who exercises the supreme powers. Not only this but they are to tell how one can reach that position. Wilson believed that to the extent possible the powers should be decentralised to the extent to which the responsibilities of authorities is reduced.

On the basis of American experience he has said that all the powers have got centralised in the Central Government which has made it very powerful. The Congress is sovereign authority in the country. He believes that those who decide the policies which the administration is to follow should be strictly accountable to the choice of majority.

Uniformity of Administrative System. According to Wilson political views and political ideologies of different countries based on their constitution can be different but in so far as principles of good administration are concerned, may be a capitalists, socialist or any other form of government these cannot be different. These are bound to be uniform. In other words, the principles of good administration for all forms of government must remain the same. He believed that administrative system under Napoleon in France and Fredrick in Russia was very good.

Objects of Administrative Study. According to Wilson main object of administrative study should be to find out what the government can successfully do and how, with utmost efficiency, economy and least possible waste of energy. Then he has said that its another objective is to rescue executive from confusion and place it on deep foundations on stable principles. He considered administration as the most dominant part of government. While discussing the causes of neglect of study of administration, he said that before 19th century population was manageable and functions of the government were not very many. In addition, administration was not complex. It was however, during 19th century that population and trade and commerce grew and with that the number of enterprises as well. Administrative system also became complex and difficult. The responsibilities of the administrators multiplied and this brought for reaching changes in the thinking all around about the role of administration.

Woodrow Wilson and Politics. Woodrow Wilson was a politician and also a Political Scientist. In 1879 he wrote 'Cabinet Government in the United States' in which he has tried to discuss the actual working of U.S. Congress. In 1885 he brought out 'Congressional Government' and in 1908 Constitutional Government in the United States. He all along believed that perfection in administrative organisation could be attained in a hierarchical ordered and professionally trained civil service.

Wilson on Methods of Study of Administration. Wilson was quite keen that scientific methods should be used for the study of administration. For the purpose he did not favour philosophical method but was in favour of use of historical and comparative methods. He said that without comparative studies in government, a prevailing misconception that administration in democratic and other states stands on different footings cannot be removed. It is comparative system which can help in knowing weak and strong points of different administrative systems. He said that from European autocracies we can learn their efficient administrative methods without importing autocratic spirit. This will help democracies to meet the challenges of autocracies and other forms of government.

Constitutional Principles and Administrative Reforms. According to Wilson administrative reforms should not be always linked with the constitution because no constitution could last for more than 10 years without changes. If both were linked together then governments will always be busy to adjust and watch changes having no time for developing details of administration. He has therefore, suggested that let the debate on constitutional principles go on, but full attention should be paid to systematic analysis and proper understanding of science of administration.

Critical Evaluation. There are different views about the contribution of Woodrow Wilson to administration thought. One view is that his views are not original. But this view does not very much hold good. It is because today the views of Wilson about administrative system are being seriously studied. It is because of his views about administrative system that today on the basis of his thinking, many theories are being developed.

Herbert Simon has however, boldly criticised Wilson. He believes that Wilson is not clear about the relationship of politics with administration. He and other critics have gone to the extent of saying that he was not very clear about the very concept of public administration. According to one of the critics of Wilson, he failed to amplify what the study of administration actually entailed, what was proper relationship between political and administrative realms and whether or not administrative studies could become abstract science akin to natural sciences.

Whereas Wilson has been adversely criticised by critics, there are many who have favourably evaluated his work. According to them it was his famous essay which gave birth of public administration as self-conscious enquiry and made it as a recognised field of study. Judged from stand point of view of development of public administration in 19th century his writings were stimulating. According to Allen Schick, through his most distinguished essay Wilson not only introduced the idea of administration but also launched public administration as generic course. The supporters of Wilson also point out that his 1887 published essay can be said as the beginning of present day U.S. public administration system.

The principles of administration enunciated by him are even today being seriously studied and favoured.

But again the critics have pointed out that Wilson has failed to clearly come out with his consistent views. Dwight Waldo has pointed out that he has tried to link administration to business methods, instituted a civil service and so on, which really confuse any careful reader of the subject. In this famous essay he has stated that he aimed at discovering what should properly and successfully, an administrator can do but actually he has dealth with the separation and non-separation of politics and administration and even on this problem his views are not very clear. His 'The Study of Administration', is too general, too broad and too vague. He has raised too many questions and provided answer to too few. He is not clear as to what public administration really is.

But even then it is accepted that it was under him that the U.S. won the war. His 14 point programme resulted in ceasefire and his views were the basis of founding of the League of Nations. He was awarded Noble Peace Prize in 1919 for bringing peace in the world. He favoured morality in administration. He never compromised with his principles. He was known for leading a disciplined life. To the public he generally was impersonal and cold but at home he was humorous. He was believe to be bold and courageous. He is also considered as one of the reformist President of the U.S.A. He could inspire others to work. It was during his period that the U.S.A. became a powerful nation. He was an able political leader and also an academician of standing. He was interested in undertaking socially useful projects and activities. He loved the poor and down trodden. As President he paid full attention to administration and tried to reform that. Administrative system which he developed was followed by his successor Presidents. He appreciated the value of public opinion in administration and accepted that he was a good party leader and allowed political parties to play their part in administration.

Views about Authority

According to Barnard authority is the "character of a communication (order) in a formal organisation by virtue of which it is accepted by a contributor or member of the organisation as governing or determining what he does or is not to do in so far as organisation is concerned." It implies acceptance of communication as authority and why the communication is at all accepted by the members of the organisation.

Conditions for Acceptance of Authority

1. According to Barnard authority is accepted when four conditions are simultaneously met. One such condition is that those who are to accept the authority fully and clearly understand the communication. The orders should be clearly understandable and should be specific. Orders issued in general terms create problem both at the interpretation and implementation stage.

2. Then Barnard has said that another condition for the acceptance of authority is that the orders should be consistent with the purposes and goals of the organisation. Any order contrary to it is not likely to be accepted because of contradictions between the two. If at all there is prima facie any contradiction, it is essential that the communication should explain that to the satisfaction of contributors or members.

3. His third condition is that the communication should be compatible with personal interests. If it clashes with the interests of the individuals that is most likely not to be accepted. It should be of such a nature that it motivates the members. If the interests of the contributors are not protected they may resign, disobey or even evade obeying on one pretext or the other.

4. Then the last condition to which he has drawn attention is that it should be seen that those who are expected to obey the authority have physical and mental ability to comply with the orders. When there is no such capacity, the orders are likely to be disobeyed or disregarded.

He has said that usually in a sound organisation orders are issued taking these considerations into account and the groups also have a tendency to accept communications. But he has said that problem in every organisation always remains that superior officers do not know till the last moment whether their orders will or will not be obeyed. This uncertainty can prove dangerous for any organisation. He is of the view that every subordinate has two alternatives before him *i.e.* whether to accept or not to accept the communication. He fully understands that obedience means reward and disobedience can lead to punishment.

Zone of Indifference. While dealing with the problem of cooperation in an organisation. Barnard has drawn attention to zone of indifference. He has said that each individual will gladly accept subordination provided the order falls within his definite jurisdiction. It is decided by the officers whose orders are happly accepted. If his orders are not fully obeyed, the extent to which these are disobeyed to that extent his authority gets reduced. It is therefore, desirable that those orders which cannot be obeyed should not be issued. When such orders are issued which apparently cannot be obeyed for that before issue some inducements should be made so that authority is not challenged.

Problems of Cooperation. Barnard has said that from the conditions for the obedience of orders it becomes clear that a subordinate is to decide whether he is to obey the orders or not. This means that cooperation of individual to organisation is uncertain. He has said that this cooperation can be obtained when all the four conditions mentioned above are met and when the orders fall within the zone of indifference.

Categories of Orders. While elaborating his point further Barnard has said that on the basis of acceptability the orders can be placed under three categories namely those which will not at all be accepted; which may or may not be accepted and which will be gladly acceptable. The orders of the last category fall in the zone indifference.

But this zone of indifference will depend on such factors as to what type of inducement the organisation provides and what type of sacrifices the members are required to make. It is in the interest of executive that it should ensure that orders fall within the zone of indifference. The efficiency of authority depends on the degree to which orders are obeyed.

The Fiction of Authority. It is presumed that in an organisation for various reasons the individuals will accept authority. One reason being that they want to avoid making issue of such orders and also desire to avoid loss of personal status with their colleagues. The fiction of superior authority is necessary because that enables the individual to delegate responsibility and also because it is understood that goodwill of the organisation is at stake. Barnard has said that any action which results in intentional disobeyance of orders is an act of hostility and every organisation must take punitive action against such offenders.

Morality Concept of Responsibility. Responsibility and accountability convey almost the similar meaning. But both have difference connotations. Accountability is a legal term which has close link with organisational procedures. It is part of control procedures. On the other hand, responsibility is close to morality. Thus a person is accountable but at the same time is morally bound as well for his actions and activities. Responsibility is self-interpretive. It is not decided by any code but is combination of several factors which include morality, legality and technicality etc. Barnard has challenged the idea of equality of responsibility and authority on the plea that on several occasions the individuals are placed in such a situation in which they are prepared to take responsibility but have no authority for that.

Barnard has said that there are several personal factors which influence his behaviour. He believes that every worry or struggle is because of the outcome of circumstances. The organisation is however, very much influenced by these as well *e.g.* the individual remains in tension when he is disappointed because of which he losses self-confidence and stands on the way of acceptance of orders. He may even disagree with a code, which may, ultimately result to his disadvantage. Barnard has tried to link morality with responsibility in his analysis. He has said that every individual has his moral code but when that becomes part of function, then the individual is to reconcile the both.

❐

7

George Elton Mayo

George Elton Mayo carried out several experiment with a view to finding out the factors which influence the behaviour of the workers and their effects on production. Some of the important problems which he studied included industrial accidents, fatigue, rest pauses and working conditions of the workers in the factories.

It was first major research experiment which was carried out by Mayo, while he was at Harvard. The experiment was in a textile mill near Philadelphia in 1923. The mill was considered a model organisation and provided many facilities to the workers. The employers were quite cooperatives but even then mule spinning department was creating problems for the management where turn over was about 25%. In order to come over difficulties the management introduced some incentive schemes but the labourers did not stick to this department of the mill. Even financial incentives introduced in consultation with efficiency engineer, did not produce the desire results.

The Problems of Workers. Mayo studied the problem from different angles and found that Piecer in the department suffered from foot trouble. He also found that each worker was required to take care of 10 to 14 machines and he felt miserable while attending to his work. The Piecers in the same section were located far apart and practically there was no communication between them. There was terrific noise of the machines. The workers complained that they were too fatigued to enjoy social evenings after hard work put by them.

Mayo's Solution. After studying the problem he started his experiment by introducing rest periods of ten minutes each time in the morning and afternoon with every team of piecers. He found that the results were encouraging. The problem of physical fatigue appeared to have been come over. The labour turn over now almost did not exist and morale of the workers improved. In addition, production went up. The system of earning bonus was introduced by which those workers who produced more than a certain percentage were paid bonus proportionate to their extra production.

After some time for some reasons the scheme of rest pauses was abandoned with the result that within a week production decreased and the workers showed their unhappiness. The fatigues reappeared. This alarmed the President of the mill who ultimately decided that spinning department of the mill should be shut down for ten minutes each, four times a day. It was found that production again picked up. In order to earn bonus the workers also began to put extra labour. The control of rest periods was placed in the hands of the workers, who began to consult each other.

Hawthorne Experiments

These experiments were carried out by Mayo and his colleagues and changed radically the thinking of the management. The experiments were carried out for about 8 years between 1924-1932 in Hawthorne works of Western Electric Company of the U.S.A. These were carried out jointly by Western Electric Company and Graduate School of Business

Administration of Harward University under the auspices of National Research Council.

The Company employed about 30,000 workers and was located in Chicago city. The management of the company believed that there was cause-effect relationship between the physical work, the environment, the well-being and productivity of the workers. It also believed that given proper ventilation, temperature, lighting and other physical conditions alongwith wage incentive schemes, the production will go up. It believed that main causes responsible for reduced production were improper job design, fatigue, less illumination of work place etc. The first experiment to be carried out was to find out relationship of illumination with efficiency of workers.

Need for Experiment. It may however, be mentioned that at the time of carrying out of experiments management properly looked after the interests of the workers. They had fixed working hours, paid reasonably good wages and there was provision for a good canteen and hospital. They also had scope for entertainment. During the last 25 years, the workers had not gone on strike even once. They had no good social life and were always suffering from one disease or the other.

Following experiments were then carried out:

1. **The Lighting Experiments.** Mayo and his group started experiments as early as in 1924. In one of the experiments two groups of female workers each consisting of six were selected and located in two separate rooms. The rooms were equally illuminated and the experiment to be carried out was to find out as to what was the effect of light on production. The workers in both the cases were acclamatise to room temperature and situation. In the beginning in both the rooms same conditions of work were provided but subsequently whereas in one room no change in

light was made during work hour, in the other room light was increased and decreased. The experiment was carried out for one and half year and at the end it was found that irrespective of the effect of light, production in both the cases increased.

After having experiments about light he tried to find out the effect of payment of wages, rest periods, during working hours, group incentives, individual piece rate on rise and slowing down on production. Production also went on increasing when working hours were reduced and better canteen facilities were provided to the workers. In a bid to find out the causes which adversely affected production the researchers decided to revert the old system by abolishing all the above mentioned privileges and began from the position from which the experiments had been started, except continuing individual piece rate system. But even then production went on increasing and this puzzled the research team. Thus the researchers concluded that neither light, nor incentive scheme, nor rest period had any relevance with increased production.

2. **The Relay Assembly Test Room Experiments.** These experiments which were started in 1927 continued till 1932. The outcome was some important findings. In these experiments six girls were picked up for experimentation. These were put in a small room and assigned the duty of assembling small telephone parts. These were never experts nor raw in the work allotted to them. These were average workers. An observer was appointed to observe their performance. He observed not only when they were at work but also temperature, humidity, happenings, conversations in the room and production of the girls. The workers were kept in a separate room,

during a particular period and an observer was kept to observe their work. During this period working conditions were practically not changed and it was found that production increased.

Another experiment carried out was that the workers were given five minutes rest both in the morning and in the evening and it was found that production remained unchanged. When rest pause was increased from 5 to 10 minutes there was marginal increase in production. Still one more experiment carried out was that instead of 10 minutes rest both in the morning and evening, the workers were given 5 minutes rest each 6 times during working hours.

During this period several experiments were carried out with working hours, with a view to finding out their impact on production. In the first case the work was stopped at 4.30 p.m., thus working hours were reduced by half an hour a day, but inspite of that the production increased. Then in an experiment instead 4.30 p.m. the work was stopped at 4.00 p.m. and it was found that whereas production per hour increased, but daily and weekly production somewhat came down. In still another experiment, the work began to be stopped at 5.00 p.m. again and it was found that whereas production per hour went down, but on daily and weekly basis it went up. When work was stopped on Saturday morning and thus working hours were reduced, but on the whole the production did not came down. When the Company decided to fix 48 hours a week without any rest pause and food, it was found that on the whole that the production increased.

Findings of Research. Mayo and his team thus carried out several experiments about rest pauses and working hours and found that for about one and a half year production increased and the workers were quite happy. It was also found that production increased because the management extended full cooperation to the workers and the latter had high morale. They also worked in a free atmosphere and the management did not interfere much in their style of working. Physical atmospheric conditions, it was found could as well as could not adversely effect production.

Some Other Important Findings. The researchers also found that rest periods and less working hours which helped in the removal of fatigue did not much help in the increase in production because production still increased when these facilities were withdrawn. It was also not finally established that relief from monotony always meant more production as that had nothing to do with physical environments. It was also found that it was not wage but something else that led to greater output. The Mayo also found that work satisfaction depended to a large extent on the informal social pattern of the working group. This can help in increased production. He suggested that an environment should be created by which the workers could openly tell their requirements freely to their superiors in the company. Supervision, morale and productivity go hand in hand.

3. **The Second Relay Assembly Group Test.** In this test a group of workers were kept away from their main department and made to work as a separate group. For the purpose in 1932 five workers were selected. They were assured monetary incentives and for about nine weeks their work was supervised and studied. Before selecting them complete account of their actual production was maintained. A separate

account was kept of their output after joining the group. Their working conditions were not materially changed. The only change was that these workers were not allowed to mix with the workers of their main group.

Some Other Experiments. In an experiment called Mic Splitting Group experiment some girls were kept in a separate room where their working conditions were changed five times in a year. It was found that the girls did not cherish these changes. Their wages structure was not changed and these were even required to work on over time but even then there was 15% increase in production. The researchers also found that these workers had established social contacts.

Special Study on Human Attitudes and Sentiments. The study established that when the workers were allowed to express their grievances, they felt relieved, inspite of the fact that neither their wages were increased nor any material change was made in the environment. The study also showed that there was no correlation between the nature of complaint and the facts. Mayo also found that pre-occupation of workers with personal and family problems adversely effected their performance in the industry.

The study proved that when workers were asked to express their views about policies and activities of the company and discuss their own as well as problems of the company they felt elevated and happy because they felt that they had been given equal status with the management. They were satisfied that at least they had been given an opportunity to express their grievances. It was also found that there was a change in the attitude of the supervisors, as they knew that their behaviour was being closely supervised by research team. It was also felt that without proper appreciation of the feelings and the sentiments of the workers, their problems could not be properly understood or realised.

Human Factor in Management. Mayo pointed out that each individual had certain hopes, expectations and aspirations and as such he could not be made to work under the threat or use of force. He was of the opinion that for efficiency and better production human factor played more an important role than technical factors and as such the former should be given maximum importance. He has suggested that at work place such conditions should be given which in addition to work satisfaction also provide social satisfaction. He has also said that due attention should be paid to individual problems of the workers as well, so that these do not become organisational problems and hamper production.

Management Role. Mayo was of the view that alongwith technical and economic aspects, human aspect should be given paramanent consideration in factory system. The management should have the capacity to handle human situation, motivate the workers and communicate with them. He said that concept of authority should be linked with that of securing cooperation of the workers. He did not like the existing factory system in which a worker was treated as one of the factors of production.

Absenteeism in Industries. Mayo also studied the problem of absenteeism in three industries and found that this could be considerably checked if the management encouraged formation of informal groups and treated the workers with humane understanding. He therefore, suggested the management that the workers should not be treated only as one of the factors of production but as human beings. They should not carry the impression that the management is bent upon exploiting them. The management should try to develop human relationship in industry and encourage the workers to take initiative.

Findings of Hawthorne Experiments

These experiments which were carried out for years together made Mayo and his team come to the conclusion that humane approach of the management not only increases production but also gives social satisfaction to the workers. The workers automatically do not develop group feelings but for that the management should make efforts. The demands of the workers are influenced both by internal condition prevailing in the organisation and those which prevail outside the organisation. Environmental conditions and light does not materially effect output and production. Similarly physical and environmental factors do not very adversely affect the efficiency of the workers. These also clearly established that production and output could be increased when the work of the workers was appreciated, they were provided job security and their morale was kept high. The experiments also established that the workers did not work simply for the sake of earning money but these were also several other causes for that which had not much relevance with money.

❐

8

David G. Mc Clelland

Mc Clelland is of the view that a person feels like working hard or putting in hard labour only for three reasons. Without either of these he will not feel like working. He may feel need for having power or affiliation or achievement. He has defined achievement motivation by saying it is need or desire for achievement. When a person realises that work is being assessed or is likely to be assessed on the basis of certain well established standard and quality of his work is to be appreciated then achievement motivation comes in the picture. It then becomes an important standard for efforts and hopes as well as aspirations.

When a person becomes conscious that he is responsibile for and likely to get reward for his efforts, then he keeps himself abreast with happenings outside. He then gets motivated for achieving something. It becomes then the main cause of his success or failure. When some risk is involved in the work then results of the efforts become uncertain.

Factors of Motivation. According to Clelland each individual has own capacity for achievement motivation and each one uses his own methods and means to achieve the objectives. Similarly the opportunities to achieve the same cannot be uniform. These are bound to vary. He has therefore, said that while assessing capacity to motivate or get motivated both individual and environmental factors should be taken into consideration.

He has further said that when for any work motivating factors become weak, then need for strengthening these arises. Some people get motivated when they receive monetary rewards, whereas for others money is not that important as desire to achieve something and they struggle for their goals. He has said that some person are given monetary rewards or profits because they are doing some good and useful work. Some people however, feel that monetary rewards are recognition of the quality of their work.

Characteristics of High Need Achievement Person. Clelland has said that a person with desire to achieve much has great sense of responsibility. He feels that he is accountable for his actions some one. In order to ensure that his desire to achieve may not result in failures, he takes maximum advantage of every opportunity. He does not allow any opportunity to miss. Such a person also always remain ready to take risks and tries to get feedback and assess and analyse all those factors of achievement which can be analysed. Such a person sets such goals which are realistic, no matter whether these poses a challenge. In fact he prefers challenging jobs.

Role of Environmental Factors. Clelland accepts the fact that environmental factors very much count in achievement motivation. He has come to the conclusion that persons of high need achievements are influenced by several environmental factors. These include receiving prizes from time to time because of appreciation of good work done by them. They are also influenced by middle level risks and by the feeback which is provided as a result of impartial assessment of their work. They are influenced by the extent to which they are allowed to have freedom to select methods for achieving their objectives and also by the sense of responsibility.

Need Based Motivation. Many politicians, social workers and leaders of the dissidents are of the opinion that environmental factors can be improved by providing opportunities to earn more money. Thus those who have monetary problems these can be solved. It has also been found that those who need power; they are always careful about their control and influence. Gradually they try to go ahead on the path of leadership. Those who wish to maintain contacts they try to ensure that their contacts with others are very happy and cordial. They wish that their social group should always help them. But in every case the one who wishes to achieve something, he always like to have some success in his efforts. He wants to go near to his goals and targets.

Pennsylvania Experiment. Clelland also carried an experiment on 450 unemployed persons. All the workers were in almost the same position and they were passing almost similar situations and conditions. They all wanted to have work, money and shelter. They were practically in bad need of food. They had knocked every possible door for help. Clelland found that those workers who could be placed in the category of need for achievement. n/ACH, they got more wages and quicker promotion, as compared with the others.

Achievement motivation is a continuous struggle process which needs hard work and capacity to face challenge. The achievers are prepared to work hard and for them quality is more important then quantity output. Motivating factor may differ but ultimate aim is achievement and to achieve success.

Managerial Implications of Motivation

Motivation achievement is a ticklish problem in which both environment and manager play an important role.

Achievement Motivation and Environment. Clelland is of the view that for achievement motivation environment is as important as the desire to achieve something. If an organisation does not provide any opportunity or environment, then no amount for desire to achieve can motivate a person or make any worker a success. Determination and will to achieve something can result in success only when the organisation provides him needed opportunities. He has therefore, said that the management providing proper environments can improve the level of achievement of the workers on the one hand and organisation on the other.

Managerial Implications of Motivation. Clelland is of the view that those person who have come out successful in difficult and adverse circumstances in high achievement situations their performance is always much better than those of the average person. He has said that for management, it is therefore, essential that their should be proper balancing between the individual and the work. He has further said that those who show desire for high achievement and also those who try to achieve these through personality test should be treated as under utilised. The management should remember that those who have no desire to achieve high they are not prepared to undertake challenging tasks and they also cannot do any quality work under adverse circumstances.

Qualities of High Achievement Motivator. He has said need for achievement is nothing else but desire to succeed in life. It also means excelling others in race for achieving something. He found that those who are guided by high achievement motivation possess certain qualities for protecting the interests of the management. They are willing to come forward to shoulder more responsibilities for solving problems which confront managment. They fix certain difficult targets for them to be achieved. They lay stress on feed back and wish to have an assessment of the work which they are doing. They are attracted by such management tasks which are competitive and challenging. They do not feel attracted or motivated when tasks assigned to them are simple and circumstances are normal.

Concept of Need for Power. By this he mean 'Need for Power'. According to Clelland there are people who feel happy by providing opportunities to other they feel need more power. They need power to influence other. When this power is used for constructive purposes or for the welfare of others it is called socialised power. When however, that power is misused and aims at exercising authority and control over others that is called personalised power.

Concept of Need for Affiliation. It stands for the 'Need for Affiliation'. It is used for making friends. It is felt boldly by those who become an important part of work group in which they are working or which to achieve recognisation in that way. Clelland has tried to explain close relationship between expectations of the person and need for domination. He has said that there is bell shaped relationship between expectation and motivation. He has come to the conclusion that the degree of motivation and that of expectation goes on increasing till a stage reaches when there are equal chances of suceess or failure or achievement and non-achievement. Before reaching this stage, there is tendency on the parts of some persons to leave the task, as they feel that it is too difficult for them to be accomplished.

Clelland's Contribution. Clelland's hypothesis that achievement is in part responsible for economic growth has provided an impetus for studies concerning development and social consequences of achievement. Clelland has done considerably good work in the area of achievement motivation. He has brought out three important factors of motivation namely n/POW; n/AFF and n/ACH. Clelland has also concluded that the middle class people are always more motivated to achieve something. He has also said that in economic development of a country motivation always plays a big role. Motivational process can be developed with the help of training. He has however, pointed out that an organisation for achievement of course needs highly motivated persons but these cannot always be source of producing excellent administrators.

Bureaucracy-Neutral or Committed

We in India who have inherited the British model of administration are familiar with the concept of neutrality of public services. By the end of the nineteenth century the system of recruitment into British public services through open competitive examinations, based as far as possible on merit and non-political considerations, non-political promotions and partisan neutrality of these services had been well established. There is consensus in Britain, among the political parties and public servants, that party control of the services is deterimental to good administration. Civil servants are servants of the Crown, who are bound to serve with impartiality whichever government happens to be in power. "Civil servants usually have their own views on matters of policy but are not free to indulge in their partisan sympathise freely. Their allegiance to one party or another is subordinated to the requirements of their profession. In Britain neutrality has become a concomitant of the service-career system. It is regarded as "one of the strongest bulworks of democracy."

Meaning of Neutrality. From Weber's time, who first conceptual neutrality of bureaucracy, till today numerous scholars have interneutrality. Neutral bureaucracy has been identified with various qualities like those of expertise, impartiality, stability and anonymity. "What is indicated is that with a total non-alignment with political parties should be combined a balanced appreciation of, and a reasoned sympathy with, the political aspect of the programmes of the government, an awareness of the basic philosophical and socio-economic disputations behind the programmes and decisions, and a devotion to democratic concepts." O.P. Dwivedi and R.B. Jain explain that political neutrality "not only meant the absence of political activity or bias of the part of individual members of the bureaucracy but also that the bureaucracy would respond to the will of the government, no matter what its political complexion," Joseph La Palombara is of the opinion that the administrator should not become involved in factional fights, either among political parties or within the dominant party.

Fritz Morstein Marx looks at bureaucratic neutrality from two angles—negative and positive. Negatively, the administrative neutrality does not mean an ostrich—like withdrawal of the directing cadre from the arena of governmental choice. Policy programme, and management pose countless issues on which the higher civil servant is obligated to come forth with his best judgement. He fails to do his duty if he tries to wash his hands off these questions. "He has no warrant for simply passing them to the politicians, without first contributing his special competence for professional analysis." Positively, neutrality, according to F.M. Marx, means acceptance of the discipline of working without reservation. It also means working with devotion for the success of every government lawfully in power. "Conversely it carries with it a prohibition. Permanent officers cannot allow themselves so intimate an identification with a particular policy or programmes as to create for them an emotional disability when it comes to turning in the opposite direction under a different government."

The concept of neutrality as outlined above has three implications: (*i*) public confidence in the non-political character of the public service; (*ii*) confidence of ministers belonging to any political party in the loyalty of their permanent subordinates; and (*iii*) high morale of the public servants based on the confidence that promotions would be made not on the basis of political considerations but on merit.

It must be made clear that a neutral model cannot be practised arbitrarily. Both the parties *i.e.* political parties and elected representatives including the ministers, and public servants, must accept the implications of the model. It cannot be maintained if either of the groups refuses to acknowledge its responsibilities and implications. Moreover neutrality is a state of mind and there can be no effective law to ensure it. "It is a factor in the administrative responsibility of civil service and an ingredient in the intellectual integrity of individual civil servant. It could be induced by the characteristics of the service.

Dimensions for Measuring Neutrality

The basic postulate of neutral or depoliticised bureaucracy is that the public bureaucracy by training and tradition, could be brought up to be a political institution which would implement public policies-without the influence of political views of their own. Dwivedi and Jain outline various dimensions along which the concept of neutrality can be measured. These are:

(*i*) Degree of influence in the decision-making process.

(*ii*) The degree of segregation of the political executive from the bureaucracy.

(*iii*) The extent of political interference in a public servant's work.

(*iv*) The degree of its involvement in politics; and

(*v*) The extent of confidence which the bureaucracy enjoys with the public. For a neutral or depoliticised bureaucracy, the score for the first four cases above should be zero while in the last case it should be at optimum level.

Concept of Neutrality Outdated

It could perhaps be speculated that the widespread acceptability the doctrine in England was due to peculiar circumstances of that country which among others included: concepts of ministerial responsibility and anonymity of the civil service, power being shared by two major parties both of which were not only equally committed to the principles of democracy, nationalism and imperialism but also shared similar views on government's social responsibility; the concept in Britain has never been put to any great strain. Laski felt that the top bureaucrats and those elected to the House of Commons belong to the same class horizon. The kind of attainable society the top civil servants visualise is more or less identical with the society envisaged by the political leadership. Neutrality has been acceptable to them because their ultimate principles of action have not been in conflict with the policies of the political parties in power, nor the govrnments have sought to depart from those principles in action.

The British concept of neutrality was implanted in some other countries which had imperial linked with it like Australia, Canada, Indian etc. In India one of the purpose of creating a neutral civil servant was to isolate him from the political currents prevalent in the country. "Politicisation at this time could have only been anti-British.

This concept of neutrality worked till the Second World War. Since then it has begun to be challenged. Even the British have become sceptical about the continued validity of the neutral career service in its ability to implement the objectives of a welfare state. By extending substantial political rights to eighty four per cent of their public servants, they have impliedly admitted that it is not possible in the present day circumstances to keep them fully politically neutral or isolated. There is now overwhelming evidence, empirical as well as scholarly, in support of the view that bureaucracy cannot act as a netural instrument in the conduct of public affairs. Bureaucracy is no longer regarded as value-free but a value-laden instrument of political power.

Several reasons are advanced for the refutation of the idea of neutral bureaucracy:

(*i*) The processes of policy decision-making are no longer confined to the political executives: they percolate over the entire fabric of government resulting in inescapable items of delegation and zones of such policy, where the political executive does not come into the picture at all and yet the decisions reflect the ethos of the party in power.

(*ii*) The leadership role of public bureaucracy is explicit in all political systems, but is more pronounced in the conditions of developing countries.

(*iii*) Where the state takes up large-scale welfare programme, neutrality is neither possible nor desirable.

(*iv*) At the top levels, even the performance appraisal of public bureaucracy is done by political heads; hence an element of political assessement in bound to creep into such a rating.

(*v*) In the sphere of policy advice and execution, modern bureaucracy cannot remain aloof because often political and practical considerations are indistinguishable.

(*vi*) Civil servants the product of their upbringing and certain subjective element from their judgements cannot be eliminated. They cannot be psychologically neutral on issues and problems which confront them.

(*vii*) Bureaucracy will almost invariably reproduce in microcosm many of the basic political conflicts that characterise the systems of the developing countries, and thus it is extremely difficult for it to act neutral.

(*viii*) Neutrality is really a myth where in a political system there is a wide divergence of views among the ruling political parties especially when there is no clear traditional divsion of functions between the political masters and civil servants in terms of policy and its implementation.

(*ix*) It develops its own group identity and interests and it develops its organisational objective towards self protection.

(*x*) Politicians in developing countries who are bent upon change and intellectuals who are impatient with the rate of progress finds themselves at odd with bureaucracy which is deeply steeped in the colonial tradition of law and order. Neutrality of bureaucracy will become suspect. The more conspicuous the higher civil service becomes the caretaker of the given order, the less can it expect to be judged truly nonpartisan.

POLITICISED BUREAUCRACY

Since the Weberian model of strictly neutral bureaucracy has lost its validity, the involvement of bureaucracy in political arena is now widely accepted. It is termed as politicisation. The politicised bureaucracy is one "which is involved or influences or is influenced to any degree, consciously or unconsciously, by overt or by implicit actions in the stream of the politics of the day whether of the party in power or the parties in oppoistion...In a more extended form it may also be regarded as type of bureaucracy which uses political parties in furtherance of their collective or individual objective or which is used by political parties in the achievement of party objectives.

O.P. Dwivedi and R.B. Jain conceptualise four broad categories of bureaucracy according to the extent of their politicisation:

(*i*) depoliticised bureaucracy,

(*ii*) semi-politicised bureaucracy,

(*iii*) committed bureaucracy, and

(*iv*) fully politicised bureaucracy. The characteristics of each of these categories are as under:

Depoliticised Bureaucracy

A depoliticised bureaucracy is neutral, anonymous and apolitical. There is no bureaucratic involvement in political activity. Also there is no political interference in the recruitment and promotion of public servants which are based on pure merit. The public respects public servants as a band of devoted impartial professionals.

Semi-politicised Bureaucracy

In the case of semi-politicised bureaucracy, executive dominate bureaucracy to take decisions on party lines. The public servants enjoy the right to vote. They can join a political party after resignation or retirements. There is a limited internal interference in personnel promotion transfers etc. The bureaucracy tends to perpetuate itself and attempts to serve its own ends. There is lack of public esteem.

Committed Bureaucracy

The committed bureaucracy is one which is committed to the programmes of the party in power. Public servants are allowed to become members of political parties and participate in their meetings. Political parties interfere in appointments, transfers and promotions of public employees. In other words, public services are not free from "spoils system". The public orientation towards bureaucracy is that of a corrupt civil service which toes the line of party in power.

Fully Politicised Bureaucracy

Fully politicised bureaucracy exists in single-party authoritarian structures. Bureaucracy is enormously powerful and usurps power for serving the ends of the party. There is no distinction between the structures of the party and those of government, they are interchangeable. Public servants exercise fully political rights including election to the legislature. By and large, the recruitment to bureaucracy is done from party "cadres".

❐

9

Max Weber

German sociologist, Max Weber generated the systematic study of bureaucracy. In terms of influence it has exerted and the argument it has stimulated Weber's writing on bureaucracy is more important than the sum total of the contributions of countless scholars. Halevy writes, "Weber's theory, like Marx's has attracted widespread and continued criticism, and his conception of bureaucracy has been one of its prime targets. But this is really an indication of the theory's impact. Unimportant theories are usually disregarded and quickly forgotten, only theories that have served as a landmark in the development of the discipline have been singled out for repeated onslaughts. And the more they have been attacked, the more resilient they have becomes. Weber's theory of bureaucracy is a clear case in point. Innumerable contemporary authors on bureaucracy start out with a critique of his theory."

Weber's most extensive and systematic discussion of administration occurs within his sociology of domination in Economy and Society'. 'Parliament and Government in the Newly Organised Germany' is another vital source of knowing his views on this subject.

Weber's Ideal Type

Weber used the word bureaucracy to designate a quite specific kind of administrative organisation. He insisted that modern bureaucratic organisation as a form of apparatus was sui generies. He never defined bureaucracy in an explicit way in which he defined 'class' or 'status group'. Martin Albrow observes, however, that Weber's concept of bureaucracy can be conveyed in a definition of this kind: "by bureaucracy is meant an administrative body of appointed officials." He did not include elected officials or those selected by lot, in bureaucracy. The essential feature of the bureaucratic official was that he was an appointee. Weber thought of bureaucracy as a collective term for a body of officials, a definite and distinct group whose influence can be seen in all kinds of large organisations—state, church. Political parties, trade unions, business enterprises, unversities etc.

The legal rational authority depends on the following related beliefs:

(1) A legal code can be established which can claim obedience from members of the organisation.

(2) The man exercising authority also obeys this impersonal order.

(3) Administration looks after the interests of the organisation within the limits of law which is a system of abstract rules and are applied to particular cases.

(4) That only qua member does the member obey the law.

(5) Finally, obedience is not to the person who holds authority but to the impersonal order which has appointed him to that position.

Ramesh K. Arora has excellenty summed up the characteristics and principles of the administrative staff under legal rational authority as described by Weber. These are:

(1) Legal authority in purest form utilises bureaucratic administrative staff.

(2) The characteristic of bureaucrats are:

(*i*) They are subject to authority only in official capacities.

(*ii*) They are organised in hierarchy of office.

(*iii*) Their office is their primary occupation.

(*iv*) They are paid in money; have fixed, graded salary scales and pensions.

(*v*) Bureaucracy offers a career in which promotions are by seniority and/or achievement.

(*vi*) That each office has defined competence.

(*vii*) Officials are appointed on the basis of their technical competence.

(*viii*) Offices are filled by free selection.

(*ix*) The official is separated from means of administration.

(*x*) The officials are subject to discipline in the conduct of office.

(3) Appointment is important feature because election impedes hierarchical discipline.

(4) Specialised knowledge is indispensable, even though at the top of bureaucracy there is a non-bureaucrat.

(5) Administrative bureaucratic staff in its purest form is of monocratic type.

(*i*) It is the most rational means of carrying out imperative control over human beings.

(*ii*) It can escape existing bureaucratic authority only by creating another bureaucratic authority.

(*iii*) Its primary source of superiority is technical knowledge.

(*iv*) Capitalism has been major spur towards bureaucratisation.

(*v*) Development of bureaucracy leads to social levelling and social levelling favours bureaucracy.

These characteristics of ideal type bureaucracy had been drawn by Weber from Prussian administrative theory and European administrative history. It must be remembered, however, that this is ideal type (not an ideal) which is never found in 'pure' or 'unmixed' form in reality. Administrative systems of the industrialised. Western countries largely approximate to this ideal type.

Weber disagress with Marx and Lenin on the point that bureaucracy being tied to capitalism, will disappear when the latter is overthrown by a socialist revolution. He insists that bureaucracy is an independent entity and it will survive whether the society is capitalist or socialist. This is for two reasons. First, since the rise of bureaucracy is conditioned by those factors which have created the modern society *i.e.*, capitalism, centralisation tendencies and mass democracy, it is a phenomenon which cannot be eliminated. Weber regards bureaucracy as an indispensable component of a society built on a complex distribution of labour, centralised administration and money economy. It simply cannot be done away with. Weber says, "If bureaucratic administration is, other things being equal, always the most rational type from a technical point of view, the needs of mass administration make it today completely indispensable. The choice is only that between bureaucracy and dilettantism in the field of administration." Second, bureaucracy has become a permanent social force. Its superiority is derived from its character of being an impersonal apparatus, technically competent, precise and disciplined.

Weber sees bureaucratic tendencies not only in the modern states and private capitalist enterprises, but also in the modern army, the church and the universities. Standing armies, material wealth and the consequent increasing role of public sector, modern means of communication, political factors like universal suffrage, rise of mass political parties are the factors which work towards bureaucratisation.

Bureaucracy and Capitalism

As stated earlier, Weber does not tie bureaucracy to the capitalist order of production. He no doubt explains the emergence of bureaucracy by reference to the nature of the capitalist system (wherever capitalism flourishes, bureaucracy emerges) but capitalism is only one of the several casual factors. Bureaucracy can also emerge, or continue to exist, under other conditions *e.g.* socialism. A socialist revolution cannot result in a dictatorship of the proletariat. In modern mass society it can only result in a consolidated disctatorship of the bureaucrats.

Capitalism in its present form of development requires bureaucracy, on the other hand, "capitalism is the most rational economic basis for bureaucratic administration and enables it to develop in the most rational form." Even if capitalism were abolished, bureaucracy would nevertheless remain. In a capitalist society private and public bureaucracies check each other to a degree. If private capitalism were eliminated these bureaucracies would be merged into a single hierarchy.

Consequences of Bureaucratisation

Weber was very uneasy about the social and political consequences of the contemporary, irresistible spread of bureaucracy. Martin Kryagier mentions two points for Weber's uneasiness. First is the bureaucratisation of the whole society in the sense of the permeation of bureaucratic values, ways of thought and of behaviour throughout a population. Second point of Weber's uneasiness was that those maning bureaucratic organisations might come to be the actual rulers of a state. Bengt Abrahamsson observes that Weber could see the possibility of a bureaucratic machine revolting against its masters.

Weber goes on to add that if bureaucracy chooses to act politically, its masters could easily become victims. The reason for this is that political rulers lack the necessary expertise to effectively control the reigns of bureaucracy. "It is easier for the career official to pursue his opinion *vis-a-vis* the chief of state than it is for the officials' nominal superior *i.e.* the cabinet minister." At another place Weber cautions that bureaucrats had enormous power resources at their disposal which might enable them to rule unless they were kept under political control.

Halevy mentions two more but related consequences about which Weber was worried. He saw the impact of bureaucracy on the individual within it, the bureaucrat, as the crippling of his personality. Bureaucracy creates a person who is a little cog in a big machine, and who tries to become a bigger cog. Capitalism and bureaucracy both create a technical expert who replaces the earlier cultured man and who is convinced of his own superiority. Weber says, "specialists without spirit, sensualists without heart, this nullity imagines that it has attained a level of civilisation never before reached." The critics of bureaucracy call it a dehumanised person.

Control over Bureaucracy

Weber never thought of bureaucracy as an independent social unit. He tended to view it as a machine. Hence the question of control over bureaucracy becomes easy. It subordinates itself to anyone who is able to master the economic and legal technique necessary for its proper functioning. Since Weber regarded bureaueracy as an apparatus, it can work for anyone who knows how to gain control over it. He considered it essential that non-bureaucratic leaders be selected who might control the controllers. The other checks which Weber considers necessary for reducing the influence of bureaucracy to its rightful proportions are openness, elimination of 'official secrets' and the introduction of effective parliamentary control.

Marthin Albrow groups the mechanisms of control over bureaucracy into five. These are:

Collegiality. At each stage of official hierarchy, more than one person should, as a matter of right, be involved in taking decision *e.g.* British Cabinet.

Direct Democracy. It is practicable only in local administration, and the need for expertise was a decisive counter-weight.

Amateur Administration. This system could not measure upto the demands for expertise which modern society made. Moreover, where amateurs were assisted by professional it was always the latter who made the real decisions.

Separation of Powers. Dividing responsibility for the same function between two or more bodies. This system is inherently unstable.

Representation. *i.e.* through elected representative assemblies or parliaments. It was through this medium that Weber saw the greatest possibility of a check on bureaucracy.

Weber on Bureaucracy *vis-a-vis* Democracy

Weber was ambivalent about the implications of bureaucracy for democracy. As stated earlier, bureaucracy and democracy developed side by side. Democracy promoted the development of bureaucracy by its fight against traditional notables. He says that, on the other hand, democracy creates blockages to bureaucratic organisation by means of limiting the term of office by election and dispensing with the qualifications of expertness.

Weber stressed that in a democracy, bureaucracy should be subordinated to its political master *i.e.* elected politician. But he was deeply concerned that those who staffed the bureaucracy would themselves become the masters of the state. In relation to the elected political master the bureaucrat is an expert and in the course of his official duties, he acquires a great deal of concrete information. This information which is not always available to the political superior places the bureaucrat at a great advantage and is the source of his power.

A further threat to democracy lies in the code of bureaucratic secrecy. Most important spheres of bureaucratic action are withdrawn from public scrutiny. The citizens may complain to the elected representative about bureaucratic action, but secrecy of the action makes redress of the grievance difficult. Weber says that how much power bureaucracy exerts on its political superior, depends largely on the bureaucracy itself. "If it chooses to over-rule its master, there is nothing to prevent it from doing so. Against the bureaucracy the ruler remains powerless.

Pluralist Theory of Bureaucracy

The pluralist school of thought has made considerable contribution in recent times to our understanding of politics of democracy and bureaucracy. Pluralism views the state and bureaucracy as disjointed in structure and blundering in performance. It has been popular in the United States or several years especially in the 1950s and 1960s. In recent years some new versions of pluralism like pluralism in bureaucracy, governmental overload and ungovernability have come to be accepted.

Pluralism in Bureaucracy

Pluralism holds bureaucrats as one of the several veto groups which function in a political system. Like other groups it is engaged in competition for power and is a part of the pluralist structure of the state. The pluralist logic applies to the American political system the greatest of which is based on its particular tradition of checks and balances, but it is also valid in all industrialised democratic countries. The pluralists argue that bureaucrats are unable to rule alone, and yet no one else can rule without them. They cannot always achieve their goals, but they can prevent others from achieving theirs.

Power in the administration does not flow exclusively from the top. It also flows from structures of interests that enclose the administration. Thus there is no single source of power in the administration. Moreover the relevant bureaucratic agencies must create sufficient consensus, when political parties that come to power fail to do so, to permit policies to be moulded and executed. Therefore, a bureaucratic agency has a large share of responsibility for building and maintaining political support for its own programmes. Sometimes it has to organise and build up that support for its own survival and growth. Hence the legislature clientle and interest groups, media and even the general public are important whose support or lack of it can significantly effect a bureaucratic agency.

The political system is pluralist in its very structure also. The complexity of the state structure affords interest groups multiple access points at which to exert their influence. Also, state institutions provide arenas for interplay of contending internal factions which is fully exploited by the interest groups.

Therefore, contrary to its image, the bureaucracy is not a monolithic hierarchy, say the pluralists. Rather, it is a highly fragmented set of agencies that are partly interdependent but are also in competition within and among themselves for survival and primacy.

Another pluralist approach is the thesis of governmental overload. It is advocated by scholars like D. Bell, M. Crozier, S.P. Huntington, A King R. Rose and others. It is argued that recently there has been a growth of pressure on governments to meet large number of newly defined and vastly expanded demands, which result from what has been described by Bell and Crozier as revolution of entitlements. Hence the range of matters for which governments are held responsible is vastly increasing. As A. King puts it, now all grievances get dumped into the lap of government......"Once upon a time, then, man looked to God to order the world. Then he looked to the market. Now he looks to Government."

Bureaucracy Concept

Through distortion and misinterpretation, the term 'bureaucracy' has come to mean, in words of John A. Veig, officiousness, bungling, arbitrariness, regimentation and westefulness. According to G.B. Shaw, "bureaucracy consists of functionaries; the aristocracy of idols; the democracy of idolaters". In the words of H.J. Laski, "bureaucracy is the term usually applied to a system of Government, the control of which is so completely in the hands of the officials that their power jeopardizes the liberties of the ordinary citizen".

Mosher Kingsley and Stahl define bureaucracy as "a hierarchical administrative structure in which each official fits like a cog in a complex machine. In this organisation nothing is left to chance. All important relationships are defined in advance and the pyramid of authority is divided horizontally into levels of responsibility." E.N. Gladden defines bureaucracy as "a Government of officials". Marshall E. Dimock is of the view that "Bureaucratisation means specialisation hierarchies and long lines of communication." Max Weber portrays it as a 'system of administration characterised by expertness'. Impartiality and the absence of humanity."

Technically the term is used in two senses. In its larger sense it is used "to describe any personnel system where the employees are classified in a system of administration composed of a hierarchy of sections, divisions, bureaus, departments, and the like." In its restricted sense it is used to describe "a body of public servants organised in a hierarchical system which stands outside the sphere of effective public control."

Max Weber in his Essays on Sociology has given three characteristics of bureaucracy:

(1) The authority to give the commands required for the discharge of these duties is distributed in a stable way and is strictly delimited by rules concerning the coercive means, physical sacerdotal, or otherwise, which may be placed at the disposal of officials.

(2) The regular activities required for the purposes of the bureaucratically governed structure are distributed in a fixed way as official duties.

(3) Methodical provision is made for the regular and continuous fulfilment of these duties and for the execution of the corresponding rights.

Weber further says that there is hierarchical principle in all bureaucratic structure; a reliance on written documents files, records, and the apparatus of modern office management; the formulation of general rules or practices for the management of the office.

Prof. Friedrich gives six primary criteria of bureaucracy. These are differentiation of functions; qualifications for office; hierarchical organisation and discipline; objectively of method; precision, consistency or continuity involving adherence to rules and keeping of records; and lastly the exercise of discretion involving secrecy in regard to certain aspects of government.

Marx has used the terms four senses:

(1) Bureaucracy as an Ailment of Organisation Obstructing Good Management. Laski has also described characteristics of Bureaucracy as—a passion for routine in administration, the sacrifice of flexibility to rule, delay in the making of decision and a refusal to embark upon experiment. In this sense, Bureaucracy may be identified as a rigid, mechanical, wooden, inhuman, formal and soulless approach.

(2) Bureaucracy in the Sense of Big Government. We live in the era of the big institutions. According to Pfiffner also, "size alone is perhaps the basic cause of bureaucracy. Where large scale enterprise exists, there bureaucracy will be found".

(3) Bureaucracy as a Particular Form of Organisation More Specifically as a General Design For the Conduct of Public Administration. Pfiffner also has used the term in this sense. Gladden also defines the term to mean "a regulated administrative system organised as a series of interrelated offices."

(4) Bureaucracy Thought of as a Blight, Always for the Worse Falling on Liberty. Bureaucracy is defined as a government by the civil service for its own aggrandisement. Laski also is of the view that "bureaucracy is a system of government the control of which is so completely in the hands of officials that their power jeopardises the liberties or ordinary citizens."

An analysis of all these views prompts us to conclude that bureaucracy may be defined as a type of administrative organisation or a government by civil servants for their own aggrandisement or a professional class hierarchically organised. In the latter sense, bureaucracy is indispensable for democracy. However, if it is to be interpreted as a government by irresponsible and unresponsive civil servants, it may be considered as a sheer anachronism in this age of representative government.

Evils of Bureaucracy

As remarked above bureaucracy is looked upon with ridicule and the civil servants are contemptuously called 'Bureaucrats'. Harold Laski defined bureaucracy as "a system of government the control of which is so completely in the hands of the officials that their power jeopardises the liberties of the ordinary citizens". Ramsay Muir in his book 'How Britain is Governed' says, "Bureaucracy thrives under the cloak or Ministerial responsibility.... It is ruinous when it becomes the master." Prof. W. A. Robson has summarised its defects in the following words: "The maladies from which bureaucracy most frequently suffers are an excessive sense of self-importance on the part of officials or an undue idea of the importance of their office; an indifference towards the feeling or the convenience of individual citizens; an obsession with the binding and inflexible authority of departmental decisions, precedents, arrangements or forms, regardless of how badly or with what injustice they may work in individual cases; a mania regulations and formal procedure; a pre-occupation with the activities of particular units of administration and an inability to consider the Government as a whole; a failure to recognise the relations between the governors and the governed as an essential part of democratic process."

The defects of bureaucracy may be briefly summarised as follows:

(1) Circumlocution. The greatest criticism of bureaucracy is levelled due to its lengthy and roundabout way of doing work. Bureaucrats care very much for formal rules and regulations. However urgent the case may be, it has to run its full course of going up and down. The minutest thing is to be written down in an official way and proper procedure is followed. Sometimes files lose their importance as the matter is not decided for months together.

Charles Deckens in his novel "Little Dorrit" describes the ways and methods of the Circumlocution Office in the words.....Boards sat upon them. Secretariat minuted upon them, commissions gabbled about them, clerks registered, entered, checked and ticked them off, and they melted away. In short, all the business of the country went through the circumlocution office, except the business that never came out of it, and its name was legion."

(2) Red Tape. Closely associated with circumlocution is the defect of red-tapism which means blind following of formal rules and regulations. Though following prescribed rules is not itself bad but the dogged and blind attachment to them certainly impairs the efficiency of work because then the case will not be depended on its merits but on old and out-dated precedents. The civil servants are trained in rules and regulations. So the result is that "they cut the clothes, but do not find the body."

(3) Formalism. Another great defect of bureaucracy is its excessive adherence to formalism. Too much use of forms and formalities makes the official lose his sense of judgement and initiative. The language and the forms of official letters, and the method of making note on the file and sending it upwards all are fixed beforehand and each officer acts mechanically in the prescribed manner. W. Bagehot describing the life of an official writes, 'Entering the office young, he copied letters for five years, he made an index of papers for nine months, he made an analysis of documents for five years; more when he commenced at last to transact business it was strictly of a formal character and he was upwards of twenty years in the public service before he ever decided on anything of special importance; no wonder that he was unwilling to decide anything, that he referred everything to somebody else, that he corresponded in his best handwriting with another public office; his entries were most correct but the transaction mere normally wrong; the book-keeping was admirable but the affairs recorded feeble or inefficient."

(4) Unresponsiveness. Bureaucracy is not usually responsive to the needs of the people. It keeps on following its old standardised procedures and does not react to the changing political elimate of the country. In India after independence the attitude of some civil servants towards the people is of the same authoritativeness as was during British Rule. The official of necessity becomes esspecialist, intellectually isolated, oriented towards techniques rather than people." Bertrand Russel maintains that bureaucracy tends to develop "a negative psychology perpetually prone to prohibitions." As a result of their day-to-day routines civil servants develop special preferences, antipathies and discriminations. Their vision due to their training and experience in one particular instiutionalised activity becomes myopic.

(5) Despotism. Bureaucracy has been condemned as despotic since it eraves for power. As such, it usurps the powers of the legislature on the one hand and side-tracks the law courts on the other. Lord Hewart, a British jurist, in his book 'New Despotism' observed that British citizens shall lose their liberties under the weight of growing administrative absolutism. "A little enquiry will serve to show that there is now, and for some years past has been a persistent influence at work which, whatever the motives or the intentions that support it may be thought to be, undoubtedly, has the effect of placing a large and increasing field of departmental authority and activity beyond the reach of ordinary law." Lord Hewart believed that the liberty of the individual was in danger because 'ardent bureaucrat' has usurped the powers of legislature and executive. Similarly Ramsay Muir in his book "How Britain is Governed" has attacked the growing powers of the civil servants. In the legislative domain in civil services have come to possess the following powers—*(a)* Executive rule making which means the powers to issue a particular command; the power to license; the power to impose a penalty; the powers to inspect; the powers to enquire; *(b)* executive legislation which comprises legislation on matters of principle; power of imposing taxation; the power of amending Acts of Parliament.

(6) Corruption. Corruption is the melody of Indian bureaucracy. It has gone into the very root of the bureaucratic structure we have inherited from the Britishers. The civil services are in general prone to illegal extortion of money from the people before doing their work.

(7) Empire Building. Bureaucracy perpetuates the evil of dividing the work of government into many isolated and self-dependent sections, each pursuing its own ends and blowing its own trumpet. These units thus develop the tendency of being independent units. They cease considering themselves as parts of a bigger whole and thus consider their own little empires as ends in themselves.

(8) Yesmanship. The top bureacrats who are political favourites become perfect yesmen of their-political bosses. They in their turn, expect yesmanship from their subordinate officers. Thus a sort of vicious circle sets in. Right or wrong, the boss must be supported. Such a yesmanship is eroding efficiency and lowering the morale of straightforward honest employees who do not wrongly toe the line of the high ups—political or non-political.

(9) Self Aggrandisement. The bureaucrats are power hungry. They have lust for power. Gradually they are encroaching upon the domains of political executive, legislature and even judiciary. A critic has rightly remarked. "The permanent civil service is becoming more and more impatient of the sham facade of democracy behind which it works and is showing progressively greater skill in using the forms of parliament and the convenient doctrine of ministerial responsibility as a cover for the steady increase of the power of the Departments".

Safeguards

Though Bureaucracy seems to be a necessity in a modern welfare state, yet there is a scope to cure its melodies by keeping the following suggestions in mind:

(*a*) The Ministers should possess a dynamic personality and not play a tool in the hands of the public services.

(*b*) A maximum decentralisation of powers and authority be effected so that the sub-leaders realise their responsibility and the top leaders on account of excess of work do not sign on the dotted lines.

(*c*) Public servants should be selected and promoted on the basis of merit. No political favourite be given a high place.

(*d*) A sound system of education should be developed so that the people are intellectually advanced and the services fail to indulge in high-handedness, or are prone to corruption.

(*e*) An impartial and unbiased press can also serve as a sword of Damocles on the heads of corrupt officials.

(*f*) A system of pooling together the experience and suggestions of public servants be devised so that the knowledge so gathered be disseminated to the rest of the members of the public service.

(*g*) A research should be made on administrative methods so that efficiency and economy are effected.

If these safeguards are kept in mind there is nothing to be afraid of bureaucracy. William Beveridge correctly observed, "Democracy if it knows its business has no reason to fear bureaucracy." Morrison went to farther extreme when he suggested, "Bureaucracy is the price of parliamentary democracy."

Max Weber's Theory of Bureaucracy

Max Weber, an eminent German sociologist, gave a systematic analysis of bureaucracy. No study on bureaucracy is considered complete till Max Weber's views on bureaucracy are known. He developed a typology of authority—traditional, charismatic and legal. To him bureaucracy sustained and sanctified by the legal authority, is the most effective form of organisation. According to Weber bureaucracy has following essential characteristics:

(*i*) separation of office and its incumbent; (*ii*) selection by merit; (*iii*) fixed remuneration of officials; (*iv*) official is subjected to discipline and control during the performance of his duties; (*v*) Hierarchy of offices; (*vi*) Allocation of activities of organisation necessitated to fulfil its objectives; (*vii*) Apportioning of authority needed to discharge these activities; (*viii*) Rigid adherence to rules.

In the words of Weber "The purest type of exercise of legal authority is that which employs bureaucratic administrative staff. Only the supreme chief of the organisation occupies his position of authority by virtue of appropriation of election, or of having been designated for the succession. But even his authority consists in sphere of legal competence. The whole administrative staff under the supreme authority there consists, in the purest type of individual official, who are appointed and function according to the following critera:

(1) They are organised in a hierarchy of offices.

(2) Each office legally enjoys a clearly defined sphere of competence.

(3) The office is filled by a free contractual relationship. In a way there is free selection.

(4) They enjoy personal freedom but subjected to authority regarding impersonal official obligations.

(5) The office constitutes the career. Promotion is according to seniority or achievement or both. Promotion depends on the judgement of the superiors.

(6) The office is the sole or atleast the primary occupation of the incumbent.

(7) Candidates are selected on the basis of technical qualifications. They are appointed, not elected.

(8) They are entitled to fixed salaries and adequate pension. The salary is graded according to rank in the hierarchy. But in addition the responsibility of

the position and the requirements of the incumbents' social status are taken into consideration.

(9) The officials, work is separated from ownership of the means of administration and without appropriation of his position.

(10) The official is strictly under the disciplinary control in the conduct of official work.

At one place, Weber portrays bureaucracy as a "System of administration characterised by expertness, impartiality and the absence of humanity".

Elements of Weberian Model of Bureaucracy

Model of bureaucracy, as developed by Max Weber has certain elements. His model provides for the depersonalisation of relationship and impersonal issuance of orders and commands to subordinates and their obedience to these. Then the administrative acts, decisions and rules should be formulated and recorded in writing even where verbal discussion is the rule.

Then another feature of his model is continuous organisation of official functions bound by rules. Their rational application however, requires training. Adherence to rules has become an end in itself. The rules in bureaucracy becomes more important than the goals. It pleads separation of administrative staff from the ownership of means of production or administration. In order to check the bureaucrats from mis-using their position the model pleads for the complete absence of appropriation of official position by the incumbent. Weberian model provides for the sphere of competence which involves obligation to perform functions allotted as a part of division of labour, necessary authority to carry out the functions and clearly defined means of compulsions subject to certain conditions in their use.

According to Weber the organisation of offices follows the principle of hierarchy *i.e.* each lower office is under the control and supervision of higher one. His model attaches considerable importance to the principle of hierarchy in the organisation of offices. His model insists on the selection of technically qualified people and he has come to the conclusion that monochromatic bureaucratic organisation, from a purely technical point of view, could be capable of attaining the highest degree of efficiency.

Conditions for the Development of Bureaucracy. For the development of modern bureaucracy it is essential that the society should be economically developed on the one hand and administratively on the other. He has also said that there is close relationship between capitalism and bureaucracy. He has said that bureaucracy develops as administration becomes democratic and becomes responsive to public opinion. Thus there is close relationship between democracy and bureaucracy.

Bureaucracy has made administrative system to function smoothly but gradually bureaucrats become lethargic and too much rule conscious which retards the development of bureaucracy.

Criticism. Weber's name has very much been associated with bureaucracy but it has also been criticised on several grounds. Some of the main points of criticism advanced against him are as follows:

1. Weber has also been criticised by Talcott Parsons when he questions the internal consistency of Weber's ideal type of bureaucracy. He does not agree with Weber that high position in the hierarchy of authority will always be matched by equivalent professional skills.

2. While criticising rational legal model of democracy as developed by Weber. Merton has said the structure in which Weber has laid stress on hierarchy and rules can easily generate unexpected consequences which can prove detrimental to the attainment of objectives of an organisation.

3. Still another point of criticism made against Weber is that his insistence that every oral discussion should be recorded would result in too much formalism. His insistence on documents will make the experts in file work and reduce them to the status of a glorified clerk and reduce efficiency of organisation.

4. Then another point of criticism is that Weber has laid stress on the division of functions in an organisation. Selzrick while criticising this has said that in actual practice it has been found that each sub-unit sets up its own goals which conflict with the goals of the organisation as a whole.

5. Simon and Barnard are of the view that if Weber's structural approach is strictly followed that will lower down administrative efficiency in the organisation, which will increase through informal group relations in it.

6. The idea of impersonal orders on which Weber has laid much stress, has been criticised on the ground that in our modern times it is very difficult for a bureaucrat to be impersonal in the face of brisk political activity that goes around him.

7. According to Weber a specified sphere of competence is sufficient for development administration. But strict adherence to this principle of Weber is bound

to result in delays and inefficiency in administration. Not only this but it will provide an excuse to the officers to shirk their responsibility.

8. Phillip Selznick has also criticised Weber on another ground namely for his neglect of the fact that when a bureaucrat assumes power he is bound to use that for his own social position in the first instance and then for subverting organisation goals for increasing his own power position.

9. It has also been said that Weber is wrong when he says that impersonal order is a check on the bureaucrats in becoming power mongers.

10. Blau has criticised Weber by saying that Weberian model of bureaucracy cannot be applied to administrations of different places and times. The critics have also pointed out that Weberian model of bureaucracy does not include the orientation of members in relation to the rules of the organisation. He has also failed to lay stress on the significant influence of environmental factors on the behaviour of organisation.

11. Thus the critics have come forward with very serious drawbacks of his model of democracy. It has been said that in his model he has given less importance to human psychology and more to formal and informal relationship in an organisation. They dispute the rationality of model because of internal inconsistencies and ignoring of many hard facts of life. They do not accept valid the very basis on which Weber has constructed his ideal type model.

12. It is also said that Weberian model of bureaucracy lacks empirical validity when it is related to modern administration.

Views of Weber about Authority

Max Weber the famous German social thinker, was born in Erfurt Thurngia on April 21, 1864. His parents were quite well off and belonged to National Liberal Politician School. His father was not only a jurist but also an active politician, with the result that from his early life. Max Weber's came in contact with many famous politicians, jurists and economists, who influenced the course of his future thinking. He also graduated in law. For some time he taught law in the University of Berlin but subsequently in 1893 he worked as Professor of Political Economy at Freiburg. In 1900, he fell ill for 4 years. In 1905, he learnt Russian language and was a member of Warsaw Peace Pact. In 1918, he became visiting Professor at the University of Vienna and then became Professor at Munich University. In 1920, he suffered an attack of pneumonia and died in that year, when he was hardly fifty six years of age.

Though Max Weber died at the young age of 56, yet during his life time he produced many significant works. He was intelligent and hard working. His original works are available in German language but these have now been translated in English and in some other languages. In 1891, he published Roman Agrarian History which established him as a good writer. He wrote his thesis on 'History of Trade Companies in the Middle Ages'. In this he has tried to interpret the relationship between the jurisprudence and economics. In 1892, came out his publication entitled, 'Dia Ver Haltnisse der-landarbeiterim.'

In 'Protestant Ethics and Spirit of Capitalism', which came out in 1906, he discussed the relationship between capitalism and Protestantism. It was after this publication that he studied other religions as well. He wrote books on the sociology of Religion in India and China. 'The Hindu Social System', 'The Religion of China' and 'The Ancient

Judaism' are the books which he could complete. His another posthumous work is 'Economy and Society', in which he has compiled the essays of great contemporary sociologists. These have been translated into English by Talcott Parsons. Weber's views about sociology are available to us in his 'Essays on Sociology'.

Weber's father was an active politician and came in contact with many jurists and economists, who all influenced him in his future thinking. He was also influenced by Idealist philosophy which was quite in common discussion those days. He was also attracted by the controversy whether natural science methods could be applied to social sciences and came to the conclusion that generalisation in social sciences was a much possible in social sciences, as in natural sciences.

According to Weber authority has social relationship with social control. It can however, be legal, traditional and charismatic. According to him legal authority is one which a person enjoys because he holds a particular office. Thus a public servant tieds some authority because he occupies that position. He can use some economic goods and utilise some property, which does not belong to him, but which he can use and has an authority to use that. Traditional authority is one which one uses because traditionally that is being used. Faith in those norms is called traditional faith. He has quoted the example of father or husband exercising some authority over the family or wife, which is all traditional and that is neither legal nor any other type of authority. As regard charismatic authority, according to Weber it is an authority which is present in the individual by his own self. Such an authority can be real as well as imposed *e.g.* there are certain people who claim super natural powers *e.g.* our religious leaders and prophets have charismatic authority of their own, and that cannot be explained either in terms of law or otherwise.

Weber has however, differentiated between power, authority and control. According to him a person could be said to possess power, if in a social relationship he can carry his views inspite of resistance from others. Weber has identified authority with authoritarian power.

Types of Authority. As said above according to Weber authority is of three types namely (1) Legal authority, (2) Traditional authority and (3) Charismatic authority.

(1) Legal Authority. In every state there are certain positions which have some authority to exercise. As the person gets that position, he also gets authority with that. On the other hand, when he leaves that position with that the authority also goes away. Such a type of authority is linked with position which he holds and not because of his personal qualities and performances. He can exercise his authority within those limitations and areas are mentioned in the documents which put him on position. He can neither exceed his powers beyond what he is legally allowed to exercise.

Legal authority is an organisation means use of authority in accordance with certain well established principles and that too impartially. These principles should be applicable to all members in the organisation. These who are empowered to use this type of authority are appointed by competent authorities after following procedures as laid down under the rules. Appointing authority is always a superior authority which is always responsible for maintaining legal order. It is taken for granted that lower staff will accept and obey the authority of superior staff.

(2) Traditional Authority. It is another type of authority. It is a type of authority which one gets not because one is occupying a particular legal position or status but because traditionally authority or position of the person has all along been accepted. Because a position is traditionally accepted therefore its incumbent gets some authority. Because such authority is based on certain old traditions, it is called traditional authority *e.g.* authority of father in a patriarchal society or that of panches in a village of the ancient India.

There is a difference between legal authority and traditional authority. The former is based on certain rules and regulations, whereas the latter on traditions. Similarly whereas the former is specific and clear the latter is not specific but vogue. The former can be exercised within certain jurisdictions and limitations, but this does not apply to the latter. The persons exercising traditional authority generally are called masters and enjoy personal authority by virtue of their inherited status. Their command-carries legitimacy based on customs but their orders are based on their personal decisions. Two main important attributes of traditional authority are customs and personal attributes.

(3) Charismatic Authority. This type; of authority is based neither on traditions nor on rules and regulations but on some charisma. The persons who hold this type of authority have or possess some charismatic power or personality. The person concerned takes his personality so up and high that others begin to consider him charismatic and begin to obey his authority. He can then make the others bow before him and begin to accept his personal authority. He asks his followers to accept his objectives and ideals, as their own and makes them struggle for achieving those. In this category fall saints. Political leaders, religious and social leaders and even military heroes.

Their qualities are considered as special gifts of God given to them by Almighty and such an authority is accepted with respect and reverence. It has no legal limitations or jurisdictions. But this type of authority is absolutely temporary and for an unspecified time. It begins to lose its effect as and when the charismatic person begins to lose his charisma. At times however, this type of authority gets converted into traditional or legal authority.

Marxist view of Bureaucracy

Much before Karl Marx, Saint Simon had viewed bureaucracy as officials who governed in their own interests rather than in the interests of the governed. They sought high pay for themselves and were not merely useless but were an immense, growing and expansive crowed of incompetent parasites. "Since they had the same needs and desires, as producers, but produced nothing themselves, these people necessarily live on the work of others, either they are given or they take; in a word, they are idlers, that is to say thieves."

Karl Marx on Bureaucracy

Karl Marx used the word bureaucracy in the pejorative sense. All Marxists regard bureaucracy as tied to the capitalist state and is, therefore, a bourgeois phenomenon. Unlike Hegel, Marx did not believe that the state represents the general interests of the society. Likewise bureaucracy is not universal estate, it is particular closed society within the state serving its own, not the general interest. It is a social force through which the interests of capitalism and the bourgeois are implemented. The issue of the emergence of bureaucracy and of its continued existence is, therefore, inextricably connected with the wider topic of the character of the capitalist state.

Marx maintained that the state and its executive constitute an instruments through which the ruling class express its power, bureaucracy fulfils the function of contributing to the consolidation of class differences, and of supporting the power of the ruling class. Marx insisted that bureaucracy grew as a result of external and pathological social divisions. However independent it might appear, bureaucracy depends on existing divisions within society in two ways: (1) It depends directly on the separation between civil society and the state, without which it would have no raison d'etre. (2) It rests on the existence of divisions within civil society, of corporations, each concerned with its particular interests. In Marx's view, bureaucracy was not a class by itself in class societies. It is the servant of the classes; "not basic, but ultimately subordinate to the ruling class.

Bureaucracy shrouds all of its actions in secrecy which is preserved internally by hierarchy, and externally *i.e.* against the community, by its nature when it interacts with the world, the relationship is essentially manipulative. The only thing for which Marx praised bureaucracy was its role in centralising nations. He was not in favour of taking over control of the bureaucracy, as earlier revolutions had done, by the proletariat but he favoured that the proletariat must smash the institution. Marx had not said with clarity as to what would be the position and role of bureaucracy in the post-revolution period. With the advent of the communist society, true democracy can develop. In the communist society social and economic inequality will be eliminated. That will end exploitation, and the social classes. It is the post-revolutionary society that the state that represents the interests of the ruling class would wither away. With the end of the state as policemen comes a reduction in the number of functions and a complete change in the nature of functions carried out by the public power. "There will be no need for masses of haughty, brutal, represssive bureaucrats."

❐

10

Fredrick W. Taylor

F.W. Taylor was supporter of scientific management but he felt that for this mental revolution was absolutely necessary. It was this type of revolution which could bring a change in the approach of both the workers and the management. According to him it will develop spirit of friendly cooperation among all concerned and both the sides will then proceed in the same direction. Mutual suspicions will be replaced by good will and understanding. He is of the view that both the parties should clearly understand that the old individualistic decisions based on speculations are no longer valid and in their stead decisions based on scientific approach and research should be adopted. The aim of scientific management is to have prosperity, close collaboration and increased cooperation between the workers and the management. According to him there are certain basic principles of management. These are:

1. Development of Science of Work. Taylor is of the view that scientific approach should be adopted all through the work. In his '*The Principles of Scientific Management*' he has said that scientific management is the best way of completing the work.

Both the worker and the management must know in advance as to what constitutes a fair day's good output. It will whereas help the management in having good output the workers will be saved from unnecessary criticism of bosses. Scientific investigation is needed for finding out as to what output a worker is required to give under optimum conditions. Taylor has said that for this it is essential to have work assessment, standards of work to be followed, experimentation and decisions based on certain well established principles. It is also essential to gather traditional knowledge of workers. He has also said that all knowledge gathered and all information collected should be classified and tabulated and reduced into rules and laws so that the best way of doing a job can be found out. Taylor is fully well convinced that once this is done and a science of work is developed that will result in more production for the management and higher wages for the workers. The Company will also be benefitted.

2. Classification of Scientific Management. Taylor while dealing with science of work, has also tried to define as to what he means by scientific management. According to him scientific management has three elements namely study of every step in a particular process; select and trained employees by best approved scientific methods and development of an intimate, friendly cooperative relationship between management and men. Although today this may sound like a standard practice but 50 years ago it was a revolutionary concept. According to Taylor these being (*a*) that both should cooperate with each other in producing the largest possible surplus and (*b*) substitution of friendly cooperation and helpfulness for antagonism and strike. This according to him would constitute the first step towards scientific meanagement.

3. Placement of Employees. A worker though scientifically selected and properly trained is not likely to give maximum output unless he is properly placed. In other words, each one should be allotted a type of work which is must appropriately suited to his qualifications, taste and aptitude. The management should keep the workers inspired and that is its exclusive responsibility. He has said that it is not correct to presume that the workers are unwilling to cooperate with the management. The process of cooperation can get expedited, provided mental revolution takes place.

4. Scientific Selection. In Scientific Management Taylor has laid stress on scientific methods of selection. By this he means that before selecting and recruiting a person, a study of aptitude, nature, performance of work, he had already done and his physical and intellectual qualities need be carefully studied. The aim is that on the basis of information collected the management should try to find out both possibilities and limitations of the person concerned for future development. He was fully convinced that each one has development potentialities provided one is properly trained and opportunities are provided to him to show his potentialities. For Taylor, it was the responsibility of management to provide him opportunities and exploit his potentialities. But at the same it is equally essential that the employees should gladly accept new work methods and tools without any grudge and grumble. He has said that in the absence of scientific methods of selection efficiency of workers and their morale is bound to be adversely affected. He has said that a worker should not be viewed simply as a part of the group in which he works but as an individual worker, because each one has his own limitations and potentialities.

5. Division of Work and Responsibility. According to Taylor in traditional system the workers are made to share more responsibilities and management much less. The former are held exclusively responsible for less production which is not true. He has said that scientific system means equal sharing of responsibilities and proper division of work. The manager should be as busy as the worker. He is convinced that division of labour is bound to create more understanding among all and mutual dependence on both the workers and the management. This will also encourage cooperation and avoid conflicts and strikes. In scientific management there should be no rule of thumb but every rule must be prepared on some scientific lines. Discord should be replaced by cooperation and harmony. Individual interests should have secondary whereas collective interests should everywhere receive priority and instead of restricted output there should be optimum output.

6. Managerial Responsibilities. According to Taylor each manager has certain responsibilities to discharge. He has mentioned these in his publication entitled, "Scientific Management". One of his responsibilities is to see that instead of rule of thumb he should develop certain scientific methods of doing and completing the work. He has however, said that these unwritten rules which are based on rule of the thumb should be collected and thereafter classified and analysed. In order to do work scientifically it is essential that management should cooperate with the workers without any conditions. Then alone the workers will cooperate with each other and adopt new methods of work. The workers will also remain motivated. He has suggested the managers to make all recruitments on the basis of education, training, aptitude etc. If selection is made after careful study of the person to be selected then alone progress can be possible.

7. Standardised Work Conditions. Taylor believes that standardised working coditions are one of the basic features of scientific management. He has said that each worker should be given a day's work based on certain fixed standards. He should be provided standardised tools environments and facilities so that the work is finished properly and timely. This will enable both the management and the workers to finish their work without any worry. Not only this but every one in the organisation, from top to the bottom should have clearly daily defined tasks so that he knows clearly well targets to be achieved by him at the end of the day. If a worker fails to finish his work on well defined fixed standard, he should be ready to suffer the loss of his wages. Similarly if a worker timely finishes his work or even before time, he should be rewarded, so that every worker knows it fully well that efficiency and good production will not only bring him name and honour but also prosperity, in the form of more wages.

8. Establishment of Planning Department. In his studies Taylor has laid stress on establishment of a planning department. According to him the main fucntions of this department should be to plan in such a way that every activity in the organisation is timely completed. He has said that every aspect of every item of work of every individual and machine in the organisation should be carefully studied before hand and properly planned. This can be possible when the capacity of each individual and machine is fully assessed and there is full knowledge about the time to be taken for completing each item of work. This will check the tendency of workers to complete the work according to their choice and liking and optimum output at minimum cost shall be possible.

9. Differential Wage System. Taylor did not favour ordinary piece rate system for the payment of wages for the workers. He believed that the system is unsatisfactory because it does not provide sufficient incentives to the workers to do more work. He has laid stress on differential wage system. In this those workers who give better output are rewarded more than the others. He has said that for introducing this system it is essential that work standard should be fixed taking into consideration time and speed factors and time at which the work is to be completed. A worker should be paid less and more wages depending on the output. In it there are also high and low wage rates.

Nature of Management

The management is an essence of human activity. It applies in both the organisational and non-organisational activities. For an organisation, the management becomes of vital importance. No organisation can achieve its goals effectively and efficiently in the absence of effective and efficient management. In the absence of effective management, the resources of production remain the resources and can never become the production.

There are different ideas about the nature of management. There are some scholar who think that the management is profession. Some others look upon the subject as an art while others consider it as a science. Truly speaking, all these views are relevant and true because each of these ideas reflects different aspects of the management. For convenience, we may study the Nature of Management by presenting it into the following manner:

1. Multi-Disciplinary. Management is basically multi-disciplinary. This implies that, although management has been developed as a separate discipline, it draws knowledge and concepts from various disciplines. It draws freely ideas and concepts from such disciplines as psychology, sociology, anthropology, economics, ecology, statistics, operations research, history etc. Management integrates the ideas and concepts taken from these disciplines and presents newer concepts which can be put in practice for managing the organisations.

2. Management as Profession. Management has been regarded as a profession by many while many have suggested that it as not achieved the status of a profession. This aspect has been discussed in detail later.

3. Dynamic Nature of Principles. Principle is a fundamental truth which establishes cause and effect relationships of a function. Based on integration and supported by practical evidences, management has framed certain principles. However, these principles are flexible in nature and change with the changes in the environment in which an organisation exists. Because of the continuous development in the field, many older principles are being changed by new principles. Continuous researches are being carried on to establish principles in changing society and no principles can be regarded as a final truth.

4. Relative, Not Absolute Principles. Management principles are relative, not absolute and they should be applied according to the need of the organisation. Each organisation may be different from others. The difference may exist because of time, place, socio-cultural factors, etc. However, individual working within the same organisation may also differ. Thus a particular management principle has different strength in different conditions. Therefore, principles of management should be applied in the light of prevailing conditions.

5. Universality of Management. Management is a universal phenomenon. However, management principles are not universally applicable but are to be modified according to the needs of the situation.

6. Management Science or Art. There is a controversy whether management is science or art. However, management is both a science and an art.

The nature of management suggests that it is a multidisciplinary phenomenon; its principles are flexible, relative and not absolute. It is both science and art; it can be taken as a profession and finally it is universal. However, these aspects need further elaboration because of differing views over these aspects of management.

Management Science or Art

The controversy with regard to the nature of management, as to whether it is a science or art, is very old. This controversy, however, is not very much in the air though the controversy is yet to be settled. Specification of exact nature of management as science or art or both is necessary to specify the process of learning of management. Learning of science basically involves the assimilation of principles while learning of art involves its continuous practice.

Much of the controversy of management as science or art is on account of the fact that the earlier captains of the industry and managers have used intuition, hunches, commonsense, and experience in managing organisations. They were not trained professional managers, although they were very brilliant and had developed commonsense through which they managed well. Commonsense and science differ in the following ways:

(*i*) Commonsense is vague as compared to scientific knowledge.

(*ii*) Flagrant inconsistency often appears in commonsense whereas logical consistency is the basic of science.

(*iii*) Science systematically seeks to exaplain the events with which it deals; commonsense ignores the need for explanation.

(*iv*) The scientific method deliberately exposes claims to the critical evaluation of experimental analysis; commonsense methdos fails to test conclusions in any scientific fashion.

Science is based on logical consistency, systematic explanation, critical evaluation and experimental analysis. Thus science can be defined as follows:

Science is a body of systematised knowledge accumulated and accepted with reference to the understanding of general truths concerning a particular phenomenon, subject, or object of study. Thus science is a systematised body of knowledge.

Management as Science

Judging from the above features of formulation of theory in science, management cannot be regarded as science because it is only half-way. It may be called 'inexact science' or 'pseudo-science.' Perhaps this is true for all social sciences of which management is a branch. Management is not as exact as natural or physical sciences are. This phenomenon can be explained as follows:

1. One of the most important rules of science is that concepts have to be defined clearly in terms of the procedures involved in their measurement. One has to know exactly what one is talking about while using a particular terms. Meanings have to be clear and unambiguous to avoid confusion and erroneous classification. However, in management, various terms are not used in the same way and giving same meaning. Even the major terms like management and organisation are used in different ways. The reason for this phenomenon is quite simple. Since the second decade of this century, a number of disciplines have claimed to contribute to human knowledge of managing. The consequences has been almost unfathomable confusion over the various terms, a confusion in which ambivalence in using the various terms has played a conspicuous part.

2. In science, observations must be controlled so that causation may be imputed correctly. The most common method of eliminating a given factor as possible cause of an event is to hold it constant to keep it form varying so that it cannot operate as a source of change. This is a difficult rule to follow, specially in studying organisational phenomena. Various research studies in Management have suffered because of the bias of researches. In many

studies, for example, a variable that was thought to be irrelevant was found to exert a causal influence.

3. Science may be viewed in terms of its structure, its goals, and its methods. In terms of its structure, it is a number of scientific disciplines: physics, biology, psychology, economics, management and many others. Each of these sciences attemtps to provide a set of internally consistent hypotheses, principles, laws, and theories dealing with an aspect of total knowledge.

4. Theories in science are in terms that permit empirical confirmation. Scientific statements are testable and the tests are capable of repetition with same result. Furthermore, explanatory statements are logically consistent with other explanatory statements that have been frequently confirmed. Thus rationality of total scientific system is maintained. However, this does not happen in management exactly. Many of the management principles lack empirical evidences and are not testable. Further, these principles do not give the similar results under varying conditions and, therefore, lack universal application.

Management as an Art

Management can be regarded as an art also. The meaning of art is related with the bringing of a desired result through the application of skills. Art is concerned with the understanding of how particular work can be established. That is, art has to do with applying of knowledge or science or of expertness in performance. This is specially important in management because in many instances much creativeness and adroitness in applying the managerial efforts are necessary to achieve the desired results. Furthermore, the adequate consideration of people involved in managerial action is vital and adds to the concept of art of managing.

Science and art are complementary fields of endeavour; they are not mutually exclusive. The medical doctor requires the knowledge or science of biology, chemistry, and anatomy. But excellence in absorbing these funds of knowledge does not make him an excellent physician. He has to apply his wealth of knowledge expertly, and his skill in perceiving how and when to use his knowledge is essential to his success in preventing and controlling diseases of mankind. In management if student scores A grade and scores B grade, it does not mean that the former would be better manager than the latter. This is so because management is an art and a better manager is one who knows how to apply the knowledge in solving a particular problem. Management is an art can be seen from the following facts:

(*i*) Managment is creative like any other art. Creativity is major dimension in managerial success. It creates new situations for further improvement.

(*ii*) The process of management does involve the use of know-how and skills like any other art such as music, painting, scuplture, etc.

(*iii*) Management is personalised meaning thereby that there is no "one best way of meaning." Every man in his profession has individual approach and technique in solving the problems. The success of managerial task is related with the personality of the man apart from the character and quality of general body of knowledge.

(*iv*) The process of management is directed to achive certain concrete results as other fields of art do.

Management is an Inborn Quality

The nature of management has also been changed by the development of business. The management which was considered be an inborn quality, has now changed and the management has become a Profession. Profession involves the application of expert knowledge for the solution of a specific problem and it is controlled by a code of conduct and social responsibilities. The management has developed as an art requiring specific knowledge and skill and it has become a profession. Management fulfils all the characteristics of profession as under:

(*i*) **Special Knowledge and Skill.** Like other professions Management requires specific knowledge and skill. This knowledge and skill can be acquired only through a systematic professional course or study. The Management has its definite principles like other professions. On the basis of this principle, Management is also called a profession.

(*ii*) **Formal Training.** As the formal training is necessary for a profession, it is required for the Management. The Management requires a formal training of quite a long period under the definite system. Many institutions have been set up for the Systematic Study of Management.

(*iii*) **A Recognised Institute.** There is a recognised institute for the development of Management, as for the development of all other professions. In India there is an 'All India Management Council' which carries out the research in the field of Management.

(*iv*) **Remuneration on the Basis of Demand and Supply.** Like other professions, the remuneration of managers also varies from time to time and from nature to nature on the basis of the principle of demand and supply.

(*v*) **A Code of Conduct.** As there is a code of conduct for the professionals of every profession, we find a definite code of conduct for the Management. Managers are liable to the organisation in which they work, to the employees of the organisation and to the general society.

The above discussion makes it clear that the Management fulfils all the reqirements and characteristics of a profession. Therefore, the Management may be called a profession.

Management as a Process

Now the Management is considered to be a process. First of all objects of a business enterprise are decided and then a plan is prepared keeping in view the objects of the organisation. All the functions of organisation have to go and have to be managed in accordance with the plan decided. In the process of management, all the important functions of the organisation are involved, such as—planning organisation, selection of personnel, direction, coordinations, motivation and control.

The Management is a continuous process from another point of view also. It never comes to an end. The moment, the Management find a solution of one problem, the another problem comes forward. The Function of Management states with the establishment of the organisation and ends with the dissolution of the organisation. Therefore, Management may rightly be categorised as a process.

Management is Universal

The Management is an essence of all the human activities. Management is not limited only to the activities of a business organisation. Whenever we think of the human activities, we cannot think of the absence of management. A person manages the activities of his own also. A person has to manage the affairs of his family also. A lecturer has to manage his class. A Principles has to manage his college of school. A Manager has to manage his organisation. A Politician has to manage his areas of politics. A Distt. Magistrate has to manage his district. So, the term Management is not confined to the management of the activities of business organisation, it is universal applicable at all times at all places in all circumstances, whenever the human activities are to take place.

Importance of Management in Modern Economy

The survival and growth of an organisation depends largely on the competence and character of its management. Every organisation needs repeated stimulus which only managers can provide. Management is the dynamic life giving element in every organisation. Without management the resources of production remain resoruces and can never become output. Organisation stand or fall on the quality of their managements because sound management provides the following benefits:

1. **Optimum Utilisation of Resources.** Materials, machinery and money are the physical factors of production. The efficient use of these resources depends upon the efficiency and motivation of workers. Management makes the workers efficient and motivated through training, supervision and inspiring leadership. Managers guide and motivate workers towards best performance.

2. **Stability.** Management ensures the survival of an organisation in a fast changing environment. It coordinates the activities of different deparments in an organisation and maintains team spirit amongst the personnel. Just as mind controls the body, similarly management directs and controls the organisation to keep it on the right track.

3. **Achievement of Group Goals.** Management enables an enterprise to achieve its desired objectives through proper planning and control. It decides what should be done and how. It lays down the long-term and

short-term goals keeping in mind the resources of the enterprise. Management maintains order and co-ordination and without it there will be utter chaos. Management also creates a sound organisation structure that provides specialisation. Through a well-organised system of direction and control, management keeps a close watch on the activities of the organisation.

4. **Human Development.** Management is not simply the direction of things but the development of men. It improves the personality and calibre of people to raise their efficiency and productivity. A good manager serves as a friend and guide to his subordinates.

5. **Economic Growth.** Management is the catalyst of economic growth. We no longer talk of capital and labour but of management and labour. "Development is a matter of human energies rather than of economic growth, and the generation of human energies is the task of management. Management is the mover and development is the consequences."

6. **Fulfilment of Social Obligations.** Sound management monitors the environment of business and makes necessary changes in business policies and practices so as to keep the consumers and workers satisfied. In this way managers help an enterprise to fulfil its obligations towards different sections of society. Management balances and integrates various interests in group effects.

7. **Meets the Challenge of Change.** Management is the catalystic force that enables an organisation to face the challenge of change. The environment of business has become very turbulent. Managers maintain a dynamic equilibrium.

Importance of Management in India

The importance of management becomes manyfold in India. India is an underdeveloped country, marching ahead on the path of development and self-dependence. The only way out open to India after the independence of over two centuries, in the rapid industrialisation of the country. Rapid industrialisation will only remain an imagination if we do not have the efficient managers to manage the industrial organisation. The process of industrialisation implies the use of heavy machines and production large scale, large distribution at the national and international level. All these require a lot of plans to be taken by the Management. Management was regarded as an inborn quality in India but now the time has changed and thinking has changed. The process of Management is still to be developed much more than it has developed. The importance of Management in India may be explained in the following paragraphs:

1. **To Exploit the Natural Resources.** India is a rich country inhabited by the poor. This is a statement which makes the characteristics of our economy clear. India has the vast natural resources. The nature gifted all its resources to India but we could not exploit these resources fully. Management, therefore, becomes of great importance for the exploitation of these resources.

2. **Unemployment.** India is having the largest number of unemployed person in the world. The only solution to the problem of unemployment is the industrial development of the country and the process of Industrail Development implies the need of efficient Management. Therefore, the Management is of great importance for our country to overcome the problem of unemployment.

3. **Low Rate of Capital Formation.** In India, we find only 13% rate of capital formation while this rate is as high as 30% in other developed countries of the world. Because of this rate of capital formation, the process of industrial development also suffers. Therefore, it is necessary to increase the rate of capital formation for the over all growth of our country and this requires the better Management of capital resources of the country.

4. **Domination of the Poors.** India is a country which is regarded one of the poorest countries of the world. Above 40% population of this country is still living below the line of poverty. To uplift the standard of living of the poors, it becomes crucial to manage the things in different ways.

5. **Labour Problems.** India is facing the labour problems many times more than other countries. The Indian Labourer is passing through state of dissatisfaction and the dissatisfaction of labourer becomes more because of the industrial backwardness. Therefore, proper Management of labour problems becomes the necessity for the industrial development of the country.

6. **Centralisation of Wealth.** The distribution of wealth is very imbalanced in India. Most of the wealth is centralised in the few hands. On the other hand a large number of business undertakings are facing the problem of survival. To overcome this problem, it is necessary to re-manage the distribution of wealth and to control the legislation in the manner that it may help in the equal distribution of wealth.

7. **Low Productivity.** The productivity of Indian Industries is very low when compared with the productivity of the industries of developed countries.

Possibly, the basic reason for this low productivity is mis-management of the resources of production. Therefore, the better management of the resources of production is necessary to increase the productivity.

8. **Planned Economy.** India is marching on the path of self-dependence through the rapid industrialisation of the country. Government of India has adopted the policy of planned economy, and five years plans are being implemented in India. The success of these plan depends to a large extent on the efficiency of management.

9. **Foreign Debtedness.** India got her independence in 1947 after rule by foreign power for over two centuries. Soon after achieving independence, India adopted the rapid industrialisation of the country. For this India had to import the machines, technology and some times rawmaterials also, from other developed countries. Such heavy imports resulted in the heavy indebtedness. India now-a-days, is facing a huge problem of foreign indebtedness. The solution of this lies in the industrial development of the country which requires more and more management.

Scientific Management

In the past in management system what the management considered reasonable was considered as final. Today it is known as traditional system of management. Then rule of the thumb prevailed because then desire of the owner was final word. There was then no scientific approach.

Traditional Approach. Management system which prevailed during 19th century was known as traditional system of management. It reflected socio-economic and political conditions of those days on the one hand and social culture on the other. But traditional system has become out-dated and practices and procedures followed then are now being discarded. The procedures etc. of the past were not based on any scientific principles but had their roots on the whims of the individual. The whole approach was thus individualistic and in it individual's interests received precedence over collective and organisational interests.

Obviously the approach is neither progressive nor scientific nor it has human outlook. The workers are neither given clear directions nor they are given incentives for doing good work or better output. No care is taken about the welfare of the workers and an employer for all practical purposes is a dictator. All powers and authorities are concentrated in him and he can arbitrarily use these. A worker is paid very low wages and is considered a slave.

Scientific Approach. As against traditional approach the scientific approach, which is based on certian set principles. In this system every work is done on certain principles and by following set procedures. In it collective interests receive precedence over individual interests. It establishes certain control procedures which can help in increased production. Rule of the thumb is replaced by administrative procedures and small machines and out-dated tools and instruments are replaced by standardised tools which can help in saving time, increasing in speed of work and more production.

In this approach a worker is not considered a cog in the wheel of machine. He is considered a human being and efforts are made to appreciate his personal problems. Administrative probelms are solved with the help of scientific principles and procedures so that these are solved amicably and quickly. Efforts are made to standardise everything and there is set and systematic accounting procedure.

Then in scientific management efforts are made to have happy blending of labour and capital. It is done with the help of bringing change in outlook both in the workers and the employers or what Taylor has called 'mental revolution'. This approach lays stress on collective over individual interests. It is hoped that by this many industrial conflicts will come to an end and a sense of harmony will develop among the workers.

Not only this but in this approach it is provided that the workers should be properly trained and their knowledge updated. They are involved in production and their cooperation is sought at every stage. There is clear division of work between the workers and the management. Scientific and uniform procedures are followed. Organisation's activities are planned quite in advance and these are accomplished in a planned way. In the process help and cooperation of the workers is sought.

Merits of Scientific Management System

The system has become quite popular all over the world particularly in big industries and has replaced rule of the thumb. Because of awakening in the workers they are not prepared to tolerate arbitrariness. They stress that uniform procedures based on certain well set principles should be followed. In this system since the cooperation of the workers is sought and they are involved in management activities, therefore, industrial conflicts are considerably reduced. Then since tools, instruments and machines are standardised and unnecessary expenses are checked, therefore, cost of production comes down and profits go up.

The system replaces the rule of the thumb and with that all the drawbacks of the rule also end. In this system stress is laid on training of the workers and they are given rest pauses, their working hours are fixed and working conditions are made attractive, therefore, efficiency very much increases. Their efficiency also increases becuase they are provided standardised tools. Not only this but only qualified persons are recruited and they are given such work which suits their qualifications are aptitude.

Demerits of the System

But scientific management system has several demerits as well. One of its serious disadvantages is that the system tries to reduce the number of workers already employed in an organisation with the use of standardised equipments, work, time and study methods etc. This on the one hand creates problem of unemployment, whereas on the other it creates a busting fear in the minds of workers about their being thrown out of employment. When they are sure that increased output will mean their unemployment obviously they will not put their heart and soul in the work and also will not give more production.

Then its another disadvantage is that it weakness the activities of trade unions and reduces collective bargaining power which is not in the interest of workers, who are an important part of production.

Because of standardisation and fixed regulations, there is rigidity which means lack of elasticity, which reduces human approach. It is not good for any organisation.

The system also means exploitation of workers because each one is required to give maximum output but without proportionate increase in wages. Not only this but their initiative is also killed because they know that they are to give more output without extra wages. In this system these is stress on division of labour, which in the long run means doing the same item of work again and again. It also means monotory and boredom for the workers.

A group of writers, often known as the 'scientific administration' school attempted to inquire whether there are any general principles of administration whose application could remedy the defects like inefficiency, etc., of the governmental organisation and improve its general functioning. Also they considered whether the methods of more efficient business management could have relevance for public administration. They concluded that there are indeed sound principles of organisation. They drew inspiration from the writings on industrial management by Fredrick Taylor and of industrial psychologists in Europe and America, "From these writings have stemmed the techniques of time and motion study, production control, and office organisation and methods.

The scientific management stressed rationality, predictability, specialisation and technical competence. Its focus was on the design and operation of production process on the "shop" level of the organisation. There are three assumptions of scientific management:

(*i*) That improved practice will come from the application of the scientific method of analysis to organisational problems.

(*ii*) The second assumption concerns the relation of worker to his work. "There is a primary focus on work itself and not on the particular person doing the work. The good worker is viewed as one who accepts orders, but does not initiate actions. The worker is told how to do his job based upon scientific analysis of the job. The focus is at his basic work—worker level typically in a production shop."

(*iii*) Each worker is assumed to be "economic man". He is interested in maximising his monetary income. The organisation is seen as a rational instrument of production.

Taylors Contribution

Amongst the early writers of this school in the United States, the most influential was Fredrick W. Taylor, an engineer who came into prominence towards the end of the 19th century. There was several predecessors of Taylor who used some scientific management techniques, but it was Taylor who gave them a general framework so that they could become widely available and accepted. He is, therefore deservedly called the father of scientific management. The four principles of scientific management which he described are:

(*i*) Develop a science for each element of a man's work, which replaces the old rule-of-thumb method;

(*ii*) Management should heartily cooperate with the men so as to ensure all the work being done in accordance with the principles of the science which he has developed;

(*iii*) Scientifically select and then train, teach, and develop the workman, whereas in the past he chose his own work and trained himself as best as he could;

(*iv*) There is an almost equal division of the work and the responsibility between the management and the work men. The management should take over all work for which they are better fitted than the workmen, while in the past all of the work and the greater part of the responsibility were thrown on the men.

Taylor considered the philosophy of scientific management much more important than mere mechanism. His major contributions were to techniques in the area of motion-and-time study, specialisation, standardisation planning, techniques, slide rules and other work-saving implements, work instructions, work standards, piece rates wage systems, product and implement classification systems and modern cost systems.

Taylor concentrated on intensive analysis of work processes at the level of the industrial shop and the individual workers so as to devise the 'one-best-way' to design and execute tasks. His work accelerated a movement towards rationalised factory production methods and the establishment of 'efficiency' as the guiding criterion for managerial theory and practice.

Nigro and Nigro are of the view that "one of the scientific management's enduring contributions to modern managerial thought and practice is the idea that efficiency and goal accomplishment are the products of systematic research and evaluation." Empirical research and controlled experimentation with alternative methods were central elements in scientific management. These experiments intended to discover the "best way" to carry out specific tasks. "This approach carried beyond the design of technical systems to selection and training of employees.

The present practice in the modern industry of having a specialised and trained managerial cadre, had its origin in Taylorism. Taylor argued for a management cadre serving as the intelligence or "brains" of the factory operation. He was reacting to the disorder he found in the typical plant of his where the workers themselves decided what work methods to follow and selected their own tools for each operation. That means, in fact, the workers were not being managed. They were managing themselves. The management and supervisory roles of today were largely absent then. Each worker used rule-of-thumb methods developed over years of experience in trade. Their superiors were unable to tell the workers how to do their work efficiently. They could only urge them to use their initiative so as to produce the largest possible return to the employer. This was the sort of disorder which was sought to be replaced by order lines the keystone of Taylor's managerial thought. Taylor regarded the then prevailing system as irrational and highly inefficient. He felt that even the workmen best suited for doing the work could not fully understand without the help of those "working with him or over him."

Evaluation. The most strident criticism of Taylor and the scientific management has come from the Marxists. They ridicule the theory of 'scientific labour management' or 'rational organisation of labour'. They describe the techniques of scientific management as a predominantly psychological adaptation of human mechanism to the mechanics of industry. They think that these techniques are more efficient tools to exploit the labour still more by the capitalists. B. Venkateswarlu writes that 'Taylor's axiom was that for every operation a worker has to carry out the one best way'. The worker has to do his work in accordance with the best norms, thereby economising motion, time and the money of the enterprise. In order to encourage him to conform to the norms and to faster emulation, the workers is offered a system of bonuses. Scientific management seeks to establish the conditioned reflex most profitable for the enterprise, to produce a human production automation physically conditioned and stimulated psychological spring of prestige and material spring of the bonus. And this brought the enterprise huge profit not by scientifically exploiting the labourers of their labour but also an attendant process of capitalist division of labour resulting in de-skilling that conditioned the physical and mental faculties of human beings for the sole purpose of profit making".

The Marxists quote statistics to prove that the profit of the enterprises wherein Taylor's experiments was carried out, increased much more substantially than the meagre increase in the wages of the workers which were disproportionate to rise in output. The implementation of Taylor's principle resulted in the disassociation of the labour process from the skills of the workers. Workers were made to depend not upon their abilities but entirely upon the practices of management. Work under this system is in reality "mental and physical violence on the part of the capitalist over the mass workers".

There is no doubt some truth in the above criticism although it seems to be partial and exaggerated. There are other critics also who agree that Taylor treated workers as depersonalised 'resources'. However, Nigro and Nigro hold a different opinion. They observe that Taylor "genuinely believed that the changes he proposed would greatly improve the worker's lot and make clear the underlying economic interdependence between the employee and the organisation. Through piece-rate pay systems and rationally designed and supervised production techniques, industry could tap the workers' primary motivation to make more money, and consequently combine higher profits with higher income for those who worked hard.

The scientific management did not put forward a fully developed theory of organisation or administration. The scientific managers restricted their work to level of shop floor activity. They did not pay much attention to the over all administrative structures of organisations.

As far as human motivation, scientific management made assumptions which have proved incomplete. The rational-economic man, as Taylor assumed man to be, has been replaced by "a far more complex interpretation of human behaviour and of the sources of productivity in organisational settings." The social and psychological factors which were ignored by the scientific management school have now become considerably important.

Despite this criticism, however, the scientific management has greatly influenced public administration in the following ways:

(*i*) It made considerable contribution to the acceptance of efficiency as a primary goal of administration and management.

(*ii*) Its values and methods were in tune with the movement for reforms of government and civil service such as the centralisation of authority and accountability, establishment of merit systems, freeing public administration from partisan politics etc. Throughout the period when the reform movement was active, the scientific management concepts were widely accepted by the administrators as well as the students of public administration.

If a broad view is taken, the contributions of Taylor and his companions were really outstanding because many of the features of the scientific approach have proved to be enduring.

Human Relations Movement

The three theories described earlier *i.e.,* Bureaucracy, scientific management and the administrative theory, are called the classical theories of organisations and management. The present one *i.e.,* the human relations movement has often been described as the neo-classical (or new classical) theory. It was built on the base of the classical theory. It modified, added to, and in some way extended classical theory. "The basic assumption of neoclassical theory is that psychological and social aspects of the workers as an individual and his work group ought to be emphasised."

The trace of the human relations movement can be found even in ancient literatures. But in recent times its development mostly took place in 1920s and 1930s, and it has evolved as a part of the modern theory. During this period, the Harvard Business Schoold, under the leadership of Elton Mayo (a professor in industrial sociology) and his associates conducted extended research at the Hawthorne plant of the Western Electric Company. The essence of this revolution was focus on the organisation as a social system. The organisation was defined thus "An organisation is a group of persons with a common objective. This view emphasises social factors at work (or the informal organisation) and emotions. This is in contrast with the classical view of organisation which focussed on structure, order, the formal organisation, economic factors and objective rationality. The Hawthorne studies established the informal group as a major explanation of behaviour in organisations. They extended the conceptual horizons of organisation theory to include a huge range of social-psychological variables.

The Hawthorne experiments were conducted between 1924 and 1932. The researchers established that the social or human relationships among the workers were more important in determining productivity than were changes in working conditions. This high morale of the 'test group' workers appeared to be responsible for the productivity increases. Morale appeared to be a result of the amount of individual, personal emphatic attention given to the individual worker plus the social structure of the work group. Even simple factors, such as who sat next to whom, seemed to be important. Hence the Hawthorne researchers concluded that a worker's feelings about himself and his work group were of the utmost importance. About the complaints of the workers "ventilation therapy" was seen as important. It became apparent that often workers did not want changes made; they mainly wanted to talk to an understanding person who did not criticise or advise their troubles. These experiments demonstrated that organisations have social and emotional aspects in addition to economic ones. It was also demonstrated that "regarding people as people may be as important for productivity as rest periods' physical working conditions, or even money."

"It was upon these foundations," remark Nigro and Nigro, "laid by these (above) discoveries that the human relations school or movement was constructed. On the applied level, the movements objectives were to provide management with the social and pychological insights needed to diagnose problems rooted in the informal organisation and to devise the appropriate interventions. Great emphasis was placed on the development of human relations skills which would help supervisors to effectively bridge the gap between the informal and formal organisation."

The basic conclusions of the human relations movement, therefore, are that a worker is a Social Man seeking satisfaction primarily by membership of stable work groups. The management should work through the small group rather than operating on 'atomised economic automations' by encouraging its members to develop favourable views of their situation and by avoiding creating a source of frustration or threat. Various techniques like 'expressive' supervision and worker participation were suggested which could promote a climate of good human relations in which groups could usefully function.

Elements of the Theory

The neoclassical theory challenges the economic men concept of the classical theory. It holds that every person is different (not homogenous as was the economic man philosophy), and that a persons work group and other social factors are profoundly important. The writers of this theory have concentrated on three elements—the individual, social aspect of work groups (informal organisations) and participative management.

(i) **The Individual.** The theory emphasises differences among individuals. For them each worker is unique.

Each workers brings to that job situation certain attitudes, beliefs and ways of life, as well as certain skills, technical, social and logical. Each person has certain hopes and expectations of job situation.

(ii) Work Groups (Informal Organisations). The second element of this theory is its emphasis upon social aspects of work groups. The informal organisation that exists within the structure of the formal organisation is emphasised. This theory focuses its attention of the social aspects of man whose overriding need is seen as a desire to belong, to be accepted by, and stand well in his group. Mayo concluded that man's social situation in his work group "ranked first and the work was incidental." One of the clearest contributions of neoclassical writers has been to describe the effect of work groups (informal organisation) on motivation and productivity.

(iii) Participative Management. The third element of neo-classical theory is participative management. The emergence of participative management seemed inevitable because of the increased emphasis on the individual and work groups. Participative management means participation of the workers in decision-making about their work conditions. The workers discuss with supervisors and influence decisions that effect them. It was observed that this led to increase in productivity.

The workers' participation in decision-making was a new concept of supervision and was in contrast with the concept of the scientific management wherein. Taylor held that only experts in job analysis understood enough about a job to be able to improve it.

❐

11

Rensis Likert

Rensis Likert was born in 1903 and got his education in Columbia University. In 1932, from the same university he got his Ph. D. degree. His main area of interest and work is New Pattern of Management, Human Organisation and New ways of Managerial Conflict. Likert started his career as Director of Morale Division of the United State Strategic Bombing Surrvey. In 1946, he established Survey Research Centre at the University of Michigan. He worked as Director of the Centre and he gave outlook and direction to it. Within three years the Centre was enlarged to become the Institute for Social Research which consisted of Survey Research Centres, Research Centre for Group Dynamics and Centre for Research on Utilisation of Scientific Knowledge. He was first Director of the Institute till 1970. Afterwards he was picked up as Director Emeritus of the Institute.

At the Institute, Likert and his associates carried out extensive research on management practice in American business and government. His researches which are spread over a period of 25 years by a team of 40 researchers have been compared with Hawthorne studies. The researches were carried out on the working of several industrial and commercial forums in different situations. The institutions covered included hospitals, voluntary organisations on the one hand and top scientists in the laboratories and unskilled workers in the factories on the other.

Views About Pressure Accelerating Forces. Likert, as already said, carried extensive research work which was spread over a period of 25 years. It was quite costly and consisted of a team of as many as 40 senior researchers. It also covered workers belonging to different categories and also variety of institutions both governmental and non-governmental. On the basis of his research he has come to the conclusion that there are certain forces which accelerate pressure on high performance in American business organisations. He has mentioned these in his volume entitled '*The New Pattern of Management*'. These are:

1. Growing Competition from the industrially developing countries for world market.
2. Significant increase in the educational level of labour force.
3. Changes in employee attitudes and expectations of participative style.
4. Resistance to pressure and close supervision.
5. An increasing concern on the part of workers for development of mental health.
6. Rising trend towards giving the individual more freedom and initiative.
7. Increasing need for more complex system of organising human needs.

Supervisory Styles. Likert has at length discussed supervisory styles and has said that there are several factors which are responsible for high performance in certain units and low ones in other units. He has also discussed such important issues as to why whereas some managers are successful in achieving better results the others fail to do so. Another problem to which he has paid attention is how can effectiveness of the managers be measured.

Classification of Supervisors. Likert has classified supervisors and placed them in two categories namely: (*a*) job centred and (*b*) employee centred.

Job Centred Supervisors. They concern themselves with performance of tasks assigned to them at the prescribed standards. These supervisors try to exert maximum pressure on the workers to ensure that the work is properly and timely completed. If any mistake occurs they believe in punishing the defaulters *i.e.* the workers who commit the mistakes. They do not believe in giving much freedom to the workers.

Job centred supervisors believe in the exercise of close and detailed supervision. They do not mind whether that is liked or disliked by the subordinates. Not only this but they do not have much confidence in them.

Employee Centred Supervisors. As against job centred supervisors, there are employee centred supervisors. They are mainly concerned with human aspects of their subordinates. They believe in team building and team work for the completion of quality work and that too timely. They most willingly come forward to help their subordinates, if they have any problem and as and when they commit mistakes. They do not believe in detailed and close supervision. On the other hand, they prefer general supervision. Not only this but they allow their subordinates to have their own schedule of work for the completion of tasks allotted to them. They do not exert much pressure on the subordinates and increase their achievement motivations. They try to win their trust and confidence which they very much value.

Views About Effective Supervision. Likert has paid attention to effective supervision. He has said that even if some how high and low performing managers may be identified, that does not solve problem. The problem still remains whether high or low performance is cause or effect of environment in which manager is required to work. Likert and his associates tried to find out whether it was because high performing managers were humane to their subordinates whereas low performance managers were though with them and thus could not get high performance. In order to come to some conclusion the high and low performing managers were changed into each other's jobs. Likert found that while high performing managers succeeded in improving the performance of low production units, vice versa did not happen. Likert also found that heavy pressures exerted by supervisors could produce good results only for a short while.

Likert has said that effective supervision is a regular process and needs constant adaptation to the background values and establishing inter-personal relations with the subordinates as well as superiors. He believes that supervision is specific to a particular situation under investigation.

After dealing with the types and characteristics of supervisors, Likert has given his ideas about supportive relationship in an organisation.

Likert on Supportive Relationship. His views about supportive relationship are based on his assessment of managers of high performance. He has said that in an organisation leadership and other processes should be such that there is maximum interaction with each other. In his 'New Pattern of Management' he has said that, "Each member will, in the light of his background, values and expectations, view the experience as supportive and on that builds and maintains his sense of personal worth and importance." According to him if in an organisation skills and resources are to be maximised and individuals are to be motivated to the maximum extent possible, for that it is essential to have inter-action influence system.

What is Inter-action Influence System? It is a system which is based on inter dependent processes in an organisation. It believes that no process is independent of the other, but each one is linked with the other. It is this system which integrates organisational and managerial processes in an organisation. It also helps in integration of processes like direction, coordination, decision-making, communication system etc. In every organisation manual and material resources *i.e.* man power, machines, work groups etc. have certain skills and capacities.

Critical Evaluation of Likert's Views. Likert's views in this regard have however, not been spared by the critics. They have pointed out that the system as suggested and viewed by Likert is difficult to achieve in the traditional hierarchical organisations. It is also doubted whether his organisation structure and Linking Rin model will be in a position to remove the hindrances which come on the way of present day hierarchical system. In his organisation system each individual has twin roles in two overlapping groups. In his model groups functions and processes become far more important than individual roles. His model has also been criticised for hindering development of well knit work group and cross fertilisation of ideas skills and resources for effective problem solving in traditional organisation.

Assumptions of the Motivation Theory

Each and every organisation, whether governmental, military or business wants that the workers at all levels must remain motivated. It is then that they will put in maximum labour and given high output. For this they also provide them incentives both financial and non-financial. What type of incentives should be provided to them, the views of the administrators and scholars on this differ, but all agree that unless some incentives is provided to the workers they will not feel motivated and not put their heart and soul in the work.

Modern Theories of Motivation. Almost every thinker who has dealt with the problem of organisation and administration has dealt with the problem of motivation of the workers. Maslow gave his theory of motivation; Herzberg gave his Hygiene theory of motivation in which he divided hygiene and motivation factors and also hygiene seekers and motivation seekers and Douglas Mc Gregor gave his theory 'X' and theory 'Y' about motivation. All these have been discussed separately.

Reward Theory of Motivation. Theory has been put forth by F.W. Taylor. He has said that reward and good working conditions satisfy the workers and a satsified worker feels motivated and gives better and more output. His quality of work gets improved. The more the worker is rewarded the more motivated he will feel to do the work. It is after taking this factor into account that he gave, supported and developed Differential Price Rate System about the payment of wages to the workers.

Taylor is also of the view monetary rewards very much motivate the workers in every organisation to do more work and develop in them urge to do more work. These are therefore, very important. He has also said that these should be made basis for further rising and going up in the organisation. Some scholars however, dispute this view point. According to them monetary rewards do not always motivate the workers, though to some extent and at a particular level, these become incentives and motivate the workers. They believe that these satisfy monetary needs of the workers but do not motivate them. This view point is in principle supported by Druker. These days non-financial incentives are as important as financial ones. The people at higher level usually attach much importance to non-financial incentives *e.g.* they wish that their services should be recognised in the public.

Basic Assumptions of theTheory. Motivation becomes more effective when the rewards are immediately paid. If a worker is not paid his wages or rewards timely and it is unduly delayed that dampens the spirits of the workers and they do not remain motivated. Another assumption is that more a worker is rewarded for his work, more he shall give better output. It was because of this presumption that Taylor favoured the system of Differential Price Rate System. Still another presumption is that individual motivation is more effective than group motivation because each worker feels happy for getting the rewards for the work which he has himself completed. He gets motivated because he knows that more work he will do, more he will be rewarded for the labour put in by him. But in group situation the reward is shared by the group as a whole and as such individual motivation is considerably reduced. If in a group there are some workers who are not good and rewards are distributed among fast and slow workers equally, then that is bound to result in strains and reduce motivation of good workers who put in more efforts and give better quality work.

Monistic Theory of Motivation. It is another theory of motivation. It is based on the assumption that a worker does his work simply to earn maximum wages or money. In other words money is the basis of human behaviour. The theory is based on the principle of economic man. A worker is attracted by monetary rewards and more is monetary reward, more will he be attracted to do the work. In other words more wages or salaries a worker is paid more he shall be ready to finish the work.

Pluralist Theory of Motivation. It is another theory of motivation. It is a modern concept which believes that a worker does not work having single purpose in view. On the other hand, he has several considerations in view, while doing his work. It believes that in every day life several situations arise which strain his life and make him think in a particular direction. In order to meet his needs and also to reduce his strains he does that type work which reduces his strains and meets his needs. A never ending circle is going on which begins with needs, their satisfaction and arising of another need. There are some physical and other needs which are basic to life.

Reward and Punishment Theory. This theory is combination of two theories namely 'Reward Theory' and 'Punishment Theory' of motivation. It believes that rewards and punishment should be combined for motivating a worker. It believes that a worker may be rewarded if he does some good work but one who does not achieve some minimum fixed target he should be punished as well. In other words only those workers should be rewarded whose work is above a particular fixed level or standard of work and those who fail to achieve even the minimum fixed standard should be punished.

This theory makes both reward and punishment very conditional. It is pointed out that this theory remains valid as long as a worker's physical and security needs are not met. When his basic needs are met he thinks in terms of position, status, respect etc. and at that stage this theory loses much of its validity.

Fear and Punishment Theory. It is the oldest theory about motivation. It believes that a worker can be motivated to work only with the help of punishment or keeping him under constant fear. If the worker is threatened of demotion or removal from service he will get feared and will be compelled to do more work.

This theory has however, not received much acceptability in our modern times. It was very much prevalent during the days of Industrial Revolution, when urbanisation trend had started and the labour force migrated from rural to urban areas in search of jobs. Since labour was available for work in the factories, without much difficulty, therefore, the factors owners and capitalists could use fear for getting work from the workers. They then used punishment and fear as methods for getting the work done. At that time the workers were also in such miserable conditions and in such a helpless situations that they had no other alternative but to silently bear all high handedness of the employers, who used punishment and fear as weapons for getting the work done from the workers.

Participation Theory of Motivation. This theory believes that in order to motivate the workers, it is desirable that they should be made participants in the management of the organisation because the only aim of a worker is not to earn money but he wants to have his identification in the organisation in which he is working. It believes that the workers will feel motivated if they are made to participate in planning and decision-making activities of the organisation. They will then devleop a sense of participation in the activities of the organisation and will feel motivated and by mutual cooperation and sense of understanding both will work in a spirit which is to the advantage of organisation and can result in increased production.

Individual and Organisation Need Theory. Credit for the development of this theory goes to Argyris. The theory is based on the assumption that individual and collective needs are never the same and usually every individual wishes that first of all his personal than his collective needs should be met and he struggles in this background. He has therefore, said that while meeting demands an organisation should give preference to individual rather than collective needs. If it is desired that the workers should remain motivated the organisation should meet quickly individual needs.

Path Goal Theory of Motivation. This theory is linked with production. It says that a worker feels motivated to work when he has certain goals and objectives to achieve and clearly understands these. He puts in still harder labour, if the goals to be achieved are difficult and require hard labour. If the workers accept production of quality goods and increased production as their goal, then they will try to become good producer of goods and vice-versa. Thus in this theory for motivation more stress has been laid on production. The theory also believes that the workers have many needs and they have also high objectives before them, which they wish to achieve and more the organisation keeps these factors into consideration, more the workers will feel motivated.

Likert's Employee Centred Supervision Theory of Motivation. Likert has also given his theory of motivation. He has said that in government run management agencies production depends on several factors and worker is an important factor in it. He believes that the wages which a worker gets influence his views above production, output, satisfaction and motivation. If he does not get incentives to satisfy his needs and his wages are inadequate then he does not feel satisfied. He then also does not give production to the extent to which the management desires him to produce.

Likert also believes that the worker wishes that his problems should be solved and he should be accepted and recognised as an important part of production. He also wants that he should have both social security and respect. If the worker feels that he is an insignificant cog in the machine of the organisation his morale will then come down. He will then not feel motivated and this will adversely affect production and profits. He believes that to the extent possible the managers should not be job oriented but employee oriented. The workers should be made participants in planning and execution of the work of the organisation. They should be involved in decision-making. They should also be given maximum freedom in completing their work and the way in which to finish that. Likert's theory of motivation is very much accepted these days, as a reasonable theory of motivation of workers.

COMMUNICATION SYSTEM

Communication system and actual working and performance of an organisation are closely linked with each other and this need be clearly understood.

(a) Relationship of Communication System and Performance of an Organisation. Communication system is considered an important factor in every organisation. A good and effective system is considered very important for smooth running of every organisation. Communication can both upward and downward and vice-versa. Thus it can be both one way and both ways traffic. Though communication system may appear to be a simple system yet in practice it is not so. On the other hand, it is very complex and complicated.

A good communication system is a combination of comprehension and motivation on the one hand and acceptance and non-acceptance on the other. Any adverse reaction of the worker and others to any communication system can create many problems for the organisation. An atmosphere of fear lack of confidence, hatred etc. not only checks the flow of communication and kills initiative but also distorts the communication itself. It is therefore, very essential that the communication should be such which is meaningful and develops confidence among those who work in the organisation. Communication system of an organisation favourably or adversely affects its production as well.

(b) Managing Conflicts. In every organisation conflicts are bound to arise and it is in the interest of organisation itself that these should be resolved at the earliest. Likert has develop new pattern for resolving these conflicts and has discussed a new pattern of management which is based on cooperative and supportive relationship. He is of the view that the present system of production which is based on exploitation is the main cause responsible for employer-employee conflict. It is straining relationship between the two. The conflicts are not reducing but are on the increase. These occur not only in the organisation but also among the organisations as well and as such are to be seen at all levels in the society and both at national as well as international levels.

In his 'New Ways of Managing Conflict' he has defined conflict by saying that, "It is an active striving for one's own preferred outcome, which if attained, precludes the attainment by others of their own preferred outcome thereby producing hostility". Thus for him a conflict situation is one in which there is active struggle for having some outcome for one's ownself at the cost of other.

According to him conflicts are of two types namely *(a)* Substantive Conflict and *(b)* Affective Conflict. The former, in Likert's view is linked with the substance of the task, whereas the latter is related to emotions and the relationship with the parties is inter-personal.

Features of Conflict. Likert has said that in conflict the strategy adopted is that of winning and losing. He believes that it is wrong because in organisations it very adversely affect its working. The image of the groups and people in the eyes of the people comes down. The workers at all level get divided and those who are mature are pushed to the background and aggressive tendencies raise their head. He has therefore, suggested that for managing conflict the weaknesses of present day capitalist system will have to be removed and new pattern of management based on cooperative and supportive system will have to be developed.

Critical Evaluation of Likert's Views. There is no denial that participative management is good for increased production and helpful in maintaining healthy employer-employee relations. It can also be helpful in better performance but it is only a wishful thinking that organisation will move increasingly in the same direction and that too with good understanding. As the time will pass problems are bound to arise which will strain employer-employee relationship. The whole idea developed by him is likely to slow down decision-making process.

It is also that so long as modern organisation are dominated by capitalists, introduction of participative management system in any organisation is a wishful thinking. It is also pointed out by the critics that since the values of the workers and employees differ therefore, in every organisation therefore, conflicts are inevitable. Then how can it be expected that participative management system will serve the purpose in the manner in which it has been put forth by Likert.

❐

12

Peter F. Drucker

Peter F. Drucker was born in Vienna in 1909. He had a good part of his education both in Austria and England. He started his life career in 1929 in a newspaper when he was about 20 years of age. He also served as an Economist an international bank in London, which provided him an opportunity to see the working of banking system in the country. He settled down in the U.S.A. in 1937 and since then he is there. After coming to the U.S.A. he joined a group of insurance companies as Economist. He also served in some British banks in that country. In 1940, he joined as Management Adviser in several corporations of the country. In 1942, he joined as Professor of Philosophy and Politics in Bennigton College, where he continued to work till 1949. Thereafter he joined as Professor of Administration in Graduate School of Business, New York University. He continued to work in that University for about 22 years *i.e.* 1950 to 1972.

After leaving the University he joined Claremont Graduate School, California as Professor of Social Sciences. Prof. Drucker has special interest in economic policies, management and administration. In these areas of his interest has brought out several books and contributed a number of research articles. Some of these have been translated in different languages. In 1978, Prof. Drucker also visited India for participation in an International Congress.

Some of important publications of Drucker's are: The End of Economic Man; The Future Industrial Man; The Concept of Corporation; The New Society; The Effective Executive; The Age of Discontinuity; Preparing Tomorrow's Business Leaders Today; Technology, Management and Society; Men, Ideas and Politics; Management: Tasks, Responsibilities and Practices; The Practice of Management; America's Next Twenty Years; The Landmarks of Tomorrow; Managing for Results; Management in Turbulent Times.

His well-known book entitled *'The Practice of Management'* is a thought provoking one. In it, he has dealt with such issues as structure of management, management of managers, management of work and workers, management of business etc. The book contains about 30 articles which among other issues mentioned above also deals with duties and responsibilities of managers towards the workers and the management. After studying the book the management and the manager can identify his weaknesses and also the way in which these should be or atleast can possibly be removed.

His another important book entitled *'The Age of Discontinuity'* was brought out in 1969. It is considered as one of the most important volumes in the field of management administration. In this book he has dealt with at considerable length the effects of technological changes on economic systems and policies of the government on the one hand and management system on the other. He has tried to point out that because of far reaching changes and explosions in the field of education, basic changes have come in the working system and in the outlook and approach of both the workers and also the management.

Drucker's Published Research Articles. As said above Drucker has published quite a good number of research articles which have received attention and appreciation for the ideas contained in these papers. In this connection it may be pointed out that Drucker saw before his own eyes the horrors of two world wars and inmunerable which the mankind suffered because of wars. He also studied capitalist communist and totalitarian systems of government and came to the conclusion that neither was all good.

Views about Management

Drucker's views about management are available to us in his publications entitled *'The Practice of Management'*, *'Management: Tasks, Responsibilities and Practice'* and *'Managing in Turbulent Times'*. It is in these volumes that he has discussed different aspects of management. He has prophesied that in the years to come the demand for good managers and management systems will considerably increase. He has however, not favoured bureaucratic management. On the other hand, he has laid stress on creative management. By this he means that the manager should be creative. He has said that mere managing a business is not sufficient and that a manager should not satisfy himself merely by deciding and finalising administrative policies but he should devote time and energies in doing some constructive and innovative work. In this category he has included breaking of new ideas but not altogether discarding the old ones. He has said that a good management should try to have healthy combination of both the old and the new ideas. He has also said that constructive work includes acceptance of new management ideas with come from different quarters.

Views about Automation

Drucker is of the view that a management is required to perform or should perform different types of functions. These can be broadly placed in three categories namely (*a*) Managing a Business; (*b*) Managing Managers; and (*c*) Managing workers and Work. He has said that the management of today is faced with the serious challenge of introduction of automation, which is very much opposed by the workers, because they feel that is not in their interest. He has said that automation is posing serious challenge because it is coming at a fast speed in industries inspite of opposition from different corners. He has however, prophecied that a day is not far of when need for automation will be fully realised and present day crisis will blow away and it will be considered as a solid achievement of management.

Views about Management Functions

Drucker has discussed at considerable length of management functions. In fact that was focus of some of his publications and research articles. His publication entitled, 'Management: Tasks, Responsibilities and Practice', is primarily devoted to this topic. He has divided these tasks into three categories namely; (*a*) Purpose or Mission; (*b*) Productive Work and Worker's Achievements and (*c*) Social Impact and Social Responsibilities.

About the purpose he has said that every organisation whether it is engaged in a business or not has a mission *i.e.* a purpose which it wants to achieve. In the case of business organisations it is usually economic performance on the basis of which its achievement is assessed. On the other hand, it is not the mission or purpose of non-commercial organisations like military establishments, religious bodies hospitals and universities. Their main objective is to provide the society some type of service. These also aim at raising the morale of the workers of their living standard and to contribute in national progress.

As regards second task namely productive work and workers' achievement, Drucker has said that the main aim of management should be to make the work productive and to have good workers for that. Man is a most essentially needed part of every type of organisation, whether commercial or non-commercial. Management, by making men productive can use that to achieve any target. In order to make the work productive he has laid stress on automation. To make the men productive, which in his opinion is a very essential for achieving organisational targets, he has suggested certain motivations. These include man's satisfaction, incentives, prizes, leadership, respect, promotion etc.

The another task which he feels modern management should perform is in the social field. It should discharge social responsibilities and be aware and conscious of these. The management should study social impact of its policies. He has said that every system is part of the whole social system and should be developed and organised to meet some social needs. A business or financial organisation should provide cheap and quality goods to the society. Non-business or non-financial institutions should manage their activities in such a way that these provide maximum satisfaction to the society.

Drucker has said that aim of a financial or business organisation should not be merely to earn profits or to satisfy the employees by providing them incentives or better working conditions but also to provide very satisfactorily goods and services to the consumers. Non-commercial organisation should be set up merely for providing jobs to different categories of employees but to provide services. A good management should not ignore this basic fact.

Views on Duties of Manager

Drucker has discussed functions of both management and the manager. As said earlier he has divided the functions of management in three categories namely (*a*) managing a business; (*b*) managing managers; and (*c*) managing workers and work. He has said that a decision of manager can affect all the three functions. Whereas first function is concerned with economic efficiency and it is the responsibility of manager to see that financial stability of the organisation is in no way adversely affected but maintained at all costs. As regard second function it is the duty of the management to see that human and natural resources are so consolidated and channellised that these can be used for increasing production and profits. Third function is concerned with placement of workers and giving them suitable directions and exercising proper controls over them.

He has however, said that the most important function of management is to manage business properly and efficiently that is concerned with economic and financial aspects. The other two functions are concerned with management, labour and welfare of society. The society on the whole is however, concerned with both. These functions make the management socially responsible. Drucker has however, pointed out that all the above mentioned three functions are closely linked with each other. Every action of management therefore, influences all the three functions.

Views on Federalism

Prof. Drucker favours federal type system in the setting up of modern big organisations. He does not very much support the ideas of large scale production in many organisations but instead suggests assembling of parts of different products. He feels that the system of large scale production of products has become outdated now. On the other hand, he believes that decentralisation is based on the principle of federalism. In his opinion the system of centralisation can be based when organisational set up is based on the old pattern. He has said that the system of federalism as envisaged by him can be possible only when each manager is given the fullest liberty to perform his allotted duties. He has also said that federation helps in establishing standards for measuring the work of those who are engaged in performance of same type of duty or completion of work.

According to him it is federal which helps in finding out how far the workers have succeded in achieving their objectives. Prof. Drucker was very much influenced by the working of General Motors Company of the U.S.A. which had based its functioning on federal principles. He is convinced that this type of system can solve the problems of discontinuity.

Concept of Management by Objectives

Drucker has given the concept of Management by Objective (M.B.O.). It is his real contribution to management studies. It was in 1954 that he introduced this concept in management field.

The Concept. Drucker basically believes that every manager in his field should have clear ideas and objectives which he wants to achieve. These should not be vague but should be such which can be rationally measured. These should not be ideal but practical. He has also identified areas in which targets can be fixed and objectives set fourth can be achieved. These can be

(*a*) Productivity;

(*b*) Managemerial Performance and Development;

(*c*) Market Standing;

(*d*) Physical and Financial Resources;

(*e*) Innovation and Public Accountability in which has also included workers performance and Attitude.

Drucker belives that the management should give every manager full liberty to fix the targets which it wishes to achieve—whether the targets are upto the expected level, practical to be achieved, measurable and are within the policy framework of the organisation, are to be decided and approved by the senior officers in every case. It is therefore, not desirable but also essential that about targets to be achieved each manager should hold meetings with his superior officers. Drucker has also said that there should be no rigidity about targets. It means that the targets once fixed can be changed. The management and senior officers should from time to time evaluate achievements of targets and where and when necessary these should be changed and re-fixed so that these are in keeping with changed needs and resources.

According to him it is not exercise in futility but it has its utility. It will force the management and the managers to fix some targets, which they will like to achieve. Thus they will get direction in which they are to proceed.

Stress on Measurement of Objectives. Drucker has laid stress on measurement of objectives or targets to be achieved. Thus according to him targets should be both quantitatively measureable and verifiable. He does not favour any vagueness in any way in this regard. In fact he has at times used the term measurement in place of control. He has associated or linked targets with self-control. He has tried to stress that in case manager is involved in the fixation of targets, then business targets will gradually become personal targets of the manager and he will try to achieve these at all costs. He has further said that this type of involvement is useful in another way as well.

Salient Features of Management by Objectives. M.B.O. has certain features or characteristics. It is a system of management in which targets or objectives to be achieved are fixed jointly by the management and the workers. It is thus ensured that only such targets are fixed which can be achieved. It develops among all those who are to achieve these, a sense of involvement. In this way achieving of targets becomes easy. When all concerned at different levels *i.e.* the management and employees sit together and fix objectives, then there is no feeling that something is being imposed on them. Drucker feels that in such a situation there is no need for exercising controls from outside. Self-controls, then serve the purpose in a very meaningful manner.

Quite often in every organisation several problems arise because unrealistic departmental goals are fixed. In this system since targets are fixed in consultation with the workers, therefore, the question of their being unrealistic does not arise. There is also hardly any question mark on their achieving the same. Once the targets or objectives to be achieved have been fixed these are measured in quantitive terms and performance can be assessed and analysed. In management by objective, the whole exercise and management activity becomes a corporate activity.

Drucker has also said that in M.B.O. no participant is to be kept in the dark about any target. Every objective should be clear and each one should very clearly know about his duties, responsibilities and also his rights and duties. There should be no vagueness in these. It is always desirable that each one should be assigned only such duties which he willingly accepts to perform.

One important feature of the M.B.O. is that in it objectives of each department are fixed in the same manner and on the same principles in which these are fixed at the organisation level. In both the cases the basic principle is that in the exercise both the bosses and the employees should be involved and the workers should have no feelings of super imposition. Still another feature is that even if need for revising objectives, both for upward or downward arises, that should not be done unilaterally.

In brief, according to Drucker, management by objectives is an exercise about fixation of targets to be achieved by an organisation, not unilaterally but in cooperation with and on the basis of perfect understanding between the workers and the management. There is no super imposition on any one and that every one gets involved in it. He gradually feels that in not achieving the targets his personal prestige will come down.

Changing Concept of Bureaucracy

Bureaucracy continued to be understood in the manner described above through the 19th century. But conceptions began to emerge which recognised that there are differences other than those of power and size between groups of officials and modes of organisation. One of the most important of these conceptions "transfers attention from officials as a social group to the mode of organisation of the institutions in which they serve. This use of bureaucracy is important as a forerunner of the widespread 20th century habit of applying the terms 'bureaucracies' or 'bureaucratic' to institutions rather than to the officials employed in them; these latter are thus called bureaucrats as much because they work in the institutions as because they are members of a social group."

It was Max Weber, a German sociologist, who gave the modern concept of bureaucracy. He never defined bureaucracy in the explicit way in which he defined "class" or 'status group'. He regarded bureaucracy as a universal social phenomenon, and the means of carrying "community action" over into rationally ordered "societal action". He outlined the characteristics of the 'ideal' type from functional point of view. Some of these characteristics are structural and others behavioural. He used the word bureaucracy not to refer disparagingly to rule by officials, but to designate a quite specific kind of administrative organisation.

Marshall E. Dimock identified bureaucracy with institutions and large scale organisations in society. For him "Bureaucracy is the state of society in which institutions overshadow individuals and simple family relationships; stage of development in which division of labour, specialisation, organisation, hierarchy, planning and regimentation of large groups of individuals either by voluntary or involuntary methods, are the order of the day... Bureaucracy is simply institutionalism written large. It is not some foreign substance which has been infused into the life-blood of an institution; it is merely the accentuation of characteristics found in all. It is a matter of degree, of the combination of components, and of the relative emphasis given to them." John A. Vieg says, in free translation it means 'desk government" or management by bureaus. "It denotes the sum total of the personnel apparatus and procedures by which an organisation manages its work and accomplishes its purposes.

For Prof. Charles Hyneman, bureaucracy is big organisation. "I prefer to say that bureaucracy is a word for big organisation." He considered it big enough to be bureaucratic if one has to search for finding out who is making its policies or its policies and procedures are written out, or if you think it takes too long for one part to find out what another part proposes to do. A similar definition but laying greater emphasis on functional aspect is given by Peter M. Blau and Marshal W. Mayer. They define bureaucracy as "organisation designed to accomplish large scale administrative tasks by systematically coordinating the work of many individuals." A structural view of bureaucracy as an organisation was taken by Arthur K. Davis. He used the term for denoting "an integrated hierarchy of specialised offices defined by systematic rules—an impersonal routinised structure wherein legitimatised authority rests in the office and not in the person of the incumbent." Another definition of bureaucracy is that it is"a hierarchical organisation of officials appointed to carry out certain public objectives." A three dimensional view of bureaucracy is given by Bata K. Day. From the structural aspect, it is value neutral—"neither hero nor villain", it can be treated as a phenomenon associated with any large-scale, complex organisation.

Factors for the Rise of Bureaucracy

Bureaucracy developed in the eighteenth and nineteenth centuries, first in the countries of Western Europe and then in other countries of the world. It attained new heights in the twentieth century despite the triumphs in several states of Marxist ideology which seeks to eliminate it. What factors, then have contributed to its rise?

Laski's Views. Laski attributes the rise of bureaucracy to several factors. First, it arose as a byproduct of aristocracy. In its history, a disinclination on the part of the aristocracy for active government has in some cases led to the transfer of power into the hands of permanent officials. Second, the origin of bureaucracy may be traced to the desire of the Crown to have a body of personal servants who may be set-off against the appetite of the aristocracy for power. Third, the advent of democracy helped it in two ways: (*a*) In the nineteenth century the advent of democratic government overthrew in the Western world the chance of maintaining a system whereby officials could constitute a permanent and hereditary caste. (*b*) The new conditions which accompanied democracy made it essential to have a body of experts in charge of a particular service. Fourth, the scale of the modern state and the vastness of the service it seeks to render make expert administration inevitable.

Martin Krygier's Views. Engene Kamenka and Martin Krygier discuss at length several factors which have contributed to the rise of a class of permanent state officials called bureaucracy in modern states. The important of them are: establishment of strong centralised states in many countries of Europe beginning with France industrial revolution; expansion in the activities of the state; French revolution; growth of the concept that the public officials were servants of the nation rather than of the ruler personally;

the growth of the concept that sovereignty vested in the nation and not in the person of the ruler; introduction of the system of payment of regular salaries to public servants who were, it began to be argued, answerable to the state and not personally to the ruler; etc.

Max Weber Views. There were bureaucracies in the past *e.g.* in the ancient Egyptian, Roman and Chinese administrations; and in the Roman Catholic Church since the end of the thirteenth century, but they were less bureaucratic, limited in numbers and confined to the state and church only. With the rise of absolutism in Europe and modernisation bureaucracies became more purely bureaucratic, proliferated and penetrated much wider spheres of social life. Besides the state administrations, armies, churches universities economic enterprises and political parties also became bureaucratised. Weber regards it as the result of the following causes.

1. The Creation of Money Economy. This process occurred when Europe emerged from the Middle Ages. Weber does not regard it as an absolute pre-requisite because bureaucracies had existed in countries like Egypt, Rome and China even when compensation was paid in kind. But that could not ensure dependable revenues for bureaucrats. The system of rewarding bureaucrats by grants of land and/or the collection of tax revenues from given territories in turn tended to lead to the disintegration of bureaucracies into feudal and semi-feudal domains.

2. Democracy. The other side of the growth of democratic institutions was opposing and helping to eliminate the traditional rule of nobles and feudal elements, and encouraging education and appointment to office on the basis of knowledge.

3. The Emergence of Capitalist Economy. The system of free enterprise, the essence of capitalism, fostered bureaucracy. It created the needs which only bureaucratic organisation could satisfy. Capitalism requires and encourages strong and orderly governments in its own interests. This is another way of saying that capitalism requires and encourage government based on bureaucratic organisations. Not only governments but also capitalist enterprises themselves began to follow bureacractic principles of organisation because of the requirements of rationality and calculability—the prime features of capitalism.

4. More Encompassing Trend Towards Rationality in Western Society. Modern Western society experienced the growth of rationalism in many spheres. For instance it was evident in the development of Protestant ethic which encouraged hard work and self discipline. This ethic was the basis of the spirit of capitalism which called for the rational investment of time and efforts so as to maximise profits and achievements. This spirit, in turn, was one of the preconditions for the development of rational capitalism. The general trend towards rationality was also evident in other spheres like developments of science and governance. Thus Protestantism, capitalism, science and bureaucracy are all part of one cluster of developments-the process of rationalisation.

6. Modern Forms of Communication. Modern means of communication both required and facilitated a more complex and effective type of administration, that is bureaucratic.

Weber observed that bureaucracy developed because its rationality and technical superiority made it the most appropriate tool for dealing with the tasks and problems of complex modern society. Because of this superiority bureaucracy had to become more pervasive and it is bound to become even more so in the future.

6. Growth of the European Population. Population growth multiples administrative tasks which must be coped with through larger organisations. Larger organisations on their part tend to assume bureaucratic forms.

7. Emergence of Complex Administrative Problems. Complexity of tasks to be performed by governments gives rise to large-scale bureaucratic organisation. This is what happened in ancient Egypt, a country which had first large-scale bureaucracy in history, when it faced the complex task of constructing and regulating waterways. The newly emerged centralised states in Europe in recent times had to cope with administrative tasks unknown in the past. Not only did they have to control larger territories and populations but also they had to provide social services of a nature that no previous state had to procure before. The Complexity of these tasks required expertise and effectiveness in organisation *i.e.* bureaucracy.

Weber on Bureaucracy *vis-a-vis* Democracy

Weber had clearly recognised this dilemma. He noted that democratic movements demanding equality before law and protection against arbitrary excess of legal and administrative authority helped the development of bureaucracy. These movements demanded recruitment to public services based on merit, rather than personal or political considerations. These demands on bureaucracy had a levelling effect. Another stimulus for levelling of status differences was insistence on technical qualifications rather than inherited status in recuritment and advancement in bureaucracy. However, the measure designed to protect a bureaucracy against the abuse of authority and encroachment of its privileges may also promote bureaucratic power. Thus democracy may unintentionally promote bureaucratization which he regarded as unavoidable consequence of democratic growth.

But, according to Weber, democracy is basically opposed to the rule of bureaucracy because the latter concentrates power in the hands of those who are in charge of bureaucratic machinery and that such a concentration of power is against the basic premises of the formar. It is particularly so when experts or technocrats are removed from the influence of popular public sentiments. However, he also recognised that without a civil service class, democracy could be plagued by spoils system, public waste, irregularities and lack of technical efficiency. He summed up the dilemma thus, ".... democracy has to promote what reason demands and democratic sentiments hate."

The Question Mark in Developing Societies

The dilemma, as stated above, was still more accute in the developing countries which after liberation from colonial rule, were to take up the task of rapid economic development. There appeard to be some incompatibility between rapid economic development, on the one hand, and democratic political development on the other. Riggs flatly stated that the price of democratic development might have to be slower development in the economic sphere. For several reasons bureaucracies had to be strengthened. They had to choose between centralised, efficient and strong bureaucracies, and slow economic development. The second choice was not in their national interests but first choice could pose a threat to democratic development. The problem was highlighted by Joseph La Palombara thus: "In places such as these, a powerful bureaucracy is said to be essential if one is to override the disintegrating influences of artificial political boundaries, the competitive forces of familiar and tribal structures, the difficulty for organising and financing palitical parties, the low energy output of the population, and the tendency of the population want to expend funds on the consumer gadgets rather than on capital formation. In the developing states, powerful bureaucracies are simply necessary evils that one must learn to tolerate, hoping for best from a democratic standpoint."

In many developing countries, therefore, the emergence of overpowering bureaucracies is a fact of life. Hence, Riggs suggested the development of a middle class as a vital means of limiting bureaucratic power in favour of democratic development. In Meiji Japan the dominant social class served as a check on bureaucratic excesses. In India the Congress Party, the traditions of the Indian civil service and the growth of strong and articulate local centres of political power appear to be worked as partial checks on bureaucracy. Palombara is of the view that in the developing countries the extent of bureaucracy's power may be checked by such factors as increased literacy, strong traditional institutions, and strong social elites of which the bureaucracy is not a part or into which it has not yet been absorbed.

Eva Etzioni. Halevy's Thesis

Writing on the proposition bureaucracy *vis-a-vis* democracy Eva Etzioni-Halevy puts forth three dimensions of the problem. His first thesis is that there is an intrinsic connection between bureaucracy and democracy although it is of paradoxical or self-contradictory nature. On the one hand, the growing power of bureaucracy does indeed pose a threat to democracy. On the other hand, a modern democracy cannot exist without a relatively powerful and independent bureaucracy.

Bureaucracy poses a threat to democracy because:

(*i*) It may serve as a tool for enhancing state domination (or state repression) which is made possible by the growing pervasiveness of all bureaucracies, and the evolving technology of ever more sophisticated devices of collecting, storing and retrieving ever-larger amounts of information.

(*ii*) Bureaucracy is intent upon guarding information and preserving the utmost secrecy in its own domain.

(*iii*) Because of the above, bureaucracy has increasingly gained the potential of encroaching on the autonomy, liberty and privacy of the individual.

(*iv*) Bureaucracy has increasingly gained the potential to exempt itself from the control of elected politicians and to infringe on their domain, due to monopolisation of expertise and information and due to the decline in the power of parliament.

In view of the above, it seems clear that an overpowering bureaucracy poses a threat to democracy. But what makes an independent and powerful bureaucracy necessary for democracy? Eva Etzioni-Halevy argues, "For democratic procedures to work properly, the modern state must have at its disposal an organisation that will not only allocate the resources but will do so by non-partisan criteria. Failing this, the political democratic process would necessarily be based on an exchange of material benefits....for political support." If this happens, it will lead to all sorts of political corruption which in turn, would make the electoral process a mere farce. Thus it is not the politicians (who are obliged to seek political support for reelection and therefore remain under constant political pressure) but a body of independent and permanently appointed neutral persons *i.e.* bureaucrats (not bothered about their election prospects) that is more suitable for allocating the state resources.

The second thesis of Eva Etzioni-Halevy is that democracy poses a dilemma for bureaucracy. "By democratic rules, bureaucracy is in a doule bind: it is expected to be under the control of elected politicians and yet exempt from such control; it is expected to be subject to ministerial responsibility and yet accept responsibility for its own action; it is expected to implement the policy devised by its elected political head and yet participate in the formulation of policy in its own right; it is expected to participate in the formulation of policy and yet be politically neutral; which is another way of saying that bureaucracy is expected to be politicised and non-politicised at one and the same time."

To the extent that bureaucracy takes part in the formulation of policy, at the higher level, it takes part in the allocation of resources. Therefore it takes part in the exercise of power and as such is engaged in politics. Hence also it is subject to the pressure of interest groups and must respond to or manoeuvre between such pressures. So it is a participant in the struggle for control over resources or in other words engaged in struggle for power that is, politics. In this sense bureaucracy is clearly politicised. This type of politicisation is considered ligitmate and even beneficial to democratic processes. But if a bureaucracy favours one political party over an other in matters of policy, appointments and promotion of personnel, it gives that party enormous advantage in the electoral process. This type of politicisation or partisan functioning is considered illegitimate and therefore harmful to democratic functioning.

This then is the dilemma of bureaucracy in democracy created by the ambiguity of role definition of the former. The attempts made in several countries to give clarification of the role definition of bureaucracy have not succeeded as yet. The third thesis of Eva Etzioni-Halevy is that the ambiguity of the role definition of bureaucracy is the source of considerable strain, friction and even conflict in the political system of modern democracies. It is especially so between senior bureaucrats and senior politicians (ministers and M.P.s). In the absense of clear role definition, often senior bureaucrats have been able to "branch out into the bureaucratic political no man's land which does not fall clearly within the domain of bureaucracy nor clearly outside it. This, however, is disputed territory. Its penetration by bureaucracy has therefore led at times, to an adverse reaction by politicians who lay claim to this territory as well." This is particularly so for bureaucracy's participation in politics. Whenever the bureaucracy has approached or crossed the boundary, which is always hazy, between policy and party politics, it has led to "especially severe tensions and power struggles, which sometimes contribute to the downfall of senior politicians or even entire governments, to dismissal of senior bureaucrats or even to the abolition of entire bureaucratic agencies."

❒

13

Herbert A. Simon

Herbert A. Simon born in 1916, in Wisconsin, he received his Ph. D. in Political Science from the University of Chicago. Starting his career in municipal government on which he authored quite a few books, he served with great distinction in various capacities and organisations as an academic and as a consultant. His contribution to administrative thought and its popularity in the field are evident from the number of publications on different subjects, many of which have been translated into various languages including Turkish, Persian and Chinese. His principal publications are: *Administrative Behaviour* (1947), *Fundamental Research in Administration* (1953), *Organisations* (1958), *The New Science of Management Decision* (1960), *Shape of Automation* (1960), *Sciences of the Artificial* (1969) and *Human Problem Solving* (1972). A much sought after visiting Professor, he has lectured in many universities. He is the recipient of many awards and a number of Universities have conferred honorary doctorates on him. In recognition of his outstanding contribution in analysing the decision-making process, he was awarded the Noble Prize in 1978.

Simon equates 'administration' with decision-making. He lays emphasis on how decisions are made, and how they be made more effectively. He passess a critical indictment on the narrowness and sterility of the traditional approach and argues that before one can establish any immutable 'principles' of administration, one must be able to describe, exactly how an administrative organisation looks and exactly how it works. He says that when research has been done, when a basic vocabulary to the satisfaction of many scholars has been developed, when decision-making as well as the 'doing' have been analysed, when the limits to rationality imposed by restricting abilities, habits, values, and knowledge have been explored fully—then and only then—it may be possible to have valid principles of administration and know-how to apply them. In addition to the major stress upon decision-making as the alternative to the 'principles approach' of the traditionalists, Simon recommended an empirical approach to the study of administration. Simon is critical of the traditional principles of administration and calls them as 'proverbs'. He offers a series of hypothetical propositions of empirical relevance.

Thus Simon proposed a new concept of administration based on theories and methodology of logical positivism with the focus on decision-making. He maintains that to be scientific one must exclude value judgements and concentrate attention on facts, adopt precise definition of terms, apply rigorous analysis, and test factual statements or postulates about administration. 'An administrative science, like any science is concerned purely with factual statements.

Classical Theory

Simon calls the traditional concepts of administration as proverbs and myths. These principles of work division, unity of command, and span of control have all been attacked as being ambiguous and as mere proverbs, each paired with a contradictory proverb. The reason for such an ambiguity, according to him, is the 'inadequate' diagnosis of situations and definitions of terms and lack of detailed research into real situations. Simon says that these principles are more like a series of orderly cubicles contrived according to an abstract architectural logic than of a house designed to be inhabited by the human beings. He finds no compatibility between the perfection of administrative processes as conceived in the POSDCORB formula, and their utility in the attainment of objectives. Through these attacks, Simon points to the yawning gulf, between the principles and practice.

Decision-Making

Simon views an organisation as a structure of decision-makers. According to him decisions are made at all levels of the organisation, some of them affecting many members, while others are relatively less important decisions about details. Each decision is based on a number of premises, and Simon focusses his attention on how these premises are determined. "Some of these premises pertain to the decision-maker's preference; some to his social conditioning, and some others to the communications he receives from component units of the organisation. Simon asserts that the top management cannot dictate to every member of the organisation what each decision must be, but it can influence some, perhaps the most important premises on which the decisions are based.

Simon divides the decision-making process into three phases *viz.*, intelligence activity, design activity and choise activity. The first stage involves finding occasions calling for decision. The executive tries to understand the organisations environment and identifies conditions which need fresh action. This involves spending more time and energy that the first stage. Finally, the executive selects one of the alternative courses of action available to him. Simon says that though these three stages appear to be simple and one precedes the other, in practice the sequence is more complex than what it appears to be. Each of the stages may itself involve a sequence of decision-making more complex in process, as the 'choice stage' may also involve the intelligence activity and design activity, or each stage may involve all the three stages in itself. Simon explains that decision-making basically involves choise between alternative plans of action, and choice in turn, involves facts and values. According to him, every decision consists of a logical combination of fact and value propositions. A fact is a statement of reality indicating the existing deed, act or state of things. A factual premise can be proved by observable and measurable means. Value is an expression of preference. Simon is, however, aware that most premises have both factual and value elements and his purpose of stressing this distinction is only to clarify the different criteria of correcteness that may be applied in analysing the ethical and factual elements present in a 'decision'.

Mixed issues of fact and value, then impinge upon the administration complicating the decision-process. The relevance of this impingement on administration is to be seen in the purposive character of organisation which develops groups of individuals to achieve goals ordinarily beyond their individual reach. The continuum of purposiveness includes the concept of a 'hierarchy of decisions', and Simon concludes that behaviour in an organisation—a complex network of decision processes—is, therefore, intendedly rational in character, adjusted to the goals that have erected. Speaking of the complex network of decision process Simon says that 'each decision involves the selection of a goal and a behaviour relevant to it; this goal may in turn be mediate to a somewhat more distant goal; and so on, until a relatively final aim is reached.' The ambiguous synonymity between means-ends and fact-value, is clarified through a definition that so far as decisions lead to the selection of final goals, they may be treated as 'value judgements'—*i.e.*, the value component predominates, and in so far as the decision implement such goals, they may be treated as 'factual judgements'—*i.e.*, the factual component predominates. The relationship of a decision to a set of ends remains a factual proposition. Simon does not refer to 'value decisions' and 'factual decisions'.

Rationality in Decision-Making. Having established the factoral continuum of decision-making, Simon delves further into the dynamics of decision on a different plane—the plane of rationality. Simon expounds the necessity of being rational in making a choice. He defines rationality as one concerned with the selection of preferred behaviour alternatives in terms of some system of values whereby the consequences of behaviour can be evaluated. To him it requires a total knowledge and anticipation of the consequences that will follow on each choice. It also requires a choice from among all possible alternative behaviours. He explains rationality in terms of means-ends construct. The term 'means',—instrumental purpose—refers to any state or situation which is earlier in time than some other state or situation. The term 'ends'—ultimate purpose—refers to any state or situation which is later in a purpose chain or set of chains. The same state or situation may always be a means from one point of view and an ultimate objective from another. "If appropriate means are chosen to reach desired ends, the decision is rational. However, there are many complications to this simple test of rationality. For, it is difficult to separate means from ends because an apparent end may only be a means for some future end. This is commonly referred to as the means-end chain or hierarchy." Simon points out that "the means-end hierarchy is seldom an intergrated, completely connected chain. Often the conncetion between organisation activities and ultimate objectives is obscure, or these ultimate objectives are incompletely formulated or there are internal conflicts and contradictions among the ultimate objectives, or among the means selected to attain them." Besides, seemingly rational decision based on inaccurate conclusions, may produce undesirable, sometimes, even unanticipated results.

Modes of Organisational Influence

The behaviour of organisation man is subject to two types of influences—internal and external. The former involves establishing in the operative employees himself, attitudes and habits, which lead him to reach the desired decisions. This is achieved through organisation loyalty, concern with efficiency and training. The latter involves imposing on the operative employee decisions reached elsewhere in the organisation. This is achieved through authority and advisory and informational services. The individuals accept these influences for the simple fact that the organisation objectives also indirectly become personal objectives of the individuals and acceptance of influences satisfies personal motives.

Authority is one of the means through which organisation man is made to conform to the organisational demands. However, the general impression that authority flows from above is not correct. For, the exercise of authority, in the ultimate analysis, depends upon the willingness of those who accept it. It should also be noted that authority might operate at various levels and not necessarily downwards. Organisations develop both formal and informal relations and authority is largely used to settle the disputes in the organisation. Simon says that the operative employees is said to accept authority whenever he permits his behaviour to be guided by the decision of the superior. Following Barnard's 'zone of indifference', Simon discusses about the 'zone of acceptance', and says that if exercise of authority is attempted beyond this zone, the subordinate disobeys it.

The Criterion of Efficiency

While authority and organisational loyalty influence the value premise of the individual, the criterion of efficiency influences his capacity to handle the facts. Efficiency implies adoption of shortest path and cheapest means in achieving the desired goals. "Be efficient" is one of the major influences on organisational man.

Organisational Loyalties

It is generally observed that members in an organisation identify themselves with it. Such type of loyalty is fundamental for an organisation. Organisation loyalty fulfils a most important function of making individuals in the organisation confine themselves to their tasks instead of probing into the basics of the problem. However, narrow loyalties lead to friction and over competition for the resources.

Training

Training is a vital device through which organisation man is equipped to face challenges of the organisation. An efficient training programme would facilitate greater discretion to the individual in decision-making. Training is applicable to the process of decision whenever the same elements are involved in a number of decisions. Further training supplies facts, provides frame of reference and indoctrinates desirable values. Thus, it can be used for developing effective decision-making.

Administrative Efficiency

The administrative according to Simon must be guided by the criterion of efficiency in all aspects of decision-making. However, Simon is conscious of the complicated nature of its application in governmental organisations which are not commercial in nature. The criterion of efficiency 'dictates' that choice of alternative which produces the largest results for the given application of resources. It demands, of the two alternatives having the same cost, the one that leads to the greater attainment of the organisation objective be chosen; and of the two alternatives leading to the same degree of attainment that one which entails lesser cost should be chosen. The criterion of efficiency is thus closely related to both organisation and conservation resources. It is related to the organisation objectives in so far as it is concerned with the maximisation of output and with the conservation of resources in so far as it is concerned with the maintenance of a positive balance of output over input. Where resources, costs and objectives are variable, decisions cannot be taken purely on the basis of efficiency criteria.

Advice and Information

Continuous flow of information downwards, upwards and sideways is essential for effective functioning of an organisation. However, the nature of information of advice to be tendered may change from situation to situation. Therefore, collecting dependable information and proper utilisation of it ensures greater effectiveness in the decision-making and provides adequate lines of communication and persuasion.

Through his penetrating study, Simon focusses attention on the dynamics of decision-making processes and its role in organisations. His study provides a deep insight into administrative behaviour and the interaction between decision-making processes and administrative behaviour found in organisations. But while concentrating on the processes and the role of decision-making, Simon relegates social, political, economic and cultural factors to the background although their role is no less significant in the analysis of administrative behaviour. Similarly exclusion of value premises which are integral and essential components of policy determination per se, would steer the study of public administration to mechanical, routine and less important aspects.

Simon's study of decision-making incorporates and makes use of the logical positivists' distinction between fact and value. This approach has been attacked: (*a*) as reviving in a new guise the discredited politics-administration dichotomy;

(*b*) as harmful in its effects on decision-makers; and (*c*) as irrelevant to Simon's main thesis.

Simon's efforts to construct a value free science of administration has been criticised by Norton E. Long on the ground that it may lead to the unintended and logically unwarranted result of reviving the policy-administration dichotomy in new verbage and also lead to empirically untenable and ethically unwarranted view of administration as largely instrumental. Long further observes that bureaucracy is not, and cannot be, a neutral instrument solely devoted to the unmotivated presentation of facts to, and the docile execution of orders from, political superiors. Selznick argues that radical separation of fact and value too often identified with the logical distinctions between fact statement and preference statements, encourages the divorce of means and ends.

Simon's analysis assumes that administration plays a similar role in all societies. But it is observed from experience that administrative systems in developing countries do not have similar role orientation as their counterparts in developed countries. Simon's concept of efficiency also is subject to frequent criticism. Some criticise the term equating it with economy. Others object to the use of the term of the ground that it lead to a mechanical concept of administration, and to an inconsistent relationship between means and ends. Efficiency is not, and cannot be, the only goal of administration, because there is a whole range of other major categories of organisational purposes, such as, satisfaction of various interests, the production of goods and services, mobilising resources, conforming with certain organised codes, using the most rational techniques. Anyone of these objectives, roughly or in combination, may under certain circumstances be more important than efficiency to an organisation. Further, the goal of efficiency may often decline in importance. Efficiency is relevant only to the extent of scarcity of resources, and the perception of it by members of the organisation. It is measurable in precise terms only when it is possible to quantify both inputs and outputs.

The study of decision-making encounters many difficulties. For one, executives believe that it is often unwise to reveal the reasons for a decision or the procedure followed. For another, by the time the confidential facts are released via the 'memoirs' route, the case or the matter is no longer currently important.

Simon's theory of decision-making is criticised as being extremely general and while it provides the framework, does not supply details to guide to organisation planners. Simon's concept of rationality is also criticised. For example, Argyris feels that Simon, by insisting on rationality, has not recognised the role of intuition, tradition and faith in decision-making.

The utility of Simon's study in the decision-making process in terms of search and comparison and its criteria of maximising or satisficing, despite the criticism is unquestionable. In difference to the effective use of fact value distinction by many decision-makers is no argument against its effective use by academics as a tool in the analysis of decision-making phenomena.

In spite of all the above imperfections Simon's contribution is undoubtedly a major breakthrough in the evolution of administrative theory. But it is unfortunate that after his major work on Administrative Behaviour, Simon has not written much on public administrative system but has diverted his attention to economic and business systems.

Traditional and Modern Decision Making Techniques. Simon, as said earlier, has developed the concept of programmed and non-programmed decisions. In tradition making habits play an important role. In it there are standard operating procedures and a lot of time is spent on clerical routines. There is a system of well-defined sub-goals and there are also well set informal channels in so far as programmed decisions are concerned. In non-programmed decisions there is rule of thumb. As against that in modern decision-making in programmed decisions stress is laid on operation research, mathematical analysis, computerisation, electronic data processing and computer simulation. In the area of non-programmed decisions stress is laid on training of those who are to make decisions and on constructing heunistic computer programmes.

Simon has tried on analyse decision-making processes at considerable length. He has also discussed some decision-making models.

Theory of Equilibrium of Organisation

Professor Simon has made original contribution in the field of formal organisation and administration. As already said he was very critical about traditional approach to organisation and has characterised the views of traditional theorists as proverbs and slogans. He has laid stress in the study of organisation on human values and human aspect of the problems. He has tried to understand organisational problems in the background of social and psychological problems and issues.

Organisational Structure. The views of Prof. Simon about organisation structure very much differ from scholars and thinkers. He does not agree with them that an organisation is only a formal set up based on rules and regulations. But Prof. Simon accepts organisation as a group of people, which is faced with many serious human problems.

Influences on Organisation Man. He has said that an organisation man is under two types of influences namely internal and external. In the former case the employee himself reaches a decision whereas in the latter case decision is reached elsewhere in the organisation and is imposed on the employees working in the organisation. This is done by some authority and through informational services. The employees in the organisation accept both internal and external influences because objectives of the organisation indirectly become personal objectives of the individual as well. Not only this but by accepting these influences their personal motives are also satisfied.

Work Process in Organisation. Prof. Simon is of the view that basic work processes start at the lowest level, whereas at the middle level programmed decision are taken. These are of routine nature and continue to be repeated. These are matters of day-to-day concern. Non-programmed decisions are taken at the highest level. Those are not of repetitive nature for which precedents do not exist. There are no rules and regulations on which such decisions can be based. He has viewed organisational decisions at three levels. Simon very firmly believes that these levels are not affected by the processing of figures and automation of administrative decision system. On the other hand, because of automation mutual relation of three levels of decision makers in an organisation will become clear.

Individual Behaviour and Organisation. He has further said that it is the responsibility of organisation to make the people aware and provide them information about values and objectives of the decisions. He has fully appreciated the importance of employees of the organisation, but does not agree with those scholars who try to point out that individual is the pivot of the organisation. If an individual has courage, ability and imagination he can successfully work in any organisation.

Simon on Authority. Simon has said that authority is one of the means through which an organisation man is obliged to conform to organisational demands. He does not believe that authority flows from above. Authority, training, efficiency, organisational loyalty, organisational objectives and identification are some such factors and channels through which an organisation influences the behaviour of the individuals and moulds them to accept organisational decisions. The system of influencing an individual through organisation is technically called organisational influences. It is in this background that Simon's views about authority can be properly understood and appreciated. He has said that in the ultimate analysis, exercise of authority depends on the willingness of those who are to accept authority.

Professor Simon has defined authority by saying that it is a part of decision which guides the functioning of others. Its one important feature is that it can be used when parties to the dispute lack agreement. He feels that more stress has been laid on this aspect whereas in actual practice it is usually accepted and enforced with the help of suggestions and persuations.

Simon has said that if authority is exercised certain limits that is bound to be disobeyed. He has also said that if a particular person is not accepting authority, it does not mean that he has no power or authority but for that there can be other reasons, both internal and external as well which force him not to obey authority.

The Theory of Equilibrium of Organisation. Prof. Simon views organisation as a balanced system *i.e.* a system in equilibrium which receives contribution in the form of money or efforts and offers inducements in return for these contributions. He has said that in an organisation there are three partners. They are customers, servants and entrepreneurs. All these partners continue to affiliate and associate themselves with the organisation till their activities directly or indirectly serve their interests. They in their own way contribute in the growth and retardation of organisation.

For their contribution they are paid wages or given some services. For the existence of the organisation it is essential that the contribution of the partners and others to the organisation should exceed the wages or services which it provides to them.

Organisational Loyalties. Usually in a good organisation members identify themselves with it. It is very essential both for the growth and existence of the organisation itself. But organisational loyalty Simon means workers and others linked with organisation, conforming themselves to their tasks rather than finding faults or looking into its problems. But he has warned that narrow loyalties lead to friction and over competition for the use of scarce available manual and material resources.

Simon has laid stress on training. According to him it is with the help of training that an organisation man be in a position to face challenges of the organisation. A good training programme is likely to be useful and helpful in the difficult task of decision-making. It is training which provides facts, frame of reference and inculcates desirable values. Thus training helps in over all development of organisation man and is absolutely necessary for him.

Views about Communication System

Simon fully well realised the need of communication system in an organisation. According to him continuous flow of information down wards, upwards and sideways is very essential for effective functioning of an organisation. It is a channel through which members of the organisation come to know and also communicate decisions to each other. It is an important part of organisation set up.

Methods of Communication. It can be formal as well as informal. In the former category are included written or oral orders or words whereas in the latter category are covered social relationship of members. Simon believes in informal system of communication. It is this communication system which is at times also used by the members of the organisation for promoting their interests.

Hindrances of the Way of Communication. Some hindrances too come on the way of communication. These are initiation, transmission and reception. In an organisation communication is initiated from the lower level. But that becomes inefffective till it reaches the higher level, because lower level people do not always appreciate the fact that proper and timely communication can help in taking a decision. Not only this but in communication usually difficult language is used which is even not easily understandable. Communication system is also effected by physical distances, level of person, pressure or work etc. which makes the whole work process difficult. But even then it cannot be denied that communication is very important part of organisation.

Qualities of Good Communication System. A good communication should be clear and comprehensive. It should contain all important orders and directions in such a way that these are clearly understandable. It should be complete and there should be uniformity of ideas. There should be no contradiction between the views of higher and lower level staff so that the workers do not get confused and continue to work smoothly. The Communication becomes meaningless unless it has acceptability. Therefore, the communication should be such that it is gladly accepted by the staff. It should also be issued at the proper time.

But the purpose of communication is sufficiently defeated when the language used is difficult and not properly understood by those for whom the communication is intended. It is desirable that suitable words for communicating the idea should be chosen. It should be seen what type of communication is to be issued for what category of persons, because quite often the same communication may be differently understood by different categories of persons. While issuing communication, the destination and distance should be taken into account. It should be ensured that it timely reaches the persons and there is sufficient time for implementing the decision contained in communication.

Theory of Rationality in Decision-Making

Simon while discussing the dynamics of decision-making has discussed the problem of rationality.

Types of Rationality. Usually it is believed that an administator or any one else before taking any decision takes that after giving due considerations to all facts. But Prof. Simon does not agree with this view point. He has said that there are certain situations which circumvent rationality in decision-making, *e.g.* incomplete knowledge of the situation or facts, difficulties in anticipation, limitations of behaviour alternatives etc. Each individual has certain limitations and within his limitations he can think of certain alternatives in decision-making. Because of these limitations his thinking capacity becomes limited.

According to Prof. Simon rationality is of two types namely organisational rationality in which stress is on objectives of the organisation whereas the other is personal rationality in which an administrator takes a decision after taking his personal interests into consideration.

Rationality Defined. In his 'Administrative Behaviour' Simon has defined rationality by saying that it is concerned with the selection of preferred behaviour alternatives in terms of same system of values whereby consequences of behaviour can be evaluated. It needs both total knowledge as well as anticipation of consequences that will follow, after the use of choice. He has said that when appropriate means are chosen to reach the desired ends, the decision can be said to be rational. Though this approach to rationality may appear simple yet in practice it is complex. It is because it is difficult to separate means from ends because what appears to be end may actually be means for some future end.

According to Simon this chain is seldom a completely connected chain. For this he has given various reasons. Some of these being:

Cause Responsible for Incomplete Chain :

(*i*) Quite often there is no clarity between organisation activities and its ultimate objects.

(*ii*) There may be internal conflicts about objectives.

(*iii*) Decision which may appear to have been rationally arrived at, may not be so and may have been based on inaccurate conclusions.

(*iv*) The ultimate objectives may be incompletely formulated.

(*v*) There may be contradictions about the means to be used for achieving the objectives.

(*vi*) The ends to be achieved may have been wrongly or incorrectly stated.

He has said that because of all or any one reason the chain may remain incomplete. He has also pointed out that even otherwise in actual practice separation of means from ends is usually not possible.

Kinds of Rationality. According to Simon rationality is of different kinds. When the decision is directed to the individual's goals he has called it 'Personal Rationality' whereas when the aim is to study correct behaviour for maximising given value in a given situation, it is called objective rationality. When it aims at achieving organisational goals, it is called Organisational Rationality but when efforts are made to consciously adjust means to ends, it is called Conscious Rationality. When the decision maximise attainment relative to knowledge of the subject, it is Subjective Rationality but when it is to the degree that adjustment of means to ends has been deliberately sought it is called Deliberate Rationality.

Efficiency and Decision-Making. Simon is of the view that one major consideration for an administrator should be efficiency and as such his every decision should be guided by that. He however, fully realised that administrative efficiency was bound to pose problems in governmental bodies which were not run on commercial basis. He has defined efficiency by saying that it is choice of alternative which produces that largest results for the given application of resources.

Bounded Rationality. Simon has said that total rationality in administrative behaviour is not at all possible. It is primarily because human-beings who are to take decision are neither completely rational nor absolutely irrational. He calls it bounded rationality. He has completely ruled out the possibility of total rationality and favoured the concept of bounded rationality *i.e.* the rationality which is bounded by several limitations.

Simon has practically left no aspect of administrative behaviour and as such it cannot be expected of him to leave alone the problem of organisational efficiency.

Levels of Efficiency. Simon has said that basis of administrative decision should be efficiency, which can be measured in business organisations comparatively easily because these are run with the sole aim of earning profits. But in so far as administration is concerned the problem is that of picking up an alternative which is better out of many alternatives which can help in improving working efficiency. He does not believe that efficiency is only mechanical operation. He also agrees with those who believe that efficiency pays all attention to means only and under estimates ends. He has said that an efficient administrator is one who pays equal attention both to ways and means, which is in accordance with his work. In so far as Public Administration is concerned he has said that an efficient administrator is one who can use available manual and material resources in a neutral way. But while remaining neutral many feelings and factors come on his way, which interfere other resources, which adversely effect efficiency.

He has said that efficient administrator always finds it difficult to use judiciously and impartially all manual and material resources. If a resource can be used for one purpose, that may possibly not be used for some other project. He does not believe that specialisation in organisation will always increase efficiency, though in some cases it may do so. He has said that specialisation cannot be a condition for administrative efficiency. All that he understands from specialisation is that in an organisation different people are doing different types of work and that they will always go on doing that type of work separately.

Decision-Making Approach

Venkateswarlu argues that Herbert Simon's theory of decision-making was in response to the needs of the capitalist society of the post-World War II era and had its origins in the rediscovery of Come's positivism. His argument runs like this: capitalism had entered a new costs with the Second World War. The working class had already developed into an organised force throughout the world. Consequently, there arose new problems requiring new methods and techniques for the purpose of successfully running the giant. Western capitalist organisations of the corporate business across the world. The future of an enterprise largely depended on thoroughly calculated timely decisions pertaining to various aspects of the organisation. Thus emerged, says Venkateshwarlu, the decision-making theory "whose apostle was Nobel laureate Herbert Simon".

Simon in his book "*Administrative Behaviour*" exposed the contradictions of the scientific administration school, and sought an alternative approach to administrative efficiency through the designs of a rational model of decision-making. He defines administrative efficiency thus.

"A fundamental principle of administration.......is that among several alternatives involving the same expenditure the one should always be selected which leads to the greatest accomplishment of administrative objectives; and among several alternatives that lead to the same accomplishment the one should be selected which involves the least expenditure. Since this principle of efficiency is characteristic of any activity that attempts rationally to maximise the attainment of certain ends with the use of scarce means, it is as characteristic of economic theory as it is of administrative theory. The 'administrative man' take his place alongside the classical economic man".

Before going further into the details of Simon's ideas, it will be convenient to refer first to his 'behaviour alternative model'. According to Prof. Peter self this model states that in any situation an administrator ought ideally to examine all possible courses of action open to him, trace through the consequences of each alternative course, and then separately evaluate the benefits and losses of each alternative. He should then choose that course of action which is expected to provide the greatest net satisfaction."

Simon says that his model is different from the traditional ends—means approach. He contends that determination of ends at the beginning forecloses unduly the courses that are considered by the administrator, and also, to some extent it draws the attention away from the actual situation in which he is placed. Simon believes that separation of ends from means is false, since means also entail value judgements. In fact, however, Simon's model is not much different from the logic of the end means analysis. When both are elaborated, similar elements—ends (traditional model) or satisfactions (Simon's model), means (traditional model) or alternative courses (Simon's model), and constraints figure in both models of decision-making. Moreover in both models, all decisions are necessarily made within an assumed framework of values and constraints.

Another name given to Simon's decision-making model is rational comprehensive model. It assumes complete agreement on purposes, goals and preferences regarding the outcome of decisions. There are three basic elements in decision-making: (*i*) A comprehensive understanding of the available alternative courses of action in any given situation, and other consequences. (*ii*) It takes for granted that the decision-maker will have access to all the needed information, and also has the capacity to fully analyse that information. (*iii*) It is expected that in an organisation, the top management is capable of such rationality, makes all basic decisions and sends them down the hierarchy for implementation.

There is an alternative to the above explained rational-comprehensive model. That is the concept of limited rationality. Simon believed that the concept of limited rationality describes that reality of conditions of decision-making in an organisation more truly than the above rational comprehensive model. Simon mentions the following characteristics of that reality.

(*i*) "Organisational actors frequently do not agree on basic values, goals and outcome preferences and therefore, these are often vague and contradictory;

(*ii*) More often than not, managers respond to problems on the basis of preconceived notions and habitual patterns;

(*iii*) Decision makers typically do not know all of the possible alternatives available or their consequences;

(*iv*) Organisational decision makers never have perfect information and they have, for technical and psychological reasons, only a limited capacity to analyses the information they do have;

(*v*) The motives and values which come together to define a problem and structure the search for solution have their roots in group based perspective as opposed to an organisational point of view.

In view of these factors, the capacity for rationality is limited. Hence the people will accept satisfactory decisions. A satisfactory decision is one "that allows a problem solver to achieve his or her main goals, but the process does not involve a comprehensive analysis of all possibilities and outcomes nor does it require perfect information." Simon believes that the essence of administrative decision-making is boundedly (limited) rational, satisfying behaviour.

In Simon's model of decision-making, the formal structures and processes of the organisation are very important. According to him, organisations achieve higher levels of overall rationality than individuals. Human rationality is primarily realised through participation in organisations, which structure and discipline the choices open to the individual. The objectives and values of an organisation guide the decisions of its members in two ways: (*i*) through the exercise of authority and the provision of information; and (*ii*) through the internationalisation of these values in the psychology of the individual. This process of identification, Simon believes, is essential for organisation efficiency.

❐

14

Fred W. Riggs

Fred W. Riggs born in Kuling, China, in 1917, received his doctorate in Political Science from Columbia University in 1948. He served as a research associate of the Foreign Policy Association during 1948-51, as assistant to the Director of the Public Administration Clearing House in New York between 1951-55, and as a member of the Department of Government Indian University, from 1956 through 1967. Since 1967 he has been a Professor of Political Science at the University of Hawaii. He has also been a senior specialist at the East-West Centre, University of Hawaii, and a fellow of the Centre for Advanced Study in the Behavioural Sciences, Stanford. He was also the first Chairman of comparative administration group. In Political Science and Public Administration, more specifically in comparative administration and development administration Riggs has published a number of books and papers.

The administrative theories and models, which were mostly developed before the Second World War, were generally the offshoots of industrial revolution. These theories originated in the western countries mainly in the United States of America. The developing countries of Asia, Africa and Latin America which adopted western administrative models found that these models developed in particular environments to suit particular systems were not useful and valid for all systems. The models were found to be more suitable to maintain the existing systems than for changing the systems which is the priority task of all developing nations.

These models and theories also failed to help in understanding the administrative systems in developing countries. It is in this context that the need for developing entirely new concepts arose and the result is the emergence of the concept of comparative public administration which emphasised on cross-cultural and cross-national administrative studies. In the study of comparative public administration Riggs identified three broad trends, viz., normative to empirical, ideographic to nomathetic, and non-ecological to ecological. The major focus of an empirical study is to arrive at inferences on the basis of extensive field study instead of normative descriptions. On the other hand, the nomathetic approach seeks generalisation, laws, hypotheses that assert regularity of behaviour, and correlations with variables. Further, Riggs emphasised the need to study administrative systems in the ecological perspective so as to gain a comprehensive and indepth understanding of the administrative dynamics.

Riggs depended heavily on the concepts developed in other subejects to explain the ecology of public administration. He borrowed concepts from sociology, physics and biology to propose new theories and models in public administration. He also extensively borrowed a number of new words from other subjects, apart from coining a few to convey his ideas. That is why it is correctly said that the terms used by Riggs to explain his models are peculiarly Riggsian. Riggs used three important analytical tools to explain his administrative, *viz.*, (1) ecological approach, (2) structural-functional approach and (3) ideal models.

Ecological Approach

Administration and its environment influence each other and the understanding of the dynamics of this process is necessary to understand the administration. This approach is termed ecological approach. Ecology is a term borrowed from biology. It deals with the science concerned with inter-relationship of organisms and their environment. It is concerned with the interplay of living organisms and their physical and social enviroment and how organisms and environment are kept in balance for survival and other important objectives. The ecology of public administration, being the interaction of administration and its environment, requires a deeper understanding of the society and the various factors affecting its functioning.

The ecological approach in the study of public administration was initiated by J.M. Gaus, Robert A. Dhal and Robert A. Merton long before Riggs. But it was Riggs who made a distinctive contribution to this approach. 'Ecology of public administration', according to J.M. Gaus, includes the study of 'people, area or property, physical, and social technology wants of the people, thoughts, individuality and emergency conditions'. Developing the concept further, Riggs analysed the relationship between the administration and economic, social, technological, political and communication factors in a larger perspective.

Structural-Functional Approach

In analysing the administrative systems from ecological point of view, Riggs mainly used structural-functional approach. Talcott Parsons, Robert Merton, Almond, etc., are the other thinkers who adopted this approach in their works. This approach envisages that in every society certain important functions have to be carried out by a number of structures with the application of certain specified methods. Structures may mean the administrative mechanism or any other mechanism by which the functions are discharged. Thus, the structural-functional approach is a method of analysing the functions that are carried out in a society, the structures that are responsible to discharge the functions, and the methods that are adopted in undertaking the functions. According to Riggs, in every society five important types of functions are discharged *viz.*, economic, social, communication, symbolic and political functions. The same set of functional requisites apply to an administrative sub-system in which various structures carry out a number of functions in a specified manner.

Ideal Models

Riggs developed certain models to analyse the administrative systems of developing countries. Models are highly useful in the development of public administration as a subject from the normative to an empirical study. Riggs first used his much published models in 1956, by classifying the societies into Agraria and Industria, *i.e.*, agricultural and industrial societies. These models were developed keeping in view the societies of Imperial China and United States of America. According to him all societies transform from Agraria to Industria at a given point. Riggs identified the following as the structural features of Agraria and Industria:

	Agraria	*Industria*
(1)	Ascriptive values	Achievement norms
(2)	Particularistic	Universal
(3)	Diffuse pattern	Specificity
(4)	Limited social and spatial mobility	Higher social and spatial mobility
(5)	Simple and stable occupational differences	Well developed occupational patterns
(6)	Existence of differential stratification system	Existence of egalitarian class system

Later in 1957, he developed an equilibrium model named 'transitia' which represent the transforming societies. The 'transitia' represents the traditional stage between Agraria and Industria, and possess the characteristics of both Agraria and Industria. But the typology of Agraria-Industria was criticised as having many limitations. These limitations are briefly summarised as follows:

(1) 'Agraria-Industria' typology is not helpful in studying the transitional societies, *i.e.*, those societies which are moving from the agrarian stage towards the industrial stage;

(2) The models give very little emphasis to the analysis of the administrative system per se. The major stress is on the enviornment of the administrative system;

(3) The system does not provide sufficient mechanisms to analyse mixed societies, since modern societies always have some agrarian features;

(4) The typology assumes a unidirectional movement from the agraria to the industria.

Responding to these criticisms and limitations, Riggs developed another set of models, discarding old ones, to analyse the administrative systems in developing countries. The fused-prismatic-diffracted model is the result of this effort. The ideal models of Riggs such as fused, prismatic and diffracted are hypothetical assumptions aimed at analysing the pre-historic, developing and developed societies.

The process of transition of a ray through a prism is taken symbolically to explain the process of transformation of a society. The starting point of the ray is termed as fused, the process of internal vibration of the ray within the prism is called prismatic and finally when the ray comes out of the prism it gets diffracted to project a rainbow and this process is called diffraction. On the same analogy, various social systems in the early stages of the process of development would be fused in the transitional stage prismatic, and finally, at the end they would be in a complete diffracted stage as explained by Riggs.

As discussed earlier, Riggs created models on the basis of structural and functional approach. Accordingly in a fused society a single structure carries out various functions. Contrary to this, in a diffracted society separate structures are created to carry out specific functions. But between these two there exist a number of societies, in which the characteristics of both fused and diffracted societies exist side by side. These are called prismatic societies. However, Riggs emphasises that, no society can be exclusively called either fused or diffracted; all societies are generally prismatic in nature.

X S	T X P	A X
Fused	Prismatic	Diffracted

In the above equation the letter X is placed at three positions on the scale to suggest where pure or ideal types of the fused, prismatic and diffracted models might be located. Riggs says: "if we could average the characteristics of real societies, we might be able to place them on the same scale, and I would suggest that traditional Siam might be put where I have placed the letter S, modern Thailand near T.P. would represent the Philippines and A. America. Of course, these are speculative guesses and not the result of any exact measurement, but I believe that this method lands itself to quantification." The following table indicates the broad characteristics of fused, prismatic and diffracted societies.

Table

Fused	**Prismatic**	**Diffracted**
Particularism	Selectivism	Universalism
Ascriptive values	Attainment	Achievement
Functionally diffuse	Poly-functionalism	Functional Specificity

Riggs attempted to explain various societies by using the concept of 'multi-functionality' of societal structures. He termed 'functionally diffuse' societies 'fused' and 'functionally specific's diffracted'. He further pointed out that an intermediate society between these two extremes is 'prismatic'—his most popular model. These 'fused-prismatic-diffracted' models, however, Riggs very emphatically said, these are designed to the 'ideal' types not to be found in any actual society, but perhaps approximate to some, and useful for heuristic purposes and as an aid in the organisation of data.

Riggs further explained his model societies by making use of Personian pattern of variables and formed his hypothesis to test and understand various societies. He said that diffracted societies would rank high in terms of universalism and achievement orientation, a fused society high in particularism and ascription, and the prismatic society is characterised as an intermediary between these two by 'selectivism' (scales between universalism and particularism), 'attainment' (stands between achievement and ascription) and poly-functionalism (stands between functional specificity and functional diffusensess).

Riggs in his wide ranging analysis touched on various social, cultural and political sub-systems with a detailed examination of various connected issues and problems using a number of models. But his primary interest has been to illuminate administrative problems in transitional or developing societies.

Fused Model

Riggs selected Imperial China and the pre-revolutionary Siamese Thailand as examples to represent his concept of fused society. These societies have no classification of functions and single structure carries out a number of functions. These societies heavily depend upon agriculture with no industrialisation and modernisation. Their economic system is based on law of exchange and barter system which Riggs calls as 'redistributive model'. The royal family plays a very important role in the administration of the country. The King and the officials nominated by him carry out all administrative, economic and other activities by themselves. No separate structures exist to manage the economic and administrative affairs. The relations between the government and the people are generally at a low ebb. People pay respect to the King through extending service and presentation of material goods, without expecting anything in return.

Family played a prominent role in the Siamese Kingdom. It used to carry out a variety of economic, political and social functions. Family apart from providing base to the social structure, also stands at the apex of the administration. Influenced by this, the administration in these societies strives to protect the special interests of the family and certain sects rather than aim at universal happiness and development. The administrative system is based on structure of the family and special sects and it continues to help to preserve the system. Generally these societies tend to be static with no developed communication systems. People would have no demands and never hope to raise any issue with the government. The King and his nominees enjoy the coercive and absolute power and they generally use their powers to protect their own personal interest. These societies do not differentiate between justice and injustice, formal and informal set-ups and governmental and non-governmental activities.

Diffracted Model

These societies are based on universalistic principles with no differentiation in treatment. There is a high degree of specialisation and each structure carries out a specialised function. Ascriptive values cease to exist, giving way to the attainment values in the society. The society would be highly dynamic and diffracted. Here exists open class structures represented by various associations which play a prominent role in achieving rational in the society.

The economic system is based on market mechanism. The influence of market has both direct and indirect effect on the other facets of the society. Riggs called it 'marketised society'. Various associations discharge different functions. Communications and technology are highly developed and governments give top priority to maintain cordial public relations. Governments would be responsive to the needs of the people and protected human rights. People would bring pressure on the government to get their things done and control its behaviour to a great extent. Government officers have no coercive and absolute powers. Public pay attention and give respect to the laws of the nation on their own. This facilitates the government to implement the laws and discharge its responsibilities without any difficulty.

Prismatic Model

Riggs concentrated all his efforts to explain in detail the prismatic model—the focal point of his models. According to Riggs, the prismatic society is one which has achieved a certain level of differentiation; specialisation of roles that is necessary for dealing with modern technology, but has failed to intergate these roles. Prismatic society shares the values-patterns of both fused and diffracted societies. According to

Riggs prismatic society has three important characteristic fetures *viz.*, (1) heterogenity, (2) formalism, and (3) over-lapping.

Heterogeneity

The existenec of a high degree of heterogeneity is the main characteristics feature of a prismatic society. Heterogeneity refers to 'the simultaneous presence, side by side, of quite different kinds of systems, practices and viewpoints'. Due to the parallel co-existence of a diametrically opposite viewpoints and practices, the social change in a prismatic society would be inconsistent, incomplete and irresponsive.

There are in a prismatic society, urban areas with 'sophisticated' intellectual class, western style offices and the modern gadgets of administration. There also exist a well developed communications system, skyscrapers, airconditioners, the existence of specialised agencies to discharge various social, political, economic and technical services. On the other hand, in the rural areas, people lead a highly traditional life with no facilities of modern living like use of telephones, refrigerators, etc. The village 'elders' combine various political, administrative, social, economic and religious roles. Heterogeneity exists in a prismatic society in all walks of life presenting a paradoxical picture. In the field of education, society pays high premium on the western type of education but equally proves susceptible to traditional Gurukulas. Hospitals with all modern facilities giving allopathic treatment co-exist with ayurvedic, Unani, homoeopathic and naturopathic centres.

In the prismatic societies, political and administrative offices enjoy enormous influence, power and prestige and help in making money. Although equal opportunities exist for all, only some people are privileged enough and hope to get the jobs in higher echelons. Those who fail to get jobs would waste no time in forming 'pressure groups' against the government and start agitations on some pretext or the other. Despite the existence of a government duly elected through democratic processes, it would not be in a position to control the people. The people in power would make all efforts to protect their interests and stick to power.

The problem becomes much complicated in a poly-communal society where different communities try to pull the society in different directions in furtherance of their own sectional interests. This is evident in almost all the developing countries of Asia, Africa and Latin America. Lack of integration thus forms the basic feature of a prismatic society. All these disparities, differentiations in almost all aspects of life not only influence the working of the administrative system and condition its behaviour but would also create a number of problems to the administration. The ruling class would normally try to protect the interests of 'haves' and ignore the interests of 'have nots', which, according to Riggs, would create a revolutionary atmosphere in society.

Rigg's Sala Model

Riggs has called societies as fused, diffracted and prismatic. He believes that in each society each system has sule systems *e.g.* economic, social, political and economic. In a fused society such system is called chamber, in a diffracted society it is called bureau or office whereas in a prismatic society Riggs has called these Sala system as 'Sala Model'. He has said in each type of society it has different features or characteristics.

Origin of the Term Sala. Sala is a Spanish word which has several meaning. It stands for partition, rooms, religious conference, government office etc. In East Asian countries it is also used in different senses. Sanskrit word 'Shala' is used for pathshala *i.e.* school. It has certain features of bureau of a diffracted society and chambers of a fused society.

Before dealing with his 'Sala Model' he has said that in a prismatic society one finds that in making appointments for various administrative positions nepotism, favouritism and family considerations play an important role. Administrative functions are performed to benefit the few known. Vested interests are always in the fore front. There is no care for laws and in all administrative practices love for the family and kinship is clearly to be seen. On the other hand, in a diffracted society in making public appointments there are no such considerations.

'Sala Officer'. Riggs had discussed the qualities of a Sala Officer. He is an officer who cares less for social welfare and more for his personal interests. Thus performances, activities and decisions are guided by considerations of family and kinship. He does not uniformally apply all rules and regulations. Government programmes under his guidance are so implemented that whereas interests of vast majority are conveniently ignored those of few are protected.

Love for Community. According to Riggs in this model there is love for community and this creates many problems both for the government and the administration. Though it is theoretically expected that all laws will be uniformally applied without favouritism, yet in practice all laws are implemented and all decisions are enforced by the officers with an eye on the community to which the officer concerned belongs and tires to favour that. In this exercise majorities dominant community gains the maximum and great dissatisfaction is created among other communities. In order to satisfy them reservation or quota system is introduced so that dissatisfied communities get some representation in administration but after some time this results in the division of society.

Riggs has further said that in Sala Model though an official may enter service on merit basis but when the question of promotion and career development comes he depends very much on the support and influence of officers and others of his community. The latter also violate all such norms which come on the way of the promotion of the former and go to the farthest ends to protect the interests of the latter. This attitude and approach is also followed by the public in their behaviour patterns and they also lay stress on the observance of rules uniformally but when in any issue they are personally involved they wish that they should be favoured and if necessary, rules should be set aside to the extent to which these stand on his way.

Relationship Between Sala and Elects. Riggs has also pointed to the relationship between Sala and Elects. According to Riggs elects is typical prismatic group which makes use of modern associational methods of organisation and combines the features of sects of the fused and club of diffracted society. It represents the people of a particular community or group. The officers of this community serve only the interests of their own community and ignore those of the others. When there is close relationship between the two then there is only lip service for the observance of uniform norms which are simply violated. He has also said that in a prismatic society both new and old patterns co-exist with the result that in the norms of behaviour there is lack of consensus.

Relationship Between Bureaucratic Behaviour and Administrative Output. Riggs has discussed at some length the relationship between bureaucratic behaviour and administrative output. He has said that how far political leadership in power can punish or reward an administrator on that very much depends his strength and weakness. It is very much possible that a weak political leader may not recognise the services of any official and thus may not suitably reward him for achieving the goals of the organisation. Similarly an inefficient may not be punished by him for his omissions and lapses. In the process Sala officials may get an opportunity to promote their personal interests and inefficient may flourish. Their lapses may be ignored. He has pointed out that there is thus close relationship between bureaucratic behaviour and administrative output because performance of government gets linked with level of output of Sala officials.

According to Riggs a prismatic society is unbalanced policy in which bureaucrats dominate both administrative and political systems and as such Sala officials play a very important role in decision-making in this society. The powers get concentrated in the sala officials and they usually ignore the wishes of the people. Because of this situation development of healthy political system slows down and leadership fails to control bureaucracy. The result of this weak polity and strong bureaucratic system is that legislature, public opinion and political party system becomes very weak.

Overlapping in Sala Model. While discussing specific problems of overlapping in a sala society, Riggs has said that in the power structure of prismatic society it consists of a highly centralised authority structure which overlaps a control system which is highly localised. There is officially separation of authority and control but unofficially such a separation does not exist. In practice de-jure authority bows before de facto control. Some of the structures work in a manner that these defeat the purpose for which these are created.

On the whole Riggs has said that though it very much prevails in a prismatic society but it is not good for the society. It results in nepotism, corruption, favouritism and inefficiency.

Critical Appraisal Regarding Development of Thought

The extensive references made to the views of Riggs in the literature of Public Administration itself is an indication of his tremendous influence on the discipline of Public Administration. There cannot be any study of comparative public administration and development administration without reference to the views of Riggs. But Riggs, like many other administrative theorists, was subjected to severe criticism.

Riggs liberally coined new words to explain his concepts. In addition he also gave different meanings to a number of words already in use. There is no harm in coining new words when the existing vocabulary fails to convey the meaning and clarify the concepts. There is also nothing wrong if one gives his own meaning for the effective expression of his views. But free use of new words, and words used with different meanings may create confusion instead of clarifying the concepts. Riggs in his enthusiasm to give a scientific temper to his models, borrowed most of his terminology from physical sciences.

Sometimes the usage of new words may even mislead the readers. Sison who is very critical of Riggs' models and his terminology, says that to understand the writings of Riggs one has to read them three times. First to understand his language, second time to understand his concepts and third time to know whether there is anything really to learn. Chapman, commenting on this aspect, writes that Riggs should have prepared his own dictionary to explain his terminology.

Hahn-Been Lee doubts the utility of prismatic and sala models, in view of the development administration's focus on social change. Lee feels that Riggs' models are not helpful to know the process of social change in development. He considers Riggs' model as equilibrium models. Equilibrium models would facilitate very much in preserving the system but not introducing any change in the system. Lee thus concludes that the models of Riggs are not useful when the objective of administration is to change the system, rather than the maintenance of the system.

Richard A. Chapman emphasises that one should have an open mind in analysing the Riggsian models and see how far they would be useful to understand Public Administration. Although Riggs adopted an interdisciplinary approach to analyse social systems, he has not fully worked out the implications of his theory for Public Administration. Models are intended to be heuristic devices valuable as aids to understand complex social phenomena. In applying Riggs' models to particular societies, the problem of measurement comes. In the absence of a measuring scale, the identification of prismatic or diffracted societies becomes very difficult. As the reader carefully follows Riggs' analysis, there may be a tendency for him to associate prismatic conditions with every situation he knows. Similarly Daya Krishna says, when the fused and diffracted societies are imaginary, all the societies are to be classified as prismatic at various levels of low, middle and high. But when scales to measure the levels of 'prismatism' are lacking, the low, middle and high words have no relevance. Riggs' models are mostly based on certain assumptions.

When Riggs assumes that America also is set to become a prismatic society, Daya Krishna finds no logic in the three-fold classification of the societies in the background of the concept of 'development'. If America is a prismatic society and economically backward Egypt a diffracted society, Daya Krishan feels that, all developing countries in the world would like to continue to be prismatic societies. Riggs considered differentiation and integration as two important ingredients of development. But it is a difficult task to identify the desirable level of differentiation and integration required for development. Riggs' preference for societies with low but equitable level of differentiation and integration to those with high level of differentiation and low level of integration, according to Daya Krishna, stands as an obstacle to development.

Lack of international perspective in his approach to development is another limitation of Riggs' concept. In competitive world the higher level prismatic society may exploit the lower-level diffracted society. In Daya Krishna's view, Riggs failed to recognise the role of outside or external forces in the process of development. Daya Krishna also feels that the Riggs' view of integration as the result of a penetration and participation cannot be relevant to all situations. He says that people's participation is also possible even in dictatorial countries and hence more participation cannot be considered an important variable of integration.

R.C. Tilman criticises Riggs for adopting a wrong analytical tool borrowed from physical sciences in explaining the social systems. When interdisciplinary approach is adopted, it is the primary responsibility of the researcher to select a most suitable analytical approach. Ecological models generally explain the motives of administrative behaviour. In the whole process, administration also plays an important role to influence its environment. Administration is also a tool for social change and it influences the society in different ways at different times.

Prismatic model mainly describes developing societies but fails to explain the place to administration in the society. The main reason for it was the failure on the part of Riggs to analyse the 'internal dynamics of the society'. There is wide disparity and distinction in the relation of social, economic, political and administrative system of a society. Riggs has failed to carefully recognise these distinctions. Not much work has been done in the relationship between the diffracted characters and fused characters in a prismatic society.

Arora opines that overlapping exists equally in diffracted society as in a prismatic society, but the reasons may be different. An examination of such reasons would be very useful and provide guidance to administrative actions. Riggs has only highlighted the negative impact of overlapping but did not examine the positive aspects, which may provide healthy competition among various administrative sub-systems and increase efficiency in administration.

The very concept of prismatic model has a negative character. It all looks, as though, the conditions of developing countries were analysed through the western values and concepts. Commenting on this aspect, Michael Monroe observed that Riggs examined the conditions in developing countries while taking America as a standard society. Riggs also did not give any importance to the positive character of prismatic society as much as he did to the negative characters. He projected formalism, as a negative aspect and highlighted all its bad effects. But it is also true that sometimes there would be more benefits to the people if the rules and regulations are not strictly followed. Administration may move fast if certain rules are not strictly observed. In countries like India, if there is proper leadership, formalism may play a very positive role in carrying out the works in time.

So we can conclude that classical organisational theories mainly emphasise organisational principles and behavioural theories concentrated on human behaviour in the organisation. But ecological theories emphasise the interaction of administration and its environment. Both in content and analysis, Riggs' ecological approach touches wider horizons, and takes an integrated approach of administrative system. His approach and models help us in understanding the administrative process in developing countries. Although his administrative models are difficult to find out in practice, they help us in understanding the realities. Sala model provides an opportunity to analyse and understand the administrative system in developing countries.

As Chapman has correctly observed that, in spite of many limitations, Riggs models may deepen our insight into some of the underlying problems of public administration in transitional societies. In some ways the prismatic model may be analogous to principles in administration. 'Principles may not be universal truths and they may have the defect of proverbs, that they occur in contradictory pairs, but this does not mean that principle are worthless; indeed they may be particularly useful as critieria for describing and diagnosing administrative situations.

Prismatic Model of Riggs

Prismatic model of Riggs is perhaps the most important model of Riggs. In this he has defined the characteristics of a prismatic society which is in between fused and diffracted societies. It is a type of society in which there is some specialisation of roles and differentiation has also reached some level which can be useful and helpful in dealing with modern technology but the society is not in a position to integrate these. According to Riggs the society has three important features namely (*a*) heterogeneity (*b*) formalism and (*c*) overlapping. Each one is briefly described below:

Heterogeneity. In a prismatic society there is high degree of heterogeneity which means that in the society different systems functions simultaneously. Then in this society quite opposite views and practices are in use and being followed and in many cases views very radically differ from each other. This makes the task of social change difficult. The responses to the changes are both inconsistent and incomplete. This situation equally applies to administrative system which functions under conditions of under tainties pressures.

Life in the Urban and Rural Areas. It is in the urban areas that intellectual class resides and offices are well equipped. Administrative system to some extent is responsive to public needs. There is well developed communication system and comforts of life are available. Residing to a large extent is comfortable and specialised agencies are also available to provide and perform social, economic, political and technical services.

As regards rural areas the situation is somewhat different. These are not modernised and the people still have traditional outlook. These have not been provided that facilities of modern life. Where these are available, these are only marginal. In those areas the village elders combine various political, administrative, social and economic roles.

Wide Variety of Contrasts. On the whole in the society there are wide variety of contrasts. Whereas there is desire to have modernity, there is equally keen desire to adhere to traditionality. The society wants to have the advantages of modern life, without giving up traditional approaches to every problem. This makes the task of modernisation difficult. One finds in this society desire to educate the children on western education system but is not prepared to completely give up gurukul system.

Tensions in Society. In prismatic society political and administrative offices enjoy a lot of power and prestige. They also enjoy considerable social respect. Because of powers, which are quite often misused for achieving personal ends they become currupt and earn a lot of money. Theoretically and legally all are equal and have been provided equal opportunities in all walks of life but practically these are available to few rich or those who are well placed in any walk of life or occupy high positions in government, administration and society. Those who are denied the opportunities or are not provided job they agitate against the government and try to form a powerful pressure group. Though the government claims that it represents the people yet in many cases percentage of votes polled by those who form the government and the political party in power in democracy is much less than the percentage of votes polled by the political parties in the opposition. The claim of the government to represent the masses is refuted because quite often authorities fail to control agitation of the people effectively. Those who are in power usually try to protect their own interests and pay much less attention to national interests. Not only this but they are not willing to leave power and wish to stick to it at all costs. There is also misrepresentation of facts to serve personal ends. Because of these reasons the society is always under tension and as such cannot pay much attention to constructive and developmental activities. This situation becomes still more serious when the society is multi-lingual and there are wide ethnic differences on the one hand and communal disharmony on the other.

Riggs has said that because of tensions in society, couple with wide disparities in castes and classes, the situation worsens. Whole administrative system comes under heavy pressure and is required to solve many non-constructive ticklish problems like checking of agitations, demonstrations, outbreak of communal and non-communal violences etc. etc. Both the resources and energies of administration are wasted and the common man does not feel benefitted in any way. In this society both administration and ruling class tries to protect the interests of the rich as against the poor. The gap between the rich and poor always exists to the irritation of the latter and when those in power show undue favours to the rich and atmosphere of revolution develops in the society which causes concern to the administration.

Hypocracy. Riggs has pointed out that there is considerable hypocracy in all walks of national life *e.g.* social, economic, political, cultural etc. General laws are not respected though these are meant for observance, digestive bodies go on deliberating and enacting laws but in actual practice these are not adhered. In many cases both the administrators and legislators know that many provisions of law in actual practice cannot be implemented. Provision of deterrent punishments in laws breads corruption, whereas leniency means encouragement to violation of laws. There is thus a lot of hypocracy which is not good for its health.

Formalism. It is another feature of Riggs' prismatic society, by which he means differences of discrepancies which exist in the society between formal and effective power, the differences between what is provided in the constitution legal systems and organisational charts on the one hand and what is being actually practised on the other. In other words, it means discrepancy or gap between the formally prescribed and effectively practised norms. It also means difference between state objectives and actual performance. Riggs is of the view that formalism increases when the gap between theory and practices develops.

Causes of Formalism. Riggs has also tried to discussed the causes of formalism in a prismatic society. He has said that formalism exists because there is lack of pressure on the government by the people and organisations which function in the society. Not much care is paid to the achievements of the government and their failings in achieving the promised targets are not paid much attention. Social power is so weak that it does not influence government performance and there is considerable scope for arbitrariness in administration.

Constitutional Formalism. Riggs has also dealt with the problem of constitutional formalism in a prismatic society. By this he means gap between constitutional principles and their actual implementation, *e.g.* in a parliamentary democracy constitution vests all powers in directly elected representatives of the people but in actual practice real power is exercised by a group of influential persons and political elites from outside the Parliament. In a parliamentary democracy constitutions vests powers in the head of the state *i.e.* the President but these are exercised actually by the head of the government *i.e.* the Prime Minister. Elected representatives of the people in the legislative bodies are expected to have free hand in the choice of their leader but in actual practice their choice of leadership is decided by the party bosses outside the legislature. The examples of constitutional formalism can be multiplied. He has pointed out that the main function of a legislature is enactment of laws and to undertake legislative work.

Overlapping. Still another feature of a prismatic society, according. to Riggs is overlapping. By this he means the extent to which formally differentiated structures of a diffracted society co-exist with undiffracted structures of fused type. In an administrative system administrative behaviour is actually determined by social, political, religious factors which are non-administrative in nature. In a fused society there is no overlapping because in that traditional structures perform all the functions but that is not the case in a prismatic society. In this although modern structures are created but even then old and undifferentiated structures continue to dominate the system. Though new values are accepted and new norms are valued but these are overlooked in favour of traditional values and structures which are undifferentiated. It is because of this reason that in a prismatic society the parliament and government offices perform not only political but also administrative and economic functions.

Not only this but even the behaviour of government offices and Parliament is very much influenced by such traditional organisations as family, caste and religion. There is overlapping because there is no separation of powers in strict sense of the term, though in theory it may exist.

Economic System of Prismatic Society

Riggs has paid due attention to the economic system as it prevails in a prismatic society. He calls this system as the bazar canteen model of prismatic economy.

Riggs's Views About Economic System of Prismatic Society. Riggs while discussing economic system of prismatic society has said that in so far as a diffracted society is concerned in that economic system is guided by market forces of demand and supply. The market is governed by these forces alone. On the other hand, in a fused society economic system is governed by factors other than market economy *e.g.* family, religion and social conditions. But in so far as prismatic society is concerned in that both play their role side by side. Economic system is influenced not by economic and non-economic factors. This makes the task of price fixation in prismatic society difficult because factors which influences it cannot be anticipated.

Provision of Economic Services in Prismatic Society. According to Riggs in a diffracted society economic services to all are provided on equal basis and while doing so favouritism and nepotism does not play any role. All are created on equal footings. An employee gets his wages on the basis of his work output and services which he renders, which are decided according to market value. But Riggs has said that position is different in a prismatic society. In that society relationship between public officials and their clientle is in terms of relationship which exists between a buyer and seller. The price for a service rendered is not on equal basis but varies from place to place, time to time and person to person.

Riggs has also said that members of dominant communities get services at cheap and at reduced prices whereas minority communities are charged higher prices. He has said that society is like a subsidised canteen in which those who are politically influential and belong to privileged sections of society get commodities at cheap or subsidised rates whereas like a tributary canteen they charge higher prices from those who are politically not influential or are less privileged.

Features of Economy. According to Riggs in this economic system only a small section of society enjoys almost all economic benefits. Few people control all economic systems. They monopolise means of production and distribution and are in a position to exploit vast majority of population. Those who dominate the economy are in a position to bribe the tax authorities and get rebate in taxes and pay much less taxes than what they should have paid. The state suffers heavy loses. There is parallel and sometimes even dominant black market economy. All financial estimates prepared by the administration go to the winds and in the long run the economic system is destroyed.

Role of Foreign Capital in Economy. Riggs has pointed out that in the prismatic society foreign capital plays an important role in the market economy. Production is very low and because of poverty capital formation is not encouraging. Not much attention is paid to trade and commerce by the local business community because beyond a particular point it has no resources to invest. This compels political authorities to invite foreign capital for the growth of not only capital but also in consumer industries. Thus migrants and foreign investors invest heavily in trade, commerce, industry etc. The economy becomes dependent on them and slowly their influence both in economy,politics and administration increases.

Wage Relationship in Prismatic Society. Riggs has said that in prismatic society wage relationship is not purely on merit and achievements of the person concerned but on basis of family relationship. Because of this relationship many sala officials get fat salaries without doing any hard work. Their emoluments far more exceed the nature of their work or responsibilities being handled by them. Those at the power position, because non-privileged and uninfluential are required to do more work than the senior officials who get more wages but do less work because of their being influential. The gap between the emoluments of the high and low paid official is very wide.

Sala Offcials in Prismatic Economy. As regards the role of Sala offcials in a prismatic economy Riggs has said that in such a society there is encouragement to black marketing for which favourable conditions exists. Hoardings and adulteration are common features of such economy. There is high inflation rate, which at times is galloping and the poor and unprivilege sections of society are the worst sufferers in that. Riggs has said that in this type of economy the maximum gainers are the sala officials. They successfully develop contacts both insde and outside the country. They receive bribes from them which are gladly paid by business depending on resources and position of sala officials. They misuse scarce foreign exchange resources for promoting self-financial interests. The result of all this is poverty, social and economic injustice and exploitation of weaker and unprivileged sections of society.

Rigg's Ideal Models

In order to analyse the administrative systems of developing societies Riggs has developed certain models. He first used his models in 1956. He then classified societies into agraria and industria *i.e.* agricultural and industrial societies keeping in view societies of Imperial China and the United States of America respectively. He has said that all the societies move from agraria to industria, with the passing of time.

Features of Agraria and Industria Societies. Riggs has identified certain structural features of both these types of societies. In his opinion an agraria society has ascriptive values. It is particularistic and in it differential stratification system exists. In this society there is diffused pattern and occupational differences are simple and stable. Then its another features is that in this type of society there is limited social and spatial mobility.

As against that in industria society there is existence of egalitarian class system. There are certain achievement norms. There are well developed occupational patterns and society is not particularistic but universal.

Equilibrium Model or Transitia. It was developed by Riggs in 1957, which primarily deals with transforming societies. It represents transitional stage between two types of societies. It has salient features or characteristics of both the types of societies. But the very typology of both these types of societies was criticised by F.J. Ticknet in his Comparing Administrative System and R.S. Milne in his 'Comparisons and Models in Public Administration'. Some of the main points of criticism advance against the typology of societies are as given below:

Fused Prismatic Model. Taking into consideration the view point of the critics and appreciating the value of criticism Riggs developed fused Prismatic Model for analysing the administrative systems in developing countries. In this connection it may however, be mentioned that fused, prismatic and diffracted models of Riggs are only hypothetical assumptions which aim at analysing pre-historic societies. In order to explain the process of transformation of a society from one stage to the other he has depended on the transition of a ray through a prism. He has termed starting point of ray as fused; internal variation of ray within the prism as prismatic and the rays which come out of the prism and get diffracted are called diffraction. On the same anology he has said that various social systems at the early stages would be fused, in the transitional stages prismatic and finally at the end diffracted.

Limitations of Typology of Societies. The critics have pointed out that the models developed by Riggs have laid stress on environment of the administrative system but have paid little attention to the analysis of administrative system as such. The typology of the societies assumes that there is a undirectional movement from the agraria to the industria society which is wrong. Then another point of criticism advanced is that the system does not provide sufficient mechanism which can help in analysing mixed societies.

Needless to say that modern industria societies have several agraria features. The critics also point out that the typology as developed by Riggs is not useful in studying the transitional societies *i.e.* those agraria societies which are tyring to become industria societies.

Structural Functions in Societies. Riggs is of the view that in a fused society only a single structure out all the functions of the society whereas in a diffracted society separate structures are deliberately created for carrying out specific functions. There are however, many societies in which characteristics or features of both types of above mentioned societies are found out which he calls as prismatic societies. He has very specifically stated that in our own times there can be no society which is either purely fused or diffracted but to a degree every society today is prismatic. Extent to which a society is fused or diffracted very much depends on the nature of structures of the society concerned and functions which are carried out by each structure. R.K. Arora, in the 'Comparative Public Administration: An Ecological Perspectives' has thus indicated Riggs broad characteristics of fused, prismatic and diffracted societies.

Fused Society	*Prismatic Society*	*Diffracted Society*
Particularism	Selectivism	Universalism
Ascriptive values	Attainment	Achievement
Functionally	Poly	Functionally
diffused	functionalism	specificity

While analysing social structures he has dealt with social structures. He has also dealt with social, cultural and political sub systems and studied their problems as well. He has shown particular interest in studying administrative problems of developing societies. He has extensively used fused and diffracted models for explaining prismatic phenomenon.

Comparative Public Administration

Comparative Public Administration is very simple language means study of different systems of public administrations run by the government of that country. The concept has two aspects namely broad view in which different structures, organs and rules and regulations etc. are studied. Then is Riggs's view. It narrows down the study of comparative public administration which is confined to practical experiences and basic policy principles. He believes that real comparative study is definitely based on experiences and related to environments. It is that part of administration which concerns itself with the study of structures which are put in practical use in different cultures and which can be studied and analysed on the basis of solid facts. In brief by comparative public administration is that subject of study in which two or more administrative units are studied in so far as their organisation and working is concerned. It can be at the national level in a federation *e.g.* the study of working two or more states in India or at the international level *e.g.* the study of administrative set ups of two or more nations. Such a comparative study can be not only at the political level but also at cultural and other levels.

Aims of Comparative Public Administration. Thus comparative public administration includes the study of different administrative units of a corporation, government office etc. It can be the study of certain basic principles or of a particular principle or that of a plan. Its aim can be either to find out certain basic underlying common principles or to improve the administrative set up on certain scientific lines. It also aims at developing certain scientific administrative principles.

History of Comparative Public Administration. Broadly speaking history of comparative Public Administrative started in 1950's when two important developments took place almost simultaneously. One being growing interest in the study of the subject in which stress was laid on the study of cross national administrative studies. It was now began to be realised that comparative study of bureaucracies was as important as the comparative study of executive, legislature and judiciary and people's participation in political systems. Then another development during this period was unfolding of foreign assistance programmes. After World War II U.S. policy makers wanted to provide techniques of public administration to low income regions of the world for improving implementation of their development projects. Accordingly American government sent her administrative experts and teams to reform the bureaucracies of developing countries and for training their people. But this type of intervention was not tolerated by many countries.

F.W. Riggs's Views About Public Administration. Coming of Riggs on the scene is said to be the beginning of second phase of comparative public administration. It began in 1960's. He started Comparative Administrative Group (C.A.G.) Which consisted of scholars from different countries. A jounral of Public Administration was also brought out by the Group. Some detailed case studies of national bureaucracies were undertaken. The group under the leadership of Riggs developed variety of theoretical frame-works and created favourable atmosphere for the study of comparative public administration system.

Riggs developed the theory of cultural environment of administration and models of administrative behaviour in traditional societies. He defined development with reference to administration. Riggs has said that three tendencies are commonly found in the study of comparative public administration. First is a step forward from idealism to practical experience.

Then another tendency in the study of comparative public administration is Indographic in which a particular event or a particular administrative system is studied. He has however, suggested that this tendency should be given up. In its stead alternatives should be studied which can change actual behaviours into certain rules and regulations.

Then Riggs has said that in the study of administrative systems less stress was laid on the role of environments whereas these days role of administration and administrator cannot be properly understood and appreciated without the study of environment around. He has also said that in the past every administrative system was studied in the context of economic, cultural and political systems, with the result that role of administration on environment and that of environment on administration was not properly focussed but he has said that the study of dynamic administrative systems is not possible without studying the environments.

Critical Evaluation of Riggs's Contribution. Riggs occupies a very important position in the study of comparative public administration. He has given new direction and provided a new approach to the study of administration. In fact with him a new era in the study of the subject has started. The critics have however, not spared him and have both favourably and unfavourably evaluated his views. The critics have pointed out that Riggs has not correctly assessed the mutual relationship of political parties, bureaucracy and legislature. He has said that legislature is dominated by political party in power and that it is just like putting seal of approaval on what is suggested and proposed by Bureaucracy. If that is so then one cannot expect from legislatures to give us laws or to ensure their implementation.

There are also so many administrative systems working under so vide varieties of societies and cultural systems that it is difficult to apply any sample model to all these, as suggested by Riggs. Then the critics have pointed out that Riggs in up his study has picked only those features of prismatic society which are not inkeeping with the standards of western societies *e.g.* efficiency, morality etc. A very strong and powerful point of criticism made against Riggs is that he has made public administration a dependent factor. He has said that administration is controlled by outside forces which both control as well as change it. It has no force to control the environment. He wrongly believes that whereas outside environments can change administration, the latter cannot change the former. In his models Riggs has used several new words and created several new positions which have made even simple understanding of administrative terminology difficult. In fact he should have tried to make the understanding simple.

Riggs believes that administrative issues and administrative behaviour are closely linked with each other and that for studying these one will have to study political, economic, social and psychological aspects. The critics point out that it is nothing else but an attempt on the part of Riggs to divert attention from the main issue.

DEVELOPMENT ADMINISTRATION

The concept of development administration came to focus during 1950's which it was used for the study of those changes in public administration which were needed for carrying out policies programmes and projects which aimed at improving socio-economic conditions of the people.

Before dealing with the concept of development administration or administrative development, it is essential to understand as to what is meant by term 'development'. Development is a very vague term and it is very difficult to precisely define it. It is a step towards achieving some goal and in nature it is ever changing. It is not absolute but a relative term because it is difficult to measure development. Whereas a particular activity may be considered development or a step forward in a particular society it may not be so considered in another society. Development is very much related with aspirations and expectations of the people.

In development process the people play an important role. In fact both are closely linked with each other. The former are the target of the latter and also the purpose of development.

Population is always a major component which fixing development targets and also the methods of development. It provides human and technical resources essentially needed for the development of a society. They are the manager entrepreneurs in development agencies and undertakings. For development it is very essential that the people for whom it is intended should be most willing to accept the changes which development is likely to bring with it. In order to motivate the people to accept development changes, it is very essential that developmental methods must be very attractive and not drastic. These should be gradual and keeping in view environments of society.

Traditional systems of administration were not responsive to demands of the people but only to the legislatures and other representative bodies. These did not try to end inequalities in any walk of life. On the other hand, in many cases the policies were so enforced and implemented that these increased gaps and inequalities. The main aim of various administration structures was to maintain law and order and provide essentially needed minimum security and stability to the society. The bureaucracy was highly centralised and all administrative activities were carried out in the urban areas. It was not well depressed and top officials did not share power with their subordinate colleagues. In the system the role of the specialists was under-estimated.

The term 'development administration' was used in 1955 to distinguish the focus of administration from traditional system to the process of development. It lays stress on strengthening of administration in a way that it is possible for it to implement and achieve targets which are fixed in the plans.

Development Administration: A Mechanism. It denotes the complex of agencies government establishes to achieve its developmental goals. It is a mechanism to related several components to development in order to articulate and accomplish national, social and economic objectives. It is administration of policies, programmes and projects to serve development purposes. It is adjustment on the part of bureaucracy to ever increasing different and complex governmental functions in a way that public demands for development are fully responded.

Purpose of Development Administration. Thus the purpose of development administration is to stimulate and facilitate defined and approved programmes of social and economic progress. It aims at changing and introducing innovative programmes and movements and does not unnecessarily stick to the position of status quo. In development bureaucracy becomes accountable to the people through its elected representatives. The attitude of officers engaged in the task of development administration is positive and not negative. It is persuasive rather than restrictive. It encourages innovations and changes are considered essential for completing developmental activities and discourages traditional forms and norms of work.

Development administration is at times linked with modernisation of administration by some scholars whereas other scholars have linked it with efficient administrative methdos for economic development. It aims at preparing plans for economic development and increasing national income and with these ends in view it tries to raise necessary resources and their equitable distribution.

Causes for the Rise of Development Administration. As said earlier the concept of development administration began in 1950's and thereafter it began to be commonly used. For this various causes were responsible. After World War II many new nations, which were hitherto under colonial rule got their independence. The people of these nations had many expectations from their governments and bureaucracies, particularly in the area of their economic development and ending of their poverty, backwardness, illiteracy on the one hand and providing them shelter on the other. But their hopes did not materialise and they were dissatisfied with bureaucracies, political parties and their political bosses.

Then another cause was that the new born states wanted to establish their identity as a unified and strong nation state. Each state wanted to take its independent policy decisions, both internal and external. But bureaucracy was usually inexperienced and ill equipped. It needed resources and techniques both to formulate as well as implement policies which could help in providing strength and identity. One more cause was that each such nation wanted to develop a system which could help in translating the aspirations of the people into viable policies and programmes. Each newly born state was also faced with the problem of correcting social inequalities and injustices but solution to these problems was not easily available. The task however, put heavy burden on administrative systems and the nature of work was both new and difficult.

Then came private sector. It created problems because this sector was weak and was not prepared to invest in new economic venturs. On the whole administration in these nations was not capable of solving socio-economic and political problems of their peoples. The bureaucracy was expected to deal with unfamiliar tasks and as such the need for development administration which was required to accomplish developmental tasks, almost from a straw.

Utility of Development Administration. Development Administration has its own advantages. It has been found very useful in solving and understanding socio-economic problems of the nations both developed and developing. It has also given new orientation to the concept of development on the one hand and administration on the other. New management systems have both adopted it and found it useful. The major expression of development administration is found in the tendencies of governments for decentralisation of powers and authorities, as for decentralisation of powers and authorities, as against centralisation which was quite common earlier. Thus development administration today is not only the administration of development but it is development of administration. It strengthens the capacity of bureaucracy to facilitate development.

Development Administration and Administrative Development. There is close relationship between development administration and administrative development. Both are closely linked with each other. Ordinarily in administration important changes cannot be introduced without bringing changing in the environment. Similarly no development is possible unless administrative system is on very sound footing. In the field and area of development capacity of the government to undertake developmental activities is an important variable and it can function properly when there is proper administrative development. The goals of development administration can be achieved only when administrative system and set up has fully developed.

❐

15

Frederick Herzberg

Basically Herzberg was a sociologist. He has developed his Motivation Hygiene. Theory which is based on his studies conducted by him on 200 Accountants and engineers around Pittsburg, Pennsylvania. He used critical incident method for collecting his data. Herzberg has brought out several publications, of which the most important are (*a*) The Work and Nature of Man; (*b*) The Motivation to Work which he has written alongwith B. Mausner and B. Snyderman; (*c*) One More Time: How do you Motivate Employees? Which appeared in Harvard Business Review January 1968. 'Job Enrichment Pay off which appeared in March, 1969, Harvard Business Review, in co-authorship with Paul, W.J. Jr. Robertson K.B. In 1979, in the Journal of Applied Psychology appeared his 'Relevance in the Test of Motivation and Hygiene Theory' in co-authorship with Banedict S. Grigaliunas.

In his ideas and writings he was influenced by the writings of Abraham Maslow, Douglas Mc Gregor and Chris Argyris. He studied their writings and views but developed his own ideas and views. His two factor theory is basically his own theory, for which he can take full credit.

Herzberg has paid his attention to the problem of motivation *i.e.* the factors which motivate a worker to work and those which stand on his way and do not motivate him to work. Needless to say that the need for motivating workers has all along been felt and it has always been realised by the industry that only a motivated worker can put in maximum hard work and give better produce. For a long time it was believed by the industry that every individual was an economic man and that he could be made to put in hard work and give extra output provided he was given monetary rewards.

Need for study of motivations in industry and other organisations was felt by Herzberg because of several reasons. In our modern organisations need was felt for the study of human behaviour, which was playing increasingly important role in production. Several restrictions were being imposed on industries both by governmental agencies and trade unions. Not only this but in every industrial and non-industrial activity there was everincreasing competitions on the one hand and lobbying on the other. Technology was rapidly changing because of scientific and technological advancement. But one major cause responsible was that there was increasing demand that available human resources, particularly of qualified, experienced and technical personal should be put to maximum use because of their being in short supply. The industry feels that material resources should be fully utilised and more scientifically and rationally managed.

According to Herzberg all individuals have two sets of needs namely *(i)* that every one wants to avoid needs and *(ii)* also that every one wants to have psychological growth to the maximum.

Herzberg's Two Factor Theory

Before Herzberg gave his Two Factor Theory, whenever, management was faced with any problem it considered that it arose because the workers were interested in having more wages and have accordingly created it. It tried to solve it by increasing the wages and salaries of the workers or by giving them some other financial benefits or by improving their working conditions. But the managements found that the workers were not satisfied with these measure and they did not remain motivated.

Herzberg has come out with the Two Factor Theory. According to him money, pleasant surroundings and those supervisors who extend their cooperation to the workers can be called hygiene factors because these factors are such which remove dissatisfaction of the workers and also remove their tendency of producing less. But he has said that these hygienic factors do not always provide positive incentives for work. According to him real motivating factors for the workers are sense of achievement, interesting work, a feeling that achievement, will be a factor for their development on the one hand and recognition of their work on the other.

Herzberg has developed a new concept of motivation, which is called Hygiene motivation theory. His theory is closed to Maslow's theory of self-actualisation and Mc Gregor's theory. According to this theory every one's needs have two factors namely Hygienic Factors and Motivating Factors. Both these influence human behaviour in different ways. As said earlier he has developed his theory on the basis of experience which got because of his studies which he undertook on 200 accountants and engineers. On the basis of his studies he has concluded that one of the major factors of dissatisfaction of a worker is his work environment. He has identified some factors as hygienic factors. These fall in the first category of workers needs. Important hygiene factors according to him are:

1. Company Policy and Administration.
2. Supervision.
3. Salary.
4. Interpersonal Relations.
5. Working Conditions.

When the worker is satisfied with his work he develops some sense of satisfaction. According to him those factors which provide him some satisfaction are motivating factors. These motivate the workers to do more work. In this category he has placed such factors as:

1. Achievement
2. Recognition.
3. Work itself.
4. Responsibility.
5. Advancement.

Briefly speaking Hygiene Factors and Motivation Factors are as under:

	Hygiene Factors	*Motivating Factors*
1.	Company Policy and Administration.	Achievement
2.	Supervision.	Recognition.
3.	Salary.	Work itself.
4.	Impersonal Relations.	Responsibility.
5.	Working Conditions.	Advancement.

He has said that hygiene factors try to check those tendencies which are responsible for dissatisfaction in work. These take him from dissatisfaction to satisfaction. These however, do not increase his capacity to work, satisfaction or capacity to produce more, but their role is only to see that the dissatisfaction of the workers does not increase.

On the other hand are Motivating Factors which provide the workers, satisfaction with his work and motivate him to put in more labour and hard work. These are linked with internal conditions of work. Herzberg is of view that management is more concerned with hygiene factors, which are responsible for reducing dissatisfaction of the workers.

His Views about Satisfiers and Dissatisfiers. According to him those factors which are associated with the growth of the job and give satisfaction to workers are satisfiers.

Satisfiers. According to him satisfiers are those factors which perform the role of motivators. In this category first of all he has placed Achievement *e.g.* personal satisfaction of solving problems. independently completing a task and evaluating and analysing the result of one's efforts. Then another satisfier is recognition of work completed or of any other personal achievement. In this category does not fall generalised recognition or expression of rewards. Then comes the work itself, which means satisfaction with the task content of the job and freedom from boredom. It also means acceptance of challenging jobs and performance of variety of jobs.

In this category Herzberg has also placed 'Responsibility which means entrusting a worker with full responsibility and accountability for certain types of tasks. It also means supervising the performance of others and having control over deciding how and when tasks are to be done. According to Herzberg Advancement and Growth are other satisfiers. By advancement he means advancement to a higher order of task to perform.

Needs of the Workers. On the basis of his interviews Herzberg has said that the workers have two types of needs which are not dependent on each other. These have their influence on human behaviour in different ways. When a worker feels dissatisfied with his work he pays attention to the environments in which he is placed or required to work. On the other hand, when he is satisfied with his work, then his attention is towards his work. He has said that a person feels attracted toward his work when he is provided opportunities to grow and develop. It is necessary that his nature of work should attract him and his work should be recognised.

Dissatisfiers. As against satisfiers there are dissatisfiers which according to him are hygiene factors, in which he has included five factors, as mentioned above namely; salary, supervision, working conditions, company policy and administration and inter-personal relations. He has said that these factors have little or no relationship with the motivation of a particular job relationship. On the other hand, the motivating factors, as mentioned above, motivate the workers. These determine how an employee feels about his job, whereas hygiene factors only determine how a worker feels about his company or organisation in general.

Herzberg has said that both satisfaction and dissatisfaction are not separate and also not opposed to each other. He has also said that an employee may be either be dissatisfied or not satisfied with hygiene factors. Similarly he is either satisfied or not satisfied with motivational job factors.

Role of Job Dissatisfiers and Satisfiers. As said above, Herzberg has identified job satisfiers and job dissatisfiers and believes that the latter draw considerable attention of management. In his opinion each set is different from the other. According to him in so for as dissatisfiers are concerned these produce only short-term changes in human attitudes, whereas satisfiers produce long-term changes in attitudes. the dissatisfiers tell about workers relations with the environments in which they perform their jobs and also come on the way of job satisfaction. For all practical purposes these do not create positive job attitudes. On the other hand, satisfiers are concerned with the nature of work and job contents.

He has also said that there can be situations in which a worker may not like his job and yet he continues to work there and vice versa. The reason, according to him are different factors which influence these two separate and distinct feelings. One element being how he feels about his job and the other is how he feels about his company. Whereas former are motivational, the latter are hygienic factors.

Principles of Motivation Hygiene Theory. Herzberg has said that there are three main principles of motivation-hygiene theory. Hygiene factors are unrelated to task and the factors involved in producing job satisfaction are quite separate from the factors which lead to job dissatisfaction. Then another principle is that the opposite of satisfaction on the job is not dissatisfaction. Both satisfaction and dissatisfaction are only discrete feelings. He calls these as unipolar traits. His third principle is that motivators have much lasting effect in providing satisfaction and tend to be self-sustaining and do not need constant attention of the supervisor. On the other hand, hygiene factors have less lasting effects on preventing dissatisfactions.

Herzberg has discussed at length both hygiene and motivation factors and for him as said earlier both are not opposed to each other. He has also tried to explain that the opposite of satisfaction on the job is not dissatisfaction. He has divided the people working in an organisation into two groups.

Job Enrichment

The term Job Enrichment designates a technique used by company managers to maximise in individual workers the internal motivation to work, which is the true source of job satisfaction. Basically a concept of the 1960s, founded on the work of Frederick Herzberg, job enrichment has been significantly augmented by work done at Yale University under the direction of Richard Hackman.

The job-enrichment concept designates a production and profit-oriented way of managing, as well as a means of making work experience meaningful for people. It is based upon the premise that people are not motivated by what is externally done to them by management with rewards, privileges or punishment, nor by the environment or context in which they perform their work. People develop lasting motivation only through their experience with the content of their jobs—the work itself.

Such factors as pay, fringe benefits, the work environment, working conditions, and the quality of supervision cannot be ignored or given only taken attention. Dissatisfaction with the factors can have a severely debiliating effect on a workforce. Caring properly for these needs can result in an absence of dissatisfaction.

Managers in recent years have been witnessing high-velocity change and turmoil in the patterns of employee behaviour, and are forced to cope with a host of problems including high turnover or quit rates, absenteeism, tardiness, union grievances and work stoppages, high training costs, poor production quality, and low rates of production.

Advantages of job Enrichment. Herzberg has said that job enrichment can prove very useful in solving such problems with which persent day management is faced *e.g.* high labour turn over absenteeism, work stoppage, trade union system etc. These and similar other problems invariably create turmoil and result in low and poor quality production of goods. Once job enrichment system is introduced many of these problems will automatically be solved. In brief he believes that job enrichment is nothing else but the art of re-shaping jobs.

Process of Job Enrichment. According to him first step in processing job enrichment is that a decision is to be taken by the management whether it is a full fledged programme or only an experimental project. The latter means a complete scientific study with experimental groups, in which job changes are to be introduced at the job level on the one hand and in the control group on the other. It should be seen that at this stage short-term improvements are not made and the workers are not made conscious of the on going processes. According to Herzberg as against experimental project, a programme is straight forward application of certain changes on a large group without caring for the control groups.

Whether it should be programme or experimental project much will depend on the nature of management and environment in the organisation. If the management is not interested in introducing organisational changes then in order to convince it about the utility of the whole scheme.

The Process of Enriching Jobs

First a decision should be made as to whether the effort is to take the form of an experimental project or a programme. An experimental project is essentially a scientific study complete with experimental groups, in which the job changes will be made, and control groups in which all conditions are controlled to keep them as constant as possible. In a project, great care is taken to make very little of the process known to the employees. The purpose is to reduce the chance of short-term improvements in results occurring solely because the employees are reacting to the attention heaped on them as an 'elite' group.

The programme, on the other hand, is a straightforward application affecting as large a population as possible without regard to control groups. The question of running a project or programme is often decided by the nature of the management environment in the organisation. If upper management attitudes are very hostile and skeptical about organisational change of this sort, then it is often necessary to provide indisputable proof of effectiveness by using a project model if the effect is to have any future.

Work within a Department, or an identifiable functional group should be selected as the "client" group to work with, rather than attempting to redesign problem jobs in work groups across functional lines. This is suggested to gain the advantage of having a homogeneous management team participating in workshops and subsequent work on redesigning jobs. Preferably, a basic job performed by a large number of people should be selected. Avoid the management, staff, and support jobs at first—let changes in basic jobs force changes at higher levels. Basic jobs are usually those which directly affect the product or service turned out, or they involve direct interface with the public or the customer. Careful consideration should be given to the selection of the individual who is to act as the director for the project or programme. This individual is best equipped for the job if he is highly respected and has a proven record of success as a line manager.

The chasm between conceptual generalities and job changes can be bridged in the workshop through the process of brainstorming or so called "greenlighting". "Greenlighting" is a device used to remove the usual obstacles to free thinking. When the greenlight condition is announced, the group begins tossing out ideas for getting motivators into each job as fast as possible. Everyone is warned that no "red lights" or negative comments such as "We tried that before", "That won't work", or "This isn't a good time for that", are permitted. Sorry about implementing the recommended changes should not be a concern during greenlighting.

A time table can be set for completing a detailed analysis of each proposed item for job change, and installation of items selected to start with. Then plans are made for additional meetings to continue greenlighting and evaluation of the items from the first greenlighting session.

Module of Work and Vertical Loading of the Job

Among the best ways to set up individual responsibility is to seek natural modules of work which can be individually assigned. A work module can appear in many forms. In general, a module is a set of related tasks which contribute in sequence to the completion of some function or turning out some completed item. The module of tasks can be more meaningful if it is related to some natural unit of work for which an individual has continuing responsibility.

Natural units of work may have geographic, alphabetical, or numerical grouping or other identity. That identify may also be related to serving some recipient or group of recipients. When a natural work module is first identified it may be performed by several people doing fragments of the full module with no one single responsible for the whole. To the greatest degree that is practical each individual is given the full process to perform.

The responsibility is full and individual. In one key punch job, for example, the operators were given a module of work by having them prepare all cards from a cetain geographic area or for certain kinds of reports rather than whatever cards happend to come along next.

The principle of vertical loading involves process-loading into a job, additional tasks and responsibilities which can deliver more satisfaction than the tasks in the job to begin with. This is very different from adding more tasks which may be varied but have essentially no greater substance. The process is usually vertical because the tasks of greater interest and responsibility are most often found above in the supervisory job or a job at a higher level of complexity.

Direct Feedback. The process of feedback is highly important in the enriching process. It affects the recognition motivator. The most effective feedback occurs in the transaction between employee and the task rather than in the usual transaction between employee and supervisor. Effective feedback has these characteristics:

1. It is related to task performance, not personal characteristics.
2. It occurs at short intervals.
3. It is given direct from the task to the employee, not through the supervisor.
4. It is given on a individual rather than group basis.

This is not intended to imply that supervisory feedback is ineffective or waste of time. Most people desire it, and such interpersonal feedback on performance can be of great value when done well. Direct feedback is not fettered with interpersonal problems and is less complicated. Soon after completion of a task, worker should be learning through task feedback how well he is doing, where he stands, and what he is worth. Then he should have the opportunity to do something about it himself. This is usually accomplished by making him responsible for changes and adjustments in his process and for correcting his own errors. Once a new responsibility is given, the supervisor must give consideration to what his response will be if the employee fails with it. Some failure must be expected. The supervisor should help the employee correct the error, examine why it occurred, and assist in planning to prevent recurrence.

Task Combination. Combining tasks to a complete task module has a high degree of potential. This will provide additional interest, challenge, and a feeling of responsibility for the whole piece.

"Client" Relationship. Where natural work units are groupings by customers—for example, billing or accounts receivable—the engendered sense of responsibility leads the workers to form a "client relationship" with the accounts. They start to call them "my customers" and take on a strong attitude of ownership.

Natural Work Units. Designing the work according to a logical group that is aligned with the mission allows for the personal feeling of responsibility. Workers start to identify with this group and behave accordingly.

Vertical Loading. This pushing of responsibilities down higher levels and giving the workers more control make for increased responsibility. This should be done selectively according to individual competence.

Feedback Channels. Setting up conditions for feedback from the job is very important in the transition from a 100 per cent checking job to a partial or full task module. Elimination of checking without feedback might hurt quality. Workers and supervisors must know how they are doing.

Critical Evaluation

In spite of the wide ranging application and the popularity of two factor theory, there appears a severe criticism on Herzberg's propositions. Like Taylor's Scientific Management Theory, Herzberg was also criticised for adopting an industrial engineering approach though from the opposite way than that of Taylor. His ideas are applicable more to management than the supervisors and much less to shop floor. It was argued that pay is both satisfier and dissatisfier, particularly dissatisfier to low paid employees, at the same time higher pay provides recognition and enhances self-esteem.

House and Wigdor have criticised the theory for the following reasons:

(1) The theory is methodogically egg-bound. When things are okay, that put themselves in the best

light, but when things go wrong they blame the environmental factors, *i.e.*, the hygiene factors.

(2) Rater bias.

(3) No overall measure of satisfaction was used in Pittsburg's study. For example, most people may dislike certain features of the job, but still like the job itself.

The other elements of criticism are:

(*i*) a given factor can cause job satisfaction for one and job dissatisfaction for others and vice versa;

(*ii*) intrinsic job factors are more important to both satisfying and dissatisfying job events; and

(*iii*) a given factor can cause both job satisfaction and job dissatisfaction in the same people.

It is argued that respondents did not like to appear greedy and therefore, ranked pay very low, whereas in studies of Lawler pay was ranked as satisfier. Some studies by Shepard and Herrick, Herzberg's conclusions were confirmed. Similarly, it was argued that after the initial years in employment, job satisfaction decreases but the worker continues to work for a living.

The main criticism of the motivation-hygiene concept is that initially it interpreted job and company employment factors to be totally distinct and separate set entities (House and Wigdor). Today it is recognised that these factors at times can be both "motivators" and "hygienic" in nature. Money especially seems to be a motivator in many work situations, especially those in which the employee is earning a relatively small total annual income. Motivators and hygienic factors also may vary on jobs at different organisational levels.

It was argued by Vroom (1964) that no one has investigated whether Herzberg, Mausner and Snyderman's results could be an outcome of an attributional process. Some relevant studies do indicate that this process may account for the observed data. Staw has noted that when individuals are led to believe their performance has been successful, they tend to attribute various pleasing characteristics to the work group. Others showed that regardless of the supervisor's behaviour, manipulated to be structuring or considerate, when a work group does well it tends to see the leader as considerate. In short, people select characteristics on the basis of their outcomes. Methodology adopted in any study has a bearing on the conclusions emanating from the study. One criticism against Herzberg's theory is the methodology adopted. Schwab and others have adopted same methodology as that of Herzberg but they obtained results different from what the two-factor theory would predict. In spite of the criticism on two-factor theory, many based upon empirical researches, it is unquestionable that Herzberg's contribution to work motivation is substantial.

Hygiene and Motivation

Herzberg has divided people working in an organisation into two groups namely Hygiene seekers and Motivation seekers. Each group has its own features and characteristics.

Characteristics of Hygiene and Motivation Seekers. According to Herzberg a hygiene seeker is motivated by the environment of the organisation whereas a motivation seeker is attracted by the nature of his work. Similarly, whereas the former gets dissatisfied because of such factors as increase in salary, job security and behaviour of fellow employees, the latter has more tolerance for poor hygiene factors.

When hygienic factors improve, the hygiene seekers over react to their satisfaction. On the other hand, there is less reaction to this type of satisfaction by motivation seekers.

The former can be successful on the job because of talent whereas the latter can be over achievements.

Like over reaction with satisfaction, the hygiene seekers also over react to dissatisfaction when environments do not improve. Not only this but duration of their satisfaction is for a very short period. On the other hand, the reaction of motivation seekers to non-improvement of environment is very mild.

The hygiene seekers have no positive feelings about the virtues of work and life in general. As against that motivation seekers have positive feelings and they feel that life in general is virtuous. The former also have little interest in the kind and quality of work which they are required to perform but the latter show interest in the work which they are doing and enjoy from the nature of their work. The hygiene seekers also do not derive much satisfaction from the accomplishment of work, whereas the motivation seekers derive satisfaction after the work done by them has been completed to their satisfaction as well as to the satisfaction of others.

Impact of Hygiene Seekers. Herzberg has called them as barrack soldiers. According to them they are more motivated by external rather than internal rewards and as such they are likely to lead to organisations to as is where is situation. They are likely to infuse their own motivational attitudes into their subordinates. He feels that quite often their influence is not in proportion to their long-term effectiveness. He has further said that there is no guarantee that once hygiene needs of hygiene seekers have been satisfied, they will get motivated. He accepted the fact that as long as payment made to the worker is inadequate he may feel dissatisfied, but at the same time there is no guarantee that more pay will mean more production and profits.

Herzberg is of the view that stress on hygiene factors does not essentially motivate the workers but may lead to absenteeism and may also eliminate opportunities for initiative. An organisation can easily motivate through fears of hygiene deprivation than to motivate in terms of achievements and realisation of goals. But he has cautioned that this approach about motivation is not to the advantage of organisation in the long run. He has therefore, said that if the organisation wishes to be benefitted in the long run for that it is desirable that it should pay attention to job enrichment and vertical overloading.

Impact of Motivation Seekers. Herzberg has said that motivated workers are associated with a particular work. therefore, with every specified work, there should be some motivation. Since motivated worker is linked with work, therefore, he is associated with the very nature of work and becomes its integral part. The workers are also influenced by the work itself. The change in the nature of work and relationship influences motivated workers. The principle of motivation attaches great importance to motivated workers. For the completion of every work in the organisation smoothly there is always need and necessity of motivated workers. It is very essential to motivate the workers and to make them work happily. For this it is essential that the workers should be given considerable freedom, so that they work to the fullest of their capacity. Since these workers feel satisfied with the completion of work, therefore, they try to improve the quality of work and its standard.

Hygiene and Motivation Seekers. After explaining the significance of motivation as well as hygiene factors, Herzberg divides the people working in organisations into two groups and calls them 'hygiene seekers' and 'motivation seekers'.

Successful hygiene seekers will have two types of impact on the organisation. Firstly, they will lead the organisation to 'as is where is' as they are more motivated to external rewards than internal. Borrowing the terminology from the army, Herzberg equates them as 'barrack soldiers'. Secondly, they instil their own motivational attitudes into their subordinates and set extrinsic reward atmosphere in the organisation. Often their influence can be out of proportion to their long-term effectiveness.

Inadequate pay, no doubt, contributes to dissatisfaction but more pay is no guarantee for more productivity. As Paul and Robertson have noted, 'no amount of environmental improvement can compensate for task impoverishment'. If our concern is to motivate people, we must look against at the task we ask them to do. Emphasis on hygiene factors would lead to: impeding creativity, absenteeism, frequent occurrence of failures and restriction or elimination of opportunity for initiative and achievement.

❐

Index